Hackers and Hacking

Books in the **Contemporary World Issues** series address vital issues in today's society such as genetic engineering, pollution, and biodiversity. Written by professional writers, scholars, and nonacademic experts, these books are authoritative, clearly written, up-to-date, and objective. They provide a good starting point for research by high school and college students, scholars, and general readers as well as by legislators, business-people, activists, and others.

Each book, carefully organized and easy to use, contains an overview of the subject, a detailed chronology, biographical sketches, facts and data and/or documents and other primary source material, a forum of authoritative perspective essays, annotated lists of print and nonprint resources, and an index.

Readers of books in the **Contemporary World Issues** series will find the information they need in order to have a better understanding of the social, political, environmental, and economic issues facing the world today.

Hackers and Hacking

A REFERENCE HANDBOOK

Thomas J. Holt and Bernadette H. Schell

ABC-CLIO

Santa Barbara, California • Denver, Colorado • Oxford, England

Library of Congress Cataloging-in-Publication Data

Holt, Thomas J., 1978–
    Hackers and hacking : a reference handbook / Thomas J. Holt and Bernadette H. Schell.
        pages cm. — (Contemporary world issues)
    Includes bibliographical references and index.
    ISBN 978–1–61069–276–2 (hard copy : alk. paper) — ISBN 978–1–61069–277–9 (ebook) 1. Computer hackers. 2. Computer crimes. 3. Computer security. 4. Internet–Moral and ethical aspects. I. Schell, Bernadette H. (Bernadette Hlubik), 1952- II. Title.
HV6773.H65   2013
364.16′8—dc23   2013007935

ISBN: 978–1–61069–276–2
EISBN: 978–1–61069–277–9

17 16 15 14 13   1 2 3 4 5

This book is also available on the World Wide Web as an eBook.
Visit www.abc-clio.com for details.

ABC-CLIO, LLC
An Imprint of ABC-CLIO, LLC

ABC-CLIO, LLC
130 Cremona Drive, P.O. Box 1911
Santa Barbara, California 93116-1911

This book is printed on acid-free paper ∞

Manufactured in the United States of America

Contents

List of Figures and Tables

Preface

Hackers and Hacking: A Reference Handbook examines the many forms of computer exploits—some positively motivated and some negatively motivated—from the hacking prehistory era prior to 1969 through the present. Hacking is a skill that can be used for beneficial purposes, such as protecting computer systems and ensuring the safety of personal data. At the same time, hacking can be used by malicious actors to engage in revenge, sabotage, blackmail, or pure personal gain. What is more, experts now fear that some hacks against nuclear plants and electrical grids might lead to death or devastation of large populations depending on the severity of the attack.

This book takes a novel approach to the presentation and understanding of this controversial topic in society. The term "hacker" was originally used to denote positively motivated individuals interested in stretching the capabilities of computers and networks. In contrast, the term "cracker" was more recently introduced into mainstream society to denote those negatively motivated individuals wanting to cause harm to property or persons—or to personally gain, whether reputation-wise or financially. In recent decades, media stories have tended to focus on the dark side of hacking because that kind of news sells. Nevertheless, there is growing interest by individuals in mainstream society about hacker superheroes—even female ones—such as the fictional character Lisbeth Salander, the protagonist in the hugely successful Millennium book and film series *The Girl with the Dragon Tattoo*.

Clearly, the fascination with hackers has grown over the past 15 years because of the massive damage that might be potentially caused by computer and network intrusions—including death. Our book explores the information that is known about hackers and their exploits—how they do what they do, why they do what they do, and how their unique thinking and behaving patterns make elite hackers so interesting—and so powerful. We were inspired to write this book because of the increasing use of technology across all facets of society and the controversies surrounding the issue of hacking. While many people depend on computers, mobile phones, and the Internet in their daily lives, they know less about the individuals who may compromise these resources. Thus we wrote this book to provide insight into the nature of hacking; the techniques, motives, and thoughts of hackers; and the way in which their activities are directly tied to the evolution of the technologies we use every day.

While many other books in the field consider hacking from a purely technical standpoint that may not be immediately accessible to a layperson, our work tends to discuss the phenomenon of hacking from a social perspective, while at the same time addressing the technologies that hackers exploit and manipulate in an easy-to-understand format. Additionally, this book considers the way in which hacking can be applied to engage in various forms of cybercrime, ranging from the creation of malicious software to the theft of sensitive information and fraud. In short, this book provides an in-depth exploration of the phenomenon of hacking from a multidisciplinary perspective that addresses the social and technical aspects of this unique activity.

This book has seven chapters, containing the following points of interest. Chapter 1 provides basic background and history on hacking. Basic terms, including "hacker" and" cracker," and the types of cyberexploits commonly caused by hackers are outlined. This chapter also gives an overview of the emerging fears surrounding hackers, from the 1960s through the present, including what researchers tell us about how hackers do what they do, why they do what they do, and how unique thinking and behaving patterns set them apart from members of mainstream society.

Chapter 2 outlines the issues, controversies, and solutions regarding hacking. This chapter provides readers with a more in-depth look at the means by which hackers carry out their attacks, the costs to society of various hack attacks, and legal and technological solutions that have been developed to curb these exploits and to minimize the damages caused by them.

Chapter 3 provides perspectives from cybercrime experts on important questions related to the field of hacking and the proposed means for curbing the adverse impact of hacking exploits. The essays include both original arguments made by academics who are actively researching hackers and their exploits as well as personal stakeholders in the debate. Topics are wide ranging and address protecting critical infrastructures, examining the social dynamics and malware secrets to mitigate Net-centric attacks, and the role of nation-states in cyberattacks. We would like to thank the various contributors for sharing their perspectives on various issues of interest to practitioners and the general public.

Chapter 4 provides a series of sketches of key hackers, hacker organizations, security-related companies, and leaders in the field. Profiles include such famous hackers as Mafiaboy, Kevin Mitnick, and Bernie S. Hacker-related topics like *2600: The Hacker Quarterly*, the DefCon and Black Hat hacker conferences, and hacker cells such as Anonymous are detailed.

Chapter 5 provides data regarding trends in types of hack attacks reported by U.S. industry and government IT security heads in recent years as well as the trends in costs associated with these breaches. There is also a discussion of geographical location differences in trends, such as those found in the United States versus Canada.

Chapter 6 outlines the many resources that readers may find of interest. The annotated bibliography is divided into print and nonprint resources, including but not limited to items produced by entities such as the Department of Homeland Security, the U.S. Department of Justice, the Federal Bureau of Investigation, and the National Security Administration's National Computer Security Center.

Chapter 7 presents a chronology of hacker inventions and exploits. A briefly annotated chronology listing and linking key hacking events is outlined from the 1800s through the present. The major headings include: Prehistory of Hacking (1800s–1969); The Elder Days (1970–1979); The Golden Age (1980–1989); The Great Hacker Wars and Hacker Activism (1990–2000); Fear of a Cyber-Apocalypse Era (2001–2009); and Cyberterrorism, Cyberspying, and Cyberwars (2010–Present).

Hackers and Hacking

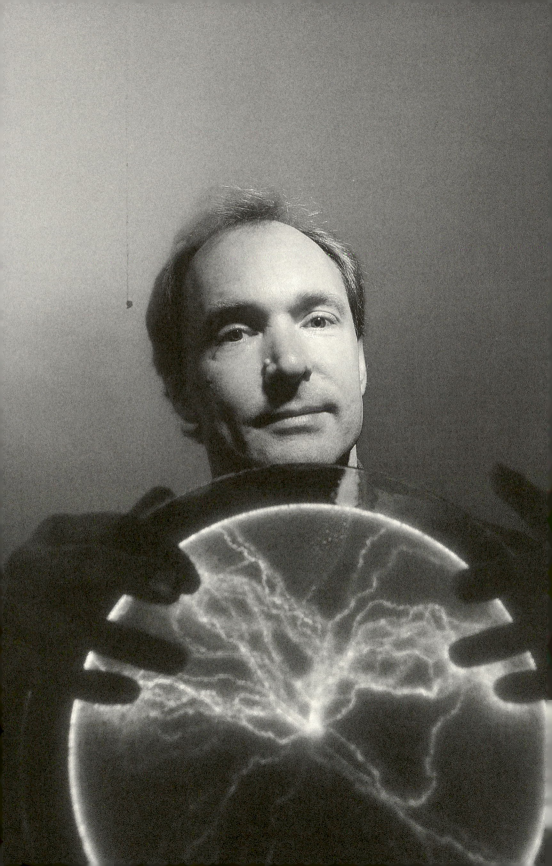

1 Background and History

This chapter begins with a discussion of the Internet—what it is and how it differs from an intranet, the history of its development in North America and elsewhere, and its present-day status in terms of the impact on economies globally. The positive effects are emphasized near the beginning of the chapter, and the negative effects—including the activities of Black Hat computer hackers—are discussed later, reflecting the reality of the Internet's development. The chapter closes with a summary of present-day challenges that are explored more fully in Chapter 2.

The Growth and Adoption of the Internet from 1969 through the Present

Internet Defined

Generally speaking, an internet (lowercase "i") is a network connecting computer systems. The Internet (capital "I") that we are all familiar with today dates back to 1969, when it was pioneered in the United States. At that time, it was a high-speed network built by the U.S. Department of Defense as a digital communications experiment that linked hundreds of defense contractors, universities, and research laboratories. This powerful computer network belonging to the U.S.

Pioneering British computer programmer Tim Berners-Lee, the father of the World Wide Web. (Catrina Genovese/Wireimagestock.com)

Advanced Research Projects Agency (ARPA) allowed highly trained artificial intelligence (AI) researchers in dispersed locations to transmit and exchange critical information with incredible speed. (A branch of computer science, AI is known for making computers behave as if they were human beings by modeling human thought processes on computers. AI is also related to the solving of complex problems using computers.)

To keep the United States and its citizens physically safe, agents working in isolated pockets needed to be able to transmit critical information over the ARPAnet rather than physically move from one geographic location to another to engage in an information exchange. The "networked" tribe arrangement that developed in those early days continues to exist in the larger online world today, allowing people to connect remotely. Nowadays, the Internet refers to a collection of networks connected by routers. The Internet is the largest network in the world and comprises backbone networks such as MILNET, mid-level networks, and stub networks (Schell and Martin 2006). Although the pioneering ARPAnet was dedicated to the U.S. military and selected contractors and universities partaking in defense research, without question its introduction hugely advanced the emerging field of information technology (IT).

It is important to emphasize that no single factor produced the powerful Internet that society enjoys today. Groundbreaking events in hardware (the mechanical parts composing the computer and computer networks) and in software (the programming language running the network and doing the necessary computations) were necessary for progress on this front to be made.

Right from the beginning, the Internet was designed to be a huge network interconnecting many smaller groups of linked computers. The Internet never had a physical or tangible entry in the same way that a door on a house provides entry to the rest of the building. Even in 1969, the Internet was designed to be a decentralized, self-maintaining group of redundant links between computers and computer networks. The beauty of the Internet even during its infancy was that it was able to send data rapidly without human intervention and with the unique capability to reroute data if one or more links became damaged or unavailable. Therefore, from a military defense perspective, even if a portion of the network were to be destroyed during a war, with a redundant system, critical data could still reach their intended destination. By design, data travel along networks not as "whole" information or messages, but rather as very small information packets. Even in ARPAnet's early days, the Internet used packet-switching protocols to allow messages to be subdivided into smaller packets of information. These packets could be sent rather independently to the required destination and automatically reassembled by the destination computer. Although packets containing information for a larger message often travel along the same path to get to the final destination, some of them may be rerouted along a different path if one or more routers along the route becomes overloaded. In addition, computers can communicate with one another through the use of a common communication protocol known as the Internet Protocol (IP). All applications utilized on the Internet are designed to make use of this protocol and have done so since the mid-1960s (Schell 2007).

Large research-intensive universities were the early adopters of the Internet, but soon technical wizards with an entrepreneurial spirit realized that online advertising, commercial software applications, and vastly marketable hardware could generate services and tools desired by the general public. This was made manifest though the emergence of the World Wide Web. Although the term "Web" is often used by those in mainstream society to signify the Internet, the World Wide Web (WWW) is just one of the applications using the Internet as a base infrastructure (Schell and Martin 2006). The www protocol became immensely popular after Tim Berners-Lee developed the HyperText Transfer Protocol (HTTP) in the early 1990s, allowing users to access and link information through a simple and intuitive user interface known as an Internet browser.

It is important to note that the Internet is different from an intranet; the latter is an information system internal to an organization or institution that is constructed with Web-based technology. Often termed "portals," intranets were initially commonly found in large firms having in excess of 15,000 employees, so that employees could access the intranet website using a browser. (Technically speaking, a browser interprets Hyper Text Markup Language [HTML]—the programming language used to code web pages into words and graphics so that users can view the pages in the intended layout and rendering.) With improved and more affordable intranet software designed by Microsoft Corporation and other firms since about 2005, intranets are nowadays found in small and medium-sized companies as well as large ones. Moreover, intranets are typically run on a private local area network (LAN) instead of on public servers. While intranet sites in firms and institutions can serve a number of functions, the primary usage seems to be to keep employees informed about upcoming events; to post company policies and procedures, including proper online etiquette; and to distribute software or application updates.

The explosive adoption of web browsers coupled with a substantive decline in the cost of technology led to widespread use of computers in industrialized nations. By the early 2000s, there was virtually no medium- or large-sized organization in developed nations without a noticeable presence on the Internet, with the bulk having at least a website and communication connectivity with email. At the same time the majority of households in these countries had access to the Internet through high-bandwidth lines. Compare this reality to the 1970s, when there were only an estimated 100,000 computers in use in the United States. Few of them were networked, and most of them were found in larger universities, businesses, or government offices—not in citizens' homes (Schell 2007). Thus, there has been a global shift in human behavior in a very short period of time, which has direct ramifications for the threat posed by the malicious hacker community.

Gaining Authorized Access to the Internet and the Modes of Communication

Given that the Internet has no entry door per se, how do Internet users gain access legally? A number of ways exist for individuals to gain legal access. One of the earliest ways was through a computer network linked directly to the Internet at an educational institution, business, or government office. The IT department would issue account numbers and passwords to legitimate users.

As more citizens purchased moderately priced personal computers (PCs) during the 1990s and beyond, users commonly paid a fee to an Internet service provider (ISP). In exchange for such payment, the user received a software package, a username, a temporary password, and an Internet access number. Equipped with a modem, the user logged on to the Internet, browsed various websites, bought things online with the click of a mouse, watched movies online, and sent and received electronic mail (email). In recent years, ISPs have offered high-speed services using DSL (a general term for any local network loop that is digital in nature) or cable modem technology. ISPs are connected to one another through network access points.

The most common ways to communicate legally and legitimately with other Internet users include the following:

Email

Listserv

Internet Relay Chat (IRC)

Telnet

Social networking sites

Remote retrieval

Email

Via email, online users can send messages to one another in real time. Compared to encrypted email, which is secure, unencrypted email is not secure, meaning that its content may be accessed, viewed, and even altered by someone with computer access. Nowadays, to see whether email sent has gotten to its intended recipient, online users can go on their systems to determine if the email sent was "delivered" and "read."

Listserv

Listserv is like an online subscription to coverage of some topic of interest to online users. Registered users can receive messages posted on the listserv by others and post their own messages on the listserv for others to read. The kind of software managing the listserv is known as a mail exploder; such a program runs on the server where the list resides. This program also gives instructions to online users about how to automatically unsubscribe from the listserv. A listserv may be classified as "open access" or "restricted access." With a moderated listserv, someone actually approves of the messages posted before sending them on to registered users.

Internet Relay Chat

Servers running IRC software allow multiple users to "talk on-line" and in real time by choosing from many activated discussion channels. A message typed on one user's computer will appear almost immediately on another user's computer monitor. To maintain privacy and to keep their real identities unknown to those in chat rooms, online users will often go under a false name (known as a moniker) like Fishgirl. Despite taking these precautions, online users of chat rooms have, on occasion, reported complaints to authorities about being harassed while online or of being cyberstalked.

Telnet

Technically, Telnet is a terminal emulation program, or one based on that protocol, that allows users to log on to the Internet. Put simply, Telnet is an Internet application that permits a user's PC to act as a terminal to a remote system. For many users connecting to the Internet, Telnet is not used because it requires knowledge of the UNIX operating system. For example, a professor at one university can use Telnet to take advantage of the extraordinary computing power of a supercomputer at some other university or a string of universities. A real-world example is Canada's Shared Hierarchical Academic Research Computing Network (SHARCNET); established in 2001, it is the largest high-performance computing consortium in Canada, now boasting 17 universities, colleges, and research institutes in Ontario, Canada. SHARCNEC (2012) works on a dedicated, private high-speed wide area network (WAN).

Social Networking Websites

Social networking websites focus on building social networks or social relationships among people. By connecting to these websites using the Internet, users can share in an online environment their ideas, events, photos, and activities of personal interest across political, economic, and geographic borders. The technology used to support social networks via computer-mediated communications was utilized in early online services such as America Online and was involved in Usenet, ARPAnet, and Listserv. Now, however, these programs may utilize various algorithms and potentially be integrated into search engines such as Google or Baidu.

A study completed several years ago by the Pew Internet and American Life Project (Leggatt 2009) found that interest in social networking sites grew exponentially after 2000, with the number of adults using social networks quadrupling from 2005 to 2009. About 90 percent of adults using social networking sites do so to remain in touch with people they already know, whereas about half of teenagers and adults are looking for new friends. Whereas 60 percent of adults are likely to restrict their online profiles so that only "trusted" friends can see them, younger online users are more likely to have fewer restrictions—making them vulnerable to cybercriminals.

Though there are myriad social networking sites in operation today, ranging from livejournal and Baidu to the recently launched Google+, the service of choice at the moment is Facebook. In 2004, when Mark Zuckerberg asked his fellow Harvard University students to try out the new idea that he called "the facebook," it was a huge success almost immediately; his online peers were able to create personal profiles, search for their friends' profiles, and invite others from the university to join the online community. After being open only to members of Harvard University for two years, Facebook was released to the general population in the fall of 2006. In that year, Facebook let anyone with a registered email address join others online. Since then, Zuckerberg and his colleagues have continued to introduce new features, one of the most novel being the creation of an application programming interface (API) for third-party developers. Consequently, programmers could design applications tapping into Facebook's huge online community—ranging from games and fun diversions like Lexulous to marketing campaigns like Burger King's Whopper Sacrifice application that asks registered users to delete 10 friends to qualify for a free Whopper sandwich. Since 2009, Facebook has been the number one social networking site with more than 10 million unique visitors (Strickland 2012).

Remote Retrieval

Nowadays, Internet users search for and retrieve information located on remote computers. There are several ways that this process can be completed. One approach is to use the File Transfer Protocol (FTP) to transfer files between systems over the network, particularly from a host (a server) to a remote computer (a client). Another way to search and retrieve is to use the Gopher protocol, released in 1991 and designed to share documents online. A third way is to use HTML.

Since February 1993, when the University of Minnesota (where the gopher protocol developers were located) announced that it would begin charging users licensing fees to use the proto-col, gopher's popularity has waned rapidly. IT experts believe that besides the licensing fees, gopher's downfall was caused by its inferior structure; compared with the free-form hypertext format-ting language of HTML, the gopher protocol was very limited.

Although information is stored in individual HTTP servers worldwide, the connection of these computers to the Internet through World Wide Web Consortium (W3C) protocols (those used to exchange information) allows the linked infor-mation to become part of a single body of information. In other words, the Internet describes a network of HTTP servers using hypertext links to find and access files. For this reason, all Internet site addresses begin with http://.

Thus, if a user types a universal resource locator (URL), such as http//:www.laurentian.ca, into the browser and presses the "Enter" key, the computer will send an HTTP request to the correct server. The server, which was developed to handle such requests, then sends the user the requested HTML page—typically containing video, text, images, and sounds and having a unique address consisting of numbers.

Flash forward to the present. Everything is data. Governments have gone online to deliver their most critical services as data, businesses have turned their business processes and competitive business secrets into data, and citizens have turned their social lives into data. In 2010, consumers and business enterprises stored in excess of 13 exabytes of data on computer drives, note-book computers, and PCs. To put this in perspective, one exa-byte is 4,000 times as much information as is stored in the Library of Congress (Tossell 2012). This expansion of data will no doubt continue as individuals increasingly move to the use of "cloud" computing, whereby data are stored remotely on serv-ers owned by corporations or other entities and accessed through the Internet. The increased use of mobile devices including tab-lets, smart phones, and laptop computers has propelled individ-uals to find ways to manage and access files without having to swap files across each device. Cloud storage enables access to and manipulation of files across multiple platforms without having to store that file on each specific device.

A Closer Look at the Adoption of the Internet in Developed Nations

In the little more than 40 years since ARPAnet was invented and the seeds of the Internet were planted, the developed world has become totally dependent on the Internet for routine daily activities. Most nations of the world, whether developed or emerging, are aware of the Internet's value for growing and maintaining their economy and potentially safeguarding their citizens. Think for a moment about all that is done on the Internet—paying bills online, filing tax returns, playing online games with players around the globe, reading electronic books, communicating with friends through social networking sites, and buying things like vacation tickets without ever leaving home.

The use of technology has a substantive impact on how individuals spend their time and interact with others. According to 2012 estimates by ComScore Inc., Canadians spend more time online than citizens in any other country, including their counterparts in highly wired societies such as the United States, China, and South Korea. The ComScore report tracks Internet usage in 11 countries, with the United States placing second behind Canada. According to these estimates, the average American spends 38.6 hours per month online, while the average Canadian spends 45 hours per month online, with the majority of time spent on social networking sites such as Facebook.

U.S. youth typically acquire their first cell phones when they are between the ages of 12 and 13 (Lenhart 2010). In fact, 75 percent of youth own either a laptop or desktop computer and 15 percent own both devices (Lenhart, Madden, and Hitlin 2005). In addition, 93 percent of American youths between the ages of 12 and 17 use the Internet, meaning that almost *all* youth have some presence on the Internet. And not only do youth have a presence, but it is a frequent presence:

88 percent of children who go online do so at least once a week (Lenhart and Madden 2007). A similar national study found that 49 percent of children are online for 5 to 7 days each week on average (Wolack, Mitchell, and Finkelhor 2006).

This voracious hunger for all things Internet has also had a positive impact on advertisers and media companies (Ladurantaye 2012). Revenue from Internet advertising in the United States hit a record $31 billion in 2011, up 22 percent from the $26 billion in such revenue in 2010, the previous record (Ladurantayne 2012). Interestingly, almost half of the ad revenue, about $15 billion, came from the "search" category of online businesses—such as Google, Bing, and Yahoo. In this category are text-based advertisements sold by the search engines that are targeted to particular search terms and other keywords frequently typed in by online users. The fastest-growing category of late has been associated with the search word *mobile*—with revenue generated from such ads totaling $1.6 billion in 2011 alone (Associated Press, April 19, 2010)

The massive revenue generated online coupled with citizen dependence on the Internet suggests that if our digital infrastructure became unavailable or was compromised by malicious actors or hackers, society might grind to a halt. All of these services would become inoperable, which is especially frightening when taking into account that critical infrastructures such as public transportation, health care, and public safety are operated, in part, by the Internet. But before going too far down this dark path, let's continue to examine the growth of the Internet in recent years in developing nations.

A Closer Look at the Adoption of the Internet in Developing Nations

The Internet has clearly had a tremendous economic and political impact on developing nations, particularly China, India, Russia, and Pakistan. Compared with the development of the Internet in developed nations—where companies like Yahoo

Exterior view of a new Apple retail store at Mianyang, China in June 2012. Internet and mobile device usage in China is exploding, and multinational companies like Apple are teaming with popular homespun efforts like search engine company Baidu to maximize market share. (Xiaofeng123/Dreamstime)

have been able to succeed because they got involved early on, had plenty of financing to hire top professionals in research and development (R&D), and had supportive governments—the "buy-in" in developing nations came later and with significantly less government encouragement. In China, for example, Baidu—a Chinese Internet search engine that emerged as a growing success story in 2005—was initially at odds with the Chinese government regarding censorship issues enforced by the government on search engines; today, however, Baidu implements China's rigorous censoring schema so that it can stay active and in business. Although relatively unknown outside of China until 2005, Baidu was founded by two Chinese gurus who had previously worked for U.S. technology firms. Baidu now dominates China's search engine market, with nearly 80 percent of the total market. In comparison, Google is said to have only a 17 percent market share in China (Tsuruoka 2012).

By 2012, China had an estimated 1 billion cell phone users and 550 million Internet surfers. In March 2012, a Chinese news website reported that the highly successful company Apple introduced Baidu as a search engine option for all Apple devices using its mobile operating system in China in early 2013. Considering the large market share in China for anything online and high tech, this decisionprovides a lucrative business opportunity for foreign companies such as Apple to expand their huge profits even more (Tsuruoka 2012).

Other developing nations, such as India, have gone after website companies on their soil that they consider to be violating their laws. In February 2012, Google India said that it removed web pages deemed to be offensive to Indian political and religious leaders to comply with a court case that has raised censorship fears in the world's largest democracy. This action followed government pressure against 22 Internet giants to remove from their websites a variety of photographs, videos, and text deemed to be "antireligious" or "antisocial"—such as pictures showing Congress party leader Sonia Gandhi and pigs running through Mecca, Islam's holiest city. A New Delhi court gave Facebook, Google, YouTube and Blogspot, as well as other websites, two weeks to present plans for policing their networks. The government also alleged that for India's 100 million Internet users, the U.S. Internet standards are just not acceptable. This case highlights the anxiety that India faces in balancing religious and political sentiments with its hope that the Internet will help spur the country's economy and increase the standard of living for 1.2 billion people (Associated Press, February 7, 2012).

Assessing the Present-Day Internet Economy on a Global Scale

In March 2012, the authors of the *Boston Consulting Group Report* attempted to estimate the present-day value and positive impact of the Internet on the global economy. While Internet growth in most advanced nations' economic sectors has been predicted to amount to "slow to no growth" now and in the years to come, the Internet economy represents a bright spot that needs to be capitalized on by developing nations, in particular. The Internet sector offers one of the world's few unfettered growth areas, according to this report. While policymakers often cite gross domestic product (GDP) growth rates of about 10 percent per year as a benchmark for developing markets, across the G20 nations the value of the Internet economy will almost double to $4.2 trillion over the next four years from $2.3 trillion in 2010–2011, representing a compounded annual growth rate from 2010 to 2016 of 10.8 percent. Although tracking the value of the Internet in developed and developing economies is, indeed, a complex and difficult task, the report produced by the Boston Consulting Group attempted to measure the Internet economy by incorporating key variables such as online consumption, investment, government spending, and net exports of all Internet-related goods and services (Grant 2012).

On this basis, the Internet is said to have contributed about $49 billion to Canada's GDP in 2010–2011, representing about 3 percent of the country's economic growth. However, the Internet's contribution is projected to grow to $76 billion by 2016, representing a compounded annual growth rate in Canada of 7.4 percent during the 2010–2016 time period. If the Internet were a currently measured sector in Canada, it would be viewed as being a greater contributor to the Canadian economy than agriculture, utilities, or hospitality (Grant 2012).

Other developed nations are projected to have slower Internet-sector growth by 2016. For example, the United States, according to the Boston Consulting Group report, is projected to have a compounded annual growth rate of 6.5 percent. In contrast, Italy is projected to have a compounded annual growth rate in the Internet sector of 11.5 percent. With a ramping up of efforts by governments and small and medium businesses to capitalize on Internet-based opportunities, affirm the report's authors, the projected compounded annual growth rates for the Internet sector are believed to be capable of climbing to very high levels in many of the developing nations. For example, the projections for growth in Internet-based revenues in Argentina, India, and Mexico through 2016 are 24.3 percent, 23 percent, and 15.6 percent, respectively. The growth rate for China is estimated to be 17.4 percent over this period (Grant 2012).

Given the massive amount of information that may be generated by the citizens of these nations, coupled with the number of devices connected to the Internet, chances are that someone connected to the Internet wants to "bend" it to meet his or her own selfish needs. In turn, we must attempt to understand who these individuals are and how they operate online.

Getting Unauthorized Network Access by Black Hat Hacking or Cracking

Hacker and Cracker Defined

Nowadays, when we hear about online users getting access to data or information on the Internet for which they do not have authorization, the label "hacker" immediately comes to mind. It is important to note that the ability to hack is a skill, involving the manipulation of technology in some way, shape, or form. Those who can successfully hack are called hackers, suggesting they have the capacity to hack. The term "hacker" has taken on many different meanings in the past 25 years, ranging from computer-savvy individuals professing to enjoy manipulating computer systems to stretch their abilities to improve systems to the malicious manipulators bent on breaking into computer systems through deceptive or illegal means with the intent to cause harm (Steele et al. 1983). Unfortunately, both definitions are correct, as the term "hacker" has been applied to both malicious and benevolent users alike. This is a consequence of the evolution of hacking in tandem with technological development over time.

Initially, hackers played a key role in the development of computer systems and the ARPAnet systems of the 1950s and 1960s. The term "hacker" was used to refer to the skilled programmers working in universities and government agencies who would speed up the then-slow processing times and create work-arounds to improve the overall user experience. In the 1970s and 1980s, home computing became popular and within the price range of the common person. Young people began to take an interest in these systems and play with computers to understand how they worked at fundamental levels. Some also began to use modems and the fledging Internet of the day to connect with other systems and people who were online. This led to the growth of malicious hacks and pranks that soon drew the attention of authorities and police. The criminalization of hacking during this period was in opposition to the perception of hacking from the 1950s. This divergence among hackers explains why the term "hacker" is fragmented and incorporates both criminal and noncriminal actors.

To differentiate between malicious and benevolent hackers, individuals within the hacker community began to use the term "cracker" to recognize individuals who engage in criminal or unethical acts using hacking techniques. This term is meant derisively, suggesting that a cracker is different from a hacker and should be treated accordingly. The use of the term "cracker" is not common outside of the hacker culture, but is extremely important to our understanding of hacking and the way in which it is viewed by those who use these skills.

Classifying Hackers by Intentions

As is obvious from the meaning and use of the terms "hacker" and "cracker," a common categorization scheme classifies hackers by their intentions. This framework can be further subdivided based on the way in which an individual applies his or her skill and knowledge to solve problems. Members of the hacker and security community often use terms derived from black-and-white western films of the 1940s and 1950s to label a hack and the hacker. Those who use their knowledge to protect and defend computer networks are often referred to as

"White Hat" hackers, in keeping with the color of the heroes' hats in films. White Hats tend to be the "do-gooders" who often work for security firms or in IT security departments in government or in industry; they are typically assigned the task of improving and securing computer services by identifying and fixing security flaws in the network.

Individuals who use hacking to engage in crime and malicious activity are sometimes referred to as "Black Hats" because of the association between the color black and villains. Generally speaking, Black Hats tend to be the "more mal-inclined online doers" who use their computer and social skills to cause problems for selected targets. Such actors may work on their own and identify targets based on their interests or knowledge, and their operations may even be incorporated by or paid through organized crime or nation states to harm a target.

Some individuals prefer to use the term "Gray Hats" to discuss those actors who may act within ethical or criminal guidelines depending on their outlook or attitude toward a specific target. This concept is a more recent development and may be used to capture the independent security experts and consultants who are often reformed Black Hats following imprisonment for hacking-related crimes (Bossler and Burruss 2011). Alternatively, they may be active hackers who choose to protect rather than harm a target, or vice versa, based on their shifting ethical beliefs.

In recent decades, media coverage of hacking has largely focused on the darker side of hacker activity because that kind of news sells. Clearly, there is growing interest by individuals in mainstream society to hear more about hackers in popular culture. In recent films hackers have gone from serving as comedic relief or supporting characters in action films to main characters and even superheroes of sorts. For instance, the protagonist of the *Matrix* trilogy, Neo, is a hacker of unparalleled skill. Similarly, Lisbeth Salander, the protagonist in the hugely successful Millennium book and 2011 film *The Girl with the Dragon Tattoo*, utilized her skills for various purposes.

As technology plays an increasingly prominent and vital role in daily life, the fascination with hackers has grown on a number of fronts, especially with the recognition that massive damage can be caused by computer and network intrusion. The increasing incorporation of Wi-Fi and connectivity in all sorts of items, ranging from passports to medical devices, has also created substantive concerns for security researchers and the general public. For example, in October 2011, Medtronic Inc. asked software-security experts in the United States to investigate the safety of its manufactured insulin pumps, as a new claim had appeared suggesting that at least one of the company's devices could be hacked to dose targeted diabetes patients with potentially lethal amounts of insulin. While to date there are no known incidents of such cyberattacks on medical devices, Medtronic publicly stated that it was prepared to do everything it could at this point to address the alleged security flaws (Finkle 2011).

Besides individuals and industry leaders, governments are growing increasingly apprehensive about the perils of mal-inclined hacking to citizens' safety and privacy. In December 2011, U.S. intelligence agencies claimed that Chinese groups sponsored by the Chinese military were responsible for rampant "cyberspying" in the United States in an attempt to obtain top-level secrets of the U.S. government. This discovery prompted some key U.S. government officials to meet with their Chinese counterparts for the purpose of warning China about the diplomatic consequences of "economic spying" using sophisticated hacking techniques. It is estimated that hundreds, if not thousands, of highly tech-savvy people are working together in distributed tribes to carry out China's apparent cyberspying mission against the U.S. government (Gorman 2011). In fact, there is evidence of an international network of compromised systems in governments, embassies, and corporate settings in 103 countries that are linked back to Chinese computer systems (Information Warfare Monitor 2009; Markoff 2009). This network, referred to as GhostNet, appears to be controlled through servers located in China and is geared toward stealing sensitive information and surreptitiously collecting data on various targets (Information Warfare Monitor 2009; Markoff 2009).

But China is not alone in hiring hackers and hacker groups to do economic spying or to cause harm. The Philippines has been cited as enlisting tech-savvy employees to break CAPTHAS, the distorted text verifying whether a user is a human (Tossell 2012). Similarly, Russia has been involved in various attacks against neighboring nation-states and large Western nations. For instance, a conflict developed between Russian and Estonian factions in April 2006 when the Estonian government removed a Russian war monument from a memorial garden (Brenner 2008; Jaffe 2006; Landler and Markoff 2007). Physical protests and violence erupted shortly after this act, followed promptly by a range of cyberattacks against government and private resources in both nations by computer hackers and citizens alike (Brenner 2008; Jaffe 2006). The substantive skills and resources leveraged by Russian actors, however, led to a shutdown of critical components of Estonia's financial and government networks (Brenner 2008; Landler and Markoff 2078). Even the United States utilized the malicious software program Stuxnet to negatively impact the development of the Iranian nuclear program. This tool specifically targeted systems within the Natanz nuclear facility to disrupt and diminish the capacity of the plant to enrich nuclear materials (Sanger 2012). Thus, cyberspace has become a hotbed of hacker activity driven by both nation-state and non-nation-state actors.

Classifying Hackers by Skill

One of the most common ways hackers are identified by those in and out of the community is by their skill and ability to use technology, as these traits are essential to the hacker subculture. For example, researchers Holt and Kilger (2008) suggest that skilled hackers who produce new materials (new scripts, tools, and products—beneficial or otherwise) should be referred to as "makecrafters," while those who are the consumers of these tools (i.e., hackers using their knowledge to repair systems or to complete a task with known tools) should be referred to as "techcrafters." "Craft" is used as a referent to the somewhat magical way that hackers "own," or control, technology.

Individuals who have an interest in hacking but who generally have little knowledge of either the culture or computer technology are commonly called "noobs" or, possibly, "n00bs," referencing their new status within the culture (Holt 2007, 2010). Their lack of skill hinders their overall capacity to hack, a reality that frequently leads them to be disparaged by more talented others. In much the same way, those who claim to be hackers but have few skills are commonly known as "script kiddies," in reference to their frequent downloading of tools from websites and hacker forums to cause damage to networks or websites (Holt 2010; Jordan and Taylor 1998; Taylor 1999). Their attacks frequently cause harm because the attacker does not understand how the tool works and may either use it incorrectly or configure it incorrectly. As a result, script kiddies often do not really understand which exploits have transpired; they simply know that they have caused harm.

In contrast, the highly sophisticated or "elite" hackers are recognized within the hacking community as the gifted segment, noted for their exceptional hacking talents and sophisticated exploits (Holt 2010; Jordan and Taylor 1998; Taylor 1999). An elite hacker must be highly skilled to experiment with command structures and explore the many files available to understand and effectively "use" the system (Schell and Dodge, with Moutsatsos 2002). In addition, they may be able to create new tools that have not been seen before or identify new vulnerabilities in software and hardware that can be manipulated (Holt 2010). The elite hackers, at the pinnacle of the community, often receive great respect from their peers because of their sophisticated hacking skills (Holt 2007). Thus, those who are considered to be "elite" or "1337" ("leetspeak" in the hacker argot, which utilizes numbers in place of letters) are frequently admired by less skilled others; the elite hackers may serve as repositories of tools and key resources for the script kiddies.

Classifying Hackers as Insiders or Outsiders

It is also important to consider the origin of an attack in the classification of an actor. Hackers employed by industry or a government agency who cause network damage are typically referred to as "insider hackers," whereas hackers not employed by industry or government agencies who cause such damage are referred to as "outsider hackers." Although this may seem like a small point, it is important to recognize that many in the general public believe intrusion attempts come largely from hackers outside of computer networks (Furnell 2002). While this is increasingly true in light of increasing Internet connectivity, research involving case studies of insider attacks suggests that hackers may operate within secure environments as trusted system administrators or security professionals (Cappelli et al. 2006; Dhillon and Moore 2001; Shaw, Post, and Ruby 1999).

One of the most talked-about insider hacker incidents in the media took place in 1996 at Omega Engineering in the United States. Timothy Lloyd, an employee at that company, planted a logic bomb in the firm's network when he discovered that he was being fired. This act of sabotage is said to have cost the company $12 million in damages to the network, forced the layoff of 80 employees, and cost the electronics firm its leading place in this very competitive and rapidly changing market (Schell and Dodge, with Moutsatsos 2002).

The actions employees take to misuse or misappropriate resources may go unnoticed, particularly by individuals with root administrative privileges (Cappelli, Moore, and Shimeall, 2006; Dhillon and Moore 2001). Insiders may surreptitiously steal information or place backdoors in programs that can be accessed to cause damage in case they are fired or mistreated (Cappelli et al. 2006; Shaw, Post, and Ruby 1999). The attacks individuals engage in may also be relatively simple in nature and exploit known flaws in internal system, though some sophisticated intrusions have been documented (Cappelli et al. 2006).

The behavior of insider attackers may be driven, in part, by their ethical perspectives and attitudes. Specifically, insiders tend to be loners who are dependent or addicted to computers and online communications (Shaw, Post, and Ruby 1999). They may also have flexible ethical outlooks, wherein they view any piece of data or file that has not been properly secured as a potential target for attack (Shaw, Post, and Ruby 1999). Finally, insiders may operate along a continuum of technical sophistication, as insider attacks have been both simple and complex depending on the types of services that have been exploited across industries (Cappelli et al. 2006).

A Cautionary Note on Hacker Classification Schemes and Overgeneralizing about Hackers

Hackers are not a homogeneous group in terms of intentions or skill sets. Accepting this reality, scholars have consistently argued over the past decade that "hacking" as an online activity can be viewed as "the unauthorized access and use or manipulation of other people's computer systems," and that hackers, in general, are part of a hacker subculture, regardless of the categorization scheme used (Bossler and Burruss 2011; Holt 2007; Holt and Kilger 2008; Jordan and Taylor 1998). Holt and Kilger (2008, p. 68) maintain that in this distinct hacking subculture known widely as the Computer Underground (CU), three norms persistently drive hacker behavior regardless of their ethical or malicious intent:

- The presence of technology, with an intimate connection to technology facilitating the ability to hack
- Secrecy, where there is a need to avoid unwanted attention from government and law enforcement agencies, coupled with a desire to brag and share accumulated knowledge
- Mastery, or the continual learning of new skills and the mastering of one's social and physical environment

These norms justify behavior and provide a way for individuals to gage their skill relative to others within the subculture. Whether an actor is a Black Hat or a White Hat, a n00b or an elite, he or she will espouse the importance of understanding technology and mastering its use in myriad ways. At the same time, hackers also stress the value of "social engineering" to gather information (Mitnick and Simon 2002; Schell and Dodge, with Moutsatsos 2002). Social engineering involves the use of nontechnical skills to manipulate and take advantage of naïve or inadequately trained employees in IT security matters. In other words, some hacking exploits are committed without much technical sophistication but rather capitalize on the "weakest link" in the system (Schell and Dodge, and Moutsatsos 2002).

Social engineering, by definition, describes the deceptive process whereby crackers "engineer" a social situation to allow them to obtain access to an otherwise closed network (Mitnick and Simon 2002). Typically, the objective of this exercise is to get others—the weakest links—to reveal information that can be used, say, to copy, change, or steal data on a network. For example, a cracker could talk a computer help desk employee into resetting a password on a stolen account. Once a password is obtained, access to the system by the cracker could be temporary or permanent, depending on the practices and policies in the company or institution in question. Similarly, a social engineering strategy could be used to gather information on the types of systems used within an organization or the names of important corporate employees such as presidents or vice presidents and their assistants.

One of the earliest known female social engineers in the CU went by the moniker Susan Thunder. According to the circulating myth, Susan Thunder was mistreated as a child and became a prostitute in her teens. In her leisure time in the 1970s, she hung out with various rock bands—where, it is said, she discovered how easy it was to get backstage passes for concerts just by calling the appropriate people and pretending to be, say, a secretary at a record company. Obviously, these acts are a form of social engineering. Susan Thunder, it is rumored, eventually applied her social engineering prowess to phone phreaking (a form of hacking), intent on getting her long-distance telephone calls for free with the help of the infamous brothers Kevin and Ron Mitnick, a hacker team active in the same period. Then and now, Susan Thunder explodes the popular myth that only males are actively involved in the CU.

Eventually the team of three cracked into U.S. Leasing's systems, deleted all of the information off one computer, filled the computer with messages like "F___ YOU F___ YOU F___ YOU," and programmed the printers to continually spit out similar insults. Among the profanities were planted the names of Kevin and Ron. This incident led to the first conviction of Kevin Mitnick (whose online moniker was Condor). Still very active in the CU, Gray Hat Kevin is a cracker who was jailed multiple times, went on the lam for a while, eventually wrote a number of books on hacking and social engineering (Schell and Dodge, with Moutsatsos 2002, 28–29), and is now a system security consultant hired by the Federal Bureau of Investigation (FBI) to solve difficult network intrusion cases (Schell 2007).

Various Types of Hacker Exploits Causing Harm and the Harm Inflicted

Black Hat hacking, or cracking, is commonly viewed as a crime committed against a computer or a network by means of a computer. The use of hacks can be classified as various forms of cybercrime based on the target of the attack and the outcome it produces for the victim in terms of property damage, economic loss, or personal harm. In fact, hacking can be organized into three of the four categories of cybercrime identified by Wall (2001): cybertrespass, deception/theft, and violence. Trespass is a common component of hacking, as the actors must breach existing boundaries of ownership, such as a network or the hard drive. Its use in theft and violence will, however, be discussed later.

If found guilty of cracking exploits causing physical or personal harm, convicted perpetrators are commonly held accountable for the damage caused, with compensation paid to victims being a likely outcome. A high-profile case that came to light in 2011 and made front-page headlines worldwide involved *News of the World*, part of the newspaper division of Rupert Murdoch's British media empire, News Corporation. The headlines claimed that key individuals employed by this newspaper engaged in widespread and illegal phone hacking in Britain.

In January 2012, six months after closing *News of the World* in a failed attempt to quiet public outrage over the excessive harm caused by the firm's hacking of the phone accounts of celebrities and newsworthy others, Murdoch, as chairman and CEO of News Corporation, and the News Group Newspapers paid out more than $1 million in compensation, plus costs, to 17 of the hacking victims—including actor Jude Law and his ex-wife Sadie Frost; the former deputy prime minister of the United Kingdom, John Prescott; and the son of Britain's most notorious serial killer, Harold Shipman. Nineteen other victims settled separately, including Shaun Russell (whose wife and daughter were killed in 1996); James Hewitt, the former cavalry officer and friend of Princess Diana; and Sara Payne (mother of murdered child Sarah Payne). Beyond the financial hit taken, the CEO and News Group Newspapers must still answer to whether the board of the newspaper division directed staff to destroy evidence of their wrongdoings (Houpt 2012).

In addition, on March 13, 2012, former News International (the British arm of Murdoch's global empire) executive Rebekah Brooks and her racehorse trainer husband Charlie were arrested in dawn raids that also nabbed four other suspects in the phone hacking scandal. The U.K. police said that the six suspects were arrested on suspicion of conspiracy to pervert the course of justice. Such a charge seems to indicate that the investigators are focusing on a possible cover-up of the degree of phone hacking that occurred rather than on the illegal hacking act. According to police, the suspects in the case ranged in age from 38 to 49. Police also said that 23 people have been arrested as part of "Operation Weeting"—as the investigation into phone hacking is labeled—with others facing charges as part of a related inquiry into corrupt relations between police and the press. The scandal actually began in 2005 when news came to light that tabloid reporters had cracked the voice mail systems of aides to the Britain's royal family, searching for inside information that would make for good stories. The scandal mushroomed in 2011 with the revelation that extensive phone hacking had occurred at Murdoch's *News of the World* tabloid (Associated Press, March 14, 2012).

Hacking Exploits in the Use of Deception and Theft of Property or Data

Hacker exploits that target computer systems or data can be viewed as acts of trespass, deception, or theft that proceed through a variety of techniques (Schell and Martin 2004):

- Flooding: a form of cyberspace vandalism resulting in denial of service (DoS) to authorized users of a website or system.
- Virus and worm production and release: a form of cyberspace vandalism causing corruption, and possibly erasing, of data.
- Spoofing: the cyberspace appropriation of an authentic user's identity by nonauthentic users, causing fraud or attempted fraud in some cases and critical infrastructure breakdowns in other cases.
- Phreaking: a form of cyberspace theft or fraud in which technology is used to make free long-distance telephone calls.
- Infringement of intellectual property rights (IPR) and copyright: a form of cyberspace theft involving the copying of a target's information or software without consent.
- Phishing: a form of fraud where the offender sends prospective victims an email from a financial institution or service

indicating that users will be cut off from services if they do not respond in a timely fashion. The information provided is then stolen and used by the offender.

Most of us with a PC have received suspicious emails that were part of an online scam aimed at tricking us into disclosing personal information or our online passwords so that others could take advantage of us. These messages may appear to come from Nigeria or northern Africa, and are commonly referred to as "419 scams," in reference to the legal code for fraud in Nigeria (Holt and Graves 2010; King and Thomas 2009). Also, the PCs of many computer users have been infected with spyware designed to capture and unwittingly report their online activities to others. Each year, hundreds of thousands of users' machines are infected by malware, or malicious software (such as a virus or Trojan horse), designed to steal information and render computers to be under the control of the cyberinvader (Comrie 2011; Symantec 2012).

Generally speaking, all of the techniques causing economic harm or loss are undesirable, but malware is among the most destructive of the various forms. This reality arises because the computer user or owner is often unaware that his or her machine has been compromised, primarily because he or she does not recognize any noticeable signs of the machine's being infected (Schell and Martin 2006; Sockel and Falk 2009).

For example, botnets, or "bots," have become a substantial problem, whereby malicious code allows an infected computer to be remote controlled by software programs acting as an agent for a third party (Bacher et al. 2005; Choo 2007; Ianelli and Hackworth 2005). Botnets are dangerous not only because they can reach into thousands or millions of infected computers worldwide, but also because they can be surreptitiously controlled by anyone around the world. Furthermore, the botnet controller has the ability to use the infected systems as an attack platform to launch distributed DoS attacks—in which a virtual army of commandeered computers bombards a website with requests until the website collapses (Bacher et al. 2005; Choo 2007). In addition, bots have been used for the distribution of spam and phishing emails around the world (Choo 2007).

Most disturbingly, the functionality afforded by botnet infrastructures can be leveraged against high-value government and private targets (Schell and Martin 2006; Sockel and Falk 2009). For example, since a spree of distributed DoS attacks against Estonian financial and academic websites began in 2007 (Kirk 2007), large businesses and government agencies around the globe have become increasingly concerned about the dangers of hack attacks and "botnets" on vulnerable networks.

What kind of hackers would want to create property-damaging bots and viruses? One individual making media headlines in 2007 in this regard was a New Zealand teen named Owen Walker, who was accused of creating a botnet gang discovered by police under Operation Bot Roast. According to Walker's mother, her son suffered from a mild form of autism known as Asperger syndrome; affected individuals often feel socially isolated from their peers but have high intelligence in specific fields such as mathematics or science. In media reports, Walker's mother said that he was often teased by his peers during his formative years because of odd behaviors associated with the syndrome. As a result, Walker dropped out of high school in grade 9; during this period, he apparently became involved in an international hacking group known as "the A-Team" (Farrell 2007).

In a hearing held in July 2008, the justice hearing the case discharged Walker without conviction on some of the most sophisticated botnet cybercrimes ever seen in New Zealand, even though the young man pleaded guilty to six charges, including accessing a computer for dishonest purposes, damaging or interfering with a computer system, possessing software for committing a crime, and accessing a computer without authorization. In his defense, Walker said that he was not motivated by maliciousness but by his intense interest in computers and his need to stretch their capabilities. As part of a ring of

21 hackers, Walker's exploits apparently cost the local economy about $20.4 million. Also, the national manager of New Zealand's police e-crime laboratory was quoted in the media as admitting that Walker had some unique abilities and that he appeared to be at the "elite" level of hacking. In the end, the judge ordered Walker to pay $11,000 in costs and damages and to assist the local police in combating online criminal activities (Gleeson 2008).

Male hackers with special talents like Walker's are not the only people making media headlines over hacking acts causing damage to property. A 19-year-old female hacker from Belgium with the online moniker Gigabyte (real-life name: Kimberley Vanvaeck) got considerable attention in 2004. This woman created the Coconut-A, Sahay-A, and Sharp-A computer viruses while studying for an undergraduate degree in applied computer science. For these exploits, Vanvaeck was arrested and charged by police with computer data sabotage, a charge that could have landed her behind prison bars for three years and drawn a fine as high as 100,000 euros.

In launching the Sahay-A worm, Gigabyte claimed to be part of the "Metaphase VX Team." When interviewed by the media, she portrayed herself as an antagonized female operating in a very male-dominated, elite virus-writing subculture (*Sophos* 2004). It seems that Gigabyte had a reputation for waging a protracted virtual war against an antivirus expert known as Graham Cluley. Oddly enough, Vanvaeck's viruses could all be identified by her antipathy toward Cluley, a senior technology consultant at the Sophos Company. In the end, Gigabyte was released by the legal system with a "slap on the wrist" and a promise to not cause trouble again.

Hacking Exploits Used in Cyberviolence

Some hacker exploits are used to engage in acts of cyberviolence targeting individuals, governments, or large populations. One of the most common forms of cyberviolence is cyberstalking, an undesirable online act whereby the Internet is used as a tool to control, harass, or terrorize a victim to the point where he or she fears harm or death, either to himself or herself or to someone close to the targeted victim (Schell and Martin 2004).

In recent years, police have been trying to educate children and adults about the perils of going online without taking the proper precautions. Nevertheless, even after taking the right measures to stay safe online, some users become the victims of unwanted behaviors such as cyberstalking and cyberpornography. Perpetrators of these acts can wreak their havoc through live chat or IRC rooms, message boards, newsgroups, and email. It is estimated that in Canada alone, at least 80,000 people are cyberstalked annually.

In 1999, the first successful prosecution under California's cyberstalking law took place. Prosecutors obtained a guilty plea from a 50-year-old ex-security guard who used the Internet to encourage the sexual assault of a 28-year-old woman who rejected his romantic advances. In fact, the charges against him included one count of cyberstalking and three counts of soliciting sexual assault. The perpetrator terrorized his target by pretending to be her in various IRC channels and online bulletin board systems, where he divulged her telephone number and address. He posted messages online indicating that she fantasized about being sexually assaulted (Grafx-Specs Design and Hosting 1999).

Considering that technology continues to evolve, making online communications with others easier year by year, cyberstalkers and cyberpornographers intent on causing harm to others have an even wider arsenal of weapons at their disposal now as compared to 2000. What is more, citizens around the world have become earlier adopters of mobile devices such as smart phones over the past decade. Cybercriminals understand this shift in adoption patterns related to evolving connectivity and are keen to use these devices to commit their acts of invasion and to gain control over targets.

Although experts have been keeping tabs on the growing numbers of citizens owning PCs in recent decades, in 2012 smart phone shipments actually surpassed those of PCs—about 488 million units in total, worldwide. In recent years, crackers have been focusing on the Android technology, in part because it is so popular in mobile phones, and in part because users can download applications (apps) from anywhere. While iPhones and iPads are less vulnerable to hack attacks than devices made by other mobile device companies (primarily because the Apple corporation is committed to installing all apps through its App Store, where its staff members screen every app by hand), "jail-broken" or altered iPhones that have had their Apple-imposed restrictions removed by adventurous owners are especially vulnerable to being hacked (Tossell 2012). Thus a present-day reality is that rogue apps could be used by a stalker to track his or her targeted victim across both virtual and on-land environments.

Beyond individual victims, hacking can be used in a larger context to engage in violent actions against nation-states or large populations (Brenner 2008; Denning 2011; Wall 2001). For instance, some hackers utilize their skills in support of activist agendas to promote their beliefs through attacks against various targets. This activity, commonly called "hacktivism" (Jordan and Taylor 2004), can have substantive consequences both online and offline, as was evident in a recent series of attacks by the group Anonymous. This collective of hackers shut down the Vatican's website, teased cabinet ministers around the world for proposed legislation deemed to be undesirable by the hacker group (including Canada's Public Safety Minister Vic Toews), released and displayed the content of hacked emails on the Internet for viewers around the world to see, and embedded themselves into national online debates (Correll 2010; Denning 2011).

Anonymous is not a centralized organization, but rather a nebulous collection of cells and splinter groups coordinating efforts in online chat rooms. Furthermore, beyond a foundational commitment to anonymity and the free flow of information, Anonymous does not seem to have a consistent philosophy or political program. The group apparently traces its origins to a message board called 4chan. Put simply, Anonymous seems to endorse a culture of creative disturbance in the pursuit of chaos, justice, retribution, and having laughs or "lulz" (Correll 2010).

On March 7, 2012, a three-pronged authority pool in Europe, North America, and South America arrested 25 suspected members of a hacking group affiliated with Anonymous called "LulzSec" or "Lulz Security." The international sweep struck a blow to Anonymous and other hacker groups, because it not only turned one of its key members into an informant but also resulted in the arrest of fellow "trusted" hackers, in a rare and significant hacking-related prosecution. Hector Xavier Monsegur, who went by the moniker "Sabu" and was a gifted person very well known in the underground hacker community, pleaded guilty to various hacking-related offenses in the summer of 2011. Afterward, he helped the FBI and police in these geographic locations to track down and arrest fellow LulzSec hackers. These arrests appeared to be a counterattack against Anonymous after the FBI and Scotland Yard were embarrassed in February 2012; at that time, LulzSec hackers apparently recorded a private conference call between members of these two law enforcement agencies and then released the contents of the call on the Internet (Keller 2012; Shane 2012).

Following these hacker arrests, members of Anonymous went online to downplay their significance, with one of the hacker affiliates stating, "#Anonymous IS an idea, not a group. There is no leader, there is no head. It will survive, before, during and after this time" (El Akkad 2012). It is important to note that a key issue with hacker groups is one of trust—or rather a lack of trust among hacker colleagues. This case serves as a prime example of a so-called trusted member of a hacker group "ratting out" his "trusted" colleagues to the authorities.

Given that the acts of Anonymous are perceived by the authorities to be relatively extreme in nature, some government authorities have begun to question whether this hacker group actually constitutes a terrorist group. Following the September 11, 2001, attacks on the World Trade Center and the Pentagon, the U.S. government and other governments globally began pondering how extremist groups could utilize the Internet to cause harm to computer networks controlling nations' critical infrastructures.

This realization, in fact, led to the U.S. government's renewed focus on combating those potentially involved in such acts, as evidenced by the passage of the controversial United and Strengthening America by Providing Appropriate Tools Required to Intercept and Obstruct Terrorism Act of 2001 (USA PATRIOT Act) six weeks after the 9/11 attacks and the Cyber Security Enhancement Act of 2002. Also in 2002, the Cyber Security Research and Development Act (CSRDA) was passed, promoting research and development in the relatively unexplored and underfunded area of cybersecurity. Furthermore, in 2003, several other U.S. bills were introduced addressing cyberterrorism issues (Raghavan 2003).

The use of the Internet by terrorist groups or extremist networks has led authorities to introduce the term "cyberterror" to refer to the premeditated, methodological, ideologically motivated dissemination of information intended to cause social, financial, physical, or psychological harm to noncombatant targets and audiences for the purpose of effecting ideological, political, or social change. This term also encompasses the utilization of digital communication or information to facilitate such actions directly or indirectly (Britz 2010).

Unfortunately, today cyberterrorism remains an option for any individual, group, or nation state wanting to use the Internet to cause harm to targeted others with the aid of skilled hackers who are capable of accomplishing such destructive feats. Put simply, while bombing physical targets in subways may attract unwanted attention and raise the risk of failure, cyberterrorist attacks can be orchestrated more accurately and easily by individuals or nation states having the necessary skills.

Also, because of their often remote locations, such perpetrators are less detectable.

Nowadays, cyberterrorism is a pressing concern for developed nations such as the United States and Canada, because computers lie at the very heart of the critical infrastructure and perform critical functions, ranging from storing vital information to controlling power delivery, communications, aviation, and financial services (Raghavan 2003). While only time will tell whether legislation passed in the United States and elsewhere to combat cyberterrorism will have the desired effects, there is no denying that governments worldwide are serious about tackling the emerging cyberterrorism problem.

In recent years, hackers have been increasingly incorporated into acts of war that directly impact relationships between nation-states (Brenner 2008; Denning 2011). When Indian border guards tortured a Bangladeshi cowherd who had crossed territorial lines in December 2011, for example, the government issued an official protest to the incident. In addition, video footage of this incident, apparently taken by one of the guards, went "viral" through the Internet. When the Dhaka government continued to play down the incident, patriotic young citizens took matters into their own hands. They launched what they labeled a "cyberwar" aimed at official and commercial websites in India. The hackers claimed to have hit more than 30,000 websites in 10 days, defacing them with Bangladeshi flags, images of civilians killed or tortured by Indian border forces, and lists of demands for the Indian government. As the hackers bragged about more hits to websites, Indian hackers began to retaliate—and at this point, the cyberwar became the focus of headlines in the Bengali media. The media generally treated the cyberwar as a bold civilian response to the lack of appropriate government action, with the inaction likely motivated by Bangladesh's fear of its more powerful neighbor India. Web experts have stated that the hacking war actually began three or four years ago, with occasional flare-ups caused by tech-savvy citizens in India, Bangladesh, and Pakistan (Nolan 2012).

The Key Elements of Criminal Liability, Conventional Crimes, and Hacking

Conventional Crimes and the Four Key Elements of Criminal Liability

In the various hacking cases cited earlier, when harm was caused, a cybercrime had technically occurred. When defining conventional crimes, Anglo-American law bases criminal liability on the coincidence of four key elements, as outlined by Susan Brenner (2001):

- A culpable mental state (*mens rea*).
- A criminal action or a failure to act when one is under a duty to do so (*actus reus*).
- The existence of certain necessary conditions or "attendant circumstances." With some crimes, it must be proved that certain events occurred, or certain facts are true, for an individual to be found guilty of a crime.
- A prohibited result, or harm.

In a conventional crime such as bigamy (i.e., multiple marriages), all four of these elements must combine to warrant the imposition of liability. To start, an individual must enter into a marriage knowing either that he or she is already married or that the person whom he or she is marrying is already married. The prohibited act is the redundant marriage (*actus reus*). The culpable mental state (*mens rea*) is the perpetrator's knowledge that he or she is entering into a redundant marriage. The attendant circumstance is the existence of a previous marriage still in force. Finally, the prohibited result, or harm to persons, is the threat that bigamous marriages pose to the stability of family life. Put simply, crimes involve conduct unacceptable by society's standards. Thus society, through its laws, imposes criminal liability (Schell and Martin 2004).

Hacking and the Four Key Elements of Criminal Liability

The following is an illustration of these four elements converging in the instance of cybertrespass involving hacking (Wall

2001). To begin, a hacker enters a computer or computer system and unlawfully takes, or exercises unlawful control over, the property—the information or the software belonging to someone else (*actus reus*). He or she enters the network with the purpose of committing an offense once inside and acts with the intention of depriving the lawful owner of the software or the information (*mens rea*). By society's standards, the hacker has no legal right to enter the computer or network in question, or to take control over what is contained therein (attendant circumstances). The hacker is, therefore, liable for his or her acts. The hacker unlawfully entered the computer network (i.e., criminal trespass) to commit an offense (i.e., theft) once inside, and as a result, the target is deprived of his or her software or information (i.e., harm is done).

Hacker Predispositions: What the Literature Tells Us

Hackers: Known Traits of Insiders

Given the concerns worldwide about increasingly sophisticated cyberexploits, what does the literature tell us about some known traits of hackers? First, we will consider the current knowledge around insider attackers, given that they account for a small but substantive proportion of the network attacker community. Then, we will consider what is known about outsider hackers.

One of the most widely recognized studies in the insider hacker area was completed by the research team of clinical psychologist Eric Shaw, psychiatrist Jerrold Post, and researcher Kevin Ruby. This team constructed behavioral profiles of insider hackers based on 100 cases that occurred from 1997 to 1999. After analyzing their study findings, Shaw, Post, and Ruby (1999) concluded that insider hackers had the following eight traits in common:

1. They are introverted, being more comfortable in their own mental world than they are in the more emotional and unpredictable mainstream world with its considerable social interaction, given that they seem to have fewer

well-developed social skills as compared to their extraverted counterparts in mainstream society.

2. They have a history of significant family problems in their early childhood, leaving them with negative feelings toward authority figures, a trait that seems to follow them into adulthood.

3. They have an online computer dependency that significantly interferes with or replaces direct social and professional interactions in their adulthood.

4. They seem to have an ethical "flexibility" that helps them to justify their exploits—a trait less typically found in the ethically driven more conventional types who, when similarly provoked, do not commit such acts.

5. They appear to have a stronger loyalty to their computer colleagues than to their employers.

6. They tend to have a sense of entitlement, seeing themselves as "special" and, therefore, owed the recognition, privilege, or exception to the normative rules governing the majority of their peers in the mainstream.

7. They tend to have a lack of empathy, with an inclination to disregard or minimize the impact of their adverse actions on others and organizations.

8. They are less likely to seek help from corporate wellness programs if stressed by home and work environment issues.

Hackers: Known Traits of Outsider/External Attackers

With a fundamental appreciation for the general predispositions of internal attackers, it is now possible to consider what is known about outsiders, or those within the hacker culture who target resources that they do not have the ability to access through legitimate channels. The profile of outsider hackers has changed over time with increased access to technology and the Internet by citizens around the world.

One of the fundamental works that helps to orient our understanding of the hacker community comes from "The

Hacker Manifesto: The Conscience of a Hacker," penned by The Mentor in 1986 (Blankenship 1986). This manifesto was popular among hackers when it was first distributed online, at a time when hacking and computer technology were just coming to the forefront. The following excerpt particularly captures the angst and rage evident among young hackers then and now:

> You bet your ass we're all alike . . . we've been spoon-fed baby food at school when we hungered for steak . . . the bits of meat that you did let slip through were pre-chewed and tasteless. We've been dominated by sadists, or ignored by the apathetic. The few that had something to teach us found us willing pupils, but those few are like drops of water in the desert. This is our world now . . . the world of the electron and the switch, the beauty of the baud. We make use of a service already existing without paying for what could be dirt-cheap if it wasn't run by profiteering gluttons, and you call us criminals. We seek after knowledge . . . and you call us criminals. We exist without skin color, without nationality, without religious bias . . . and you call us criminals. You build atomic bombs, you wage wars, you murder, cheat, and lie to us and try to make us believe it's for our own good, yet we're the criminals. Yes, I am a criminal. My crime is that of curiosity. My crime is that of judging people by what they say and think, not what they look like. My crime is that of outsmarting you, something you will never forgive me for. I am a hacker, and this is my manifesto. You may stop this individual, but you can't stop us all. After all, we're all alike.

As a composite, the preceding quotes paint a rather dark picture of the thinking and behaving patterns of those inhabiting the computer underground. Similarly, much of the research on the hacker community prior to 2000 suggests that hackers younger than the age of 30 exhibit short-term stress problems such as anxiety, anger, and depression, caused by a number of factors, including the following (Blake 1994; Caldwell 1990, 1993; Shaw, Post, and Ruby 1999):

- Childhood-inducing psychological pain rooted in peer teasing and harassment (not unlike the case of hacker Walker)
- Introverted thinking and behaving tendencies in an effort to maintain a strong inward cognitive focus
- Anger about the belief that parents and others in mainstream society misunderstand or denounce an inquisitive and exploratory nature (as is obvious in the Hacker Manifesto)
- Educational environments doing little to sate their high-cognitive and creative potential, resulting in high degrees of boredom and joy-ride-seeking (again, as is present in the Hacker Manifesto)
- A fear of being caught, charged, and convicted of hacking-related exploits (as manifested in the recent charges facing Anonymous-affiliated hackers)

More recent research has attempted to expand beyond these studies to help us to better understand the composition of the larger hacker community population. Research suggests, for example, that hackers are predominantly males younger than the age of 30, though there are older hackers working in the security community (Bachmann 2010; Jordan and Taylor 1998; Schell and Dodge 2002).

Furthermore, younger (rather than older) people may be attracted to hacking, because they have greater access and exposure to technology and have more time to spend exploring technology at deep levels. Older hackers, however, are more likely to be gainfully employed by working primarily in the computer security industry (Bachmann 2010; Schell and Dodge 2002).

Hackers also have a mix of both formal education and knowledge acquired on their own through reading and experiential learning (Bachmann 2010; Holt 2007; Holt et al. 2009). Limited evidence suggests that a proportion of skilled actors may have at least a community college education, while a small number have degrees from four-year institutions (Bachmann 2010; Holt, Soles, and Leslie 2008; Holt et al. 2009; Schell and Dodge, with Moutsatsos, 2002).

Hackers also appear to be predominantly male, though the true gender composition of the subculture is unknown (Jordan and Taylor 1998; Schell and Dodge, with Moutsatsos 2002; Taylor 1999). For instance, Schell and associates (2002) found that approximately 9 percent of their sample of hacker conference attendees were females. There is no way of knowing how many women actually engage in hacking, as they shield their identities from others online and are especially resistant to being interviewed or participating in research studies (Holt 2007). Thus it is difficult to identify the overall gender composition of the hacker community at any given point in time.

Hackers also tend to have substantive social relationships with others online and, to a lesser extent, in the real world (Bachmann 2010; Holt 2009; Holt and Kilger 2008; Meyer 1989; Schell and Dodge, with Moutsatsos 2002). These relationships are imperative in providing a source of imitation and knowledge of computer skills. These networks may form in schools or through casual associations in local technology-centered clubs like 2600 or the DefCon or DC hacker groups (Holt 2009).

Hackers also generally appear to have relatively positive psychological and emotional traits, contrary to the myths that persist in the general public. For instance, Schell and her colleagues (2002) found that hackers generally reported minimal stress levels and were generally well adjusted emotionally. In addition, recent research suggests that hackers have slightly higher levels of self-control than other offender groups and control populations (Bossler and Burruss 2010; Holt and Kilger 2008). Hackers are also able to multitask quite well due to their cognitive capabilities and overall creativity (Schell and Dodge, with Moutsatsos 2002). In fact, recent evidence suggests that hackers are in the intermediate range of the autism spectrum, which is not different from others practicing in the fields of computer science and mathematics (Schell and Melnychuk 2011). Thus, as a group, hackers appear able to adapt to the social anxieties that they may experience in certain life situations.

Conclusion

This chapter provided an overview of the development of the Internet, the economic impact of the Internal on the global economy, and different adoption rates of Internet-based services by developed and developing nations. The second part of this chapter focused on hacking—how it is defined, which types of exploits can cause harm to property or to persons, and what the literature says makes hackers "tick" (based on empirically documented studies focused on how male and female hackers seemingly think and behave).

Throughout the chapter, there were numerous mentions of the increased complexity of hacking exploits and the very real possibility that cyberwars or cyberterrorism between nations might be waged with the assistance of teams of elite hackers with special skills. A recent case of this kind of worrisome exploit was reported in the media on May 26, 2012. A computer virus called Flame was responsible for a cyberattack that targeted Iran's oil ministry and main export terminal. Flame is believed by security experts to be the most sophisticated computer worm yet developed. The virus targeted primarily a small number of organizations and individuals in Iran, Israel's West Bank, Lebanon, and the United Arab Emirates. While experts who had decoded Flame have been unable to identify the source, they affirm that only an elite team of hackers working for several months could have created it (Hopkins 2012).

The CrySys Laboratory in Hungary reported that the results of their technical analysis support the hypothesis that Flame was developed by a government agency or nation-state having a significant budget and a willingness to create harm, if not create a cyberwar. Further, experts at Symantec, another security firm, said that Flame is the most sophisticated threat that they have witnessed to date—a "backdoor" worm that searches for very specific information. Flame can "scrape" a mass of information and send it to a predetermined site—without the online user's having any idea that this is happening. What's more, the amount of information Flame can send is enormous. Likely the worm has been "working behind the scenes" for as long as two years and may have already completed its mission. Unlike Stuxnet—which was designed to identify and destroy equipment—Flame was designed to gather and send information covertly for some yet unknown mission. In 2011, *The New York Times* reported that Stuxnet was likely a joint effort by the United States and Israel to undermine Iran's efforts to create its own atomic bomb (Hopkins 2012). The next chapter focuses on laws and other measures for dealing with hacking exploits.

References

Associated Press. "Google's Following of India's Standards Hikes Fear of Censorship." *The Globe and Mail,* February 7, 2012, p. A10.

Associated Press. "Technology: Internet Ad Revenues Hit $31-Billion in U.S." *The Globe and Mail,* April 19, 2010, p. B7.

Associated Press. "U.K. Police Arrest Brooks in Hacking Probe." *The Globe and Mail,* March 14, 2012, p. B9.

Bacher, Paul, Thorsten Holz, Markus Kotter, and Georg Wicherski. *Tracking Botnets: Using Honeynets to Learn More about Bots.* Honeynet Project and Research Alliance, 2005.

http://www.honeynet.org/papers/bots/. Accessed May 5, 2007.

Bachmann, M. "The Risk Propensity and Rationality of Computer Hackers." *International Journal of Cyber Criminology* 4 (2010): 643–656.

Blake, R. *Hackers in the Mist*. Chicago: Northwestern University, 1994.

Blankenship, L. "The Hacker Manifesto: The Conscience of a Hacker." 1986. http://www.mithral.com/~beberg/manifesto.html. Accessed May 4, 2009.

Bossler, A., and G. Burruss. "The General Theory of Crime and Computer Hacking: Low Self-Control Hackers?" In *Corporate Hacking and Technology-Driven Crime: Social Dynamics and Implications,* edited by T. Holt and B. Schell, (38-67). Hershey, PA: IGI Global, 2011.

Brenner, S. W. *Cyberthreats: The Emerging Fault Lines of the Nation State*. New York: Oxford University Press, 2008.

Brenner, S. W. "Is There Such a Thing as 'Virtual Crime'?" *California Criminal Law Review* 4 (2001). http://www.boalt.org/CCLR/v4/v4brenner.htm. Accessed April 4, 2012.

Britz, M. T. "Terrorism and Technology: Operationalizing Cyberterrorism and Identifying Concepts." In *Crime On-Line: Correlates, Causes, and Context,* edited by T. J. Holt, 193–220. Raleigh, NC: Carolina Academic Press, 2010.

Caldwell, R. "Some Social Parameters of Computer Crime." *Australian Computer Journal* 22 (1990): 43–46.

Caldwell, R. "University Students' Attitudes toward Computer Crime: A Research Note." *Computers and Society* 23 (1993): 11–14.

Cappelli, D. M., A. P. Moore, and T. J. Shimeall. *Common sense guide to prevention/detection of insider threats*. Carnegie Mellon University, 2006. http://www.cert.org/archive/pdf/CommonSenseInsiderThreatsV2.1-1-070118.pdf. Accessed November 2, 2009.

Choo, Kim-Kwang Raymond. "Zombies and Botnets." *Trends and Issues in Crime and Criminal Justice.* Australian Institute of Criminology, 2007. http://www.aic.gov.au/en/publications/current%20series/tandi/321-340/tandi333/view%20paper.aspx. Accessed December 28, 2007.

Comrie, G. R. "Cybersecurity: Protecting Digital Infrastructure through CIE." *Engineering Dimensions* 32 (2011): 39–41.

Correll, S. P. "An Interview with Anonymous" *PandaLabs Blog*, 2010. http://pandalabs.pandasecurity.com/an-interview-with-anonymous/. Accessed May 10, 2011.

Denning, D. E. "Cyber-conflict as an Emergent Social Problem," In *Corporate Hacking and Technology-Driven Crime: Social Dynamics and Implications*, edited by T. J. Holt and B. Schell, 170–186. Hershey, PA: IGI-Global, 2011.

Dhillon, G. and S. Moore. "Computer crime: Theoriezing about the enemy within." *Computers and Security* 20 (2001): 715–723.

El Akkad, O. "Hacker Crackdown." *The Globe and Mail*, March 7, 2012, p. A3.

Farrell, N. "Hacker Mastermind Has Asperger Syndrome." *The Inquirer*, 2007. http://www.theinquirer.net/inquirer/news/1038901/hacker-mastermind-asperger-syndrome. Accessed April 6, 2012.

Finkle, J. "Insulin Pumps Vulnerable to Attack by Hackers." *The Globe and Mail*, October 27, 2011, p. L6.

Furnell, S. *Cybercrime: Vandalizing the Information Society.* London: Addison- Wesley, 2002.

Gleeson, S. "Freed Hacker Could Work for Police." *New Zealand Herald*, 2008. . . . http://www.google.ca/#hl=en&sclient=psy-ab&q=Gleeson+2008+Freed+hacker+could+work+for+police&oq=Gleeson+2008+Freed+hacker+could+work+for+police&aq=f&aqi=&aql=&gs_l=serp.3 . . . 3269l19500l0l20096l98l67l0l1l1l1l6l830l7401l144j20j2j6-1l68l0.frgbld.&pbx=1&bav=on.2,or.r_gc.r_pw.r_qf.,cf

.osb&fp=7e2245c602c0671&biw=1440&bih=809. Accessed
April 6, 2012.

Gorman, S. "U.S. Calls Out China on Cyberspying." *The Globe and Mail*, December 13, 2011, p. B11.

Grant, T. "Canada Lags Peers in 'Internet Economy'." *The Globe and Mail*, March 19, 2012, p. B3.

Grafx-Specs Design and Hosting. "Cyberstalking: A Real Life Problem." 1999. http://www.grafx-specs.com/News/ Cybstlk.html. Accessed May 23, 2012.

Holt, T.J. "Subcultural evolution? Examining the influence of on- and off-line experiences on deviant subcultures." *Deviant Behavior*, 28 (2007): 171–198.

Holt, T. J. "Examining the Role of Technology in the Formation of Deviant Subcultures." *Social Science Computer Review* 28 (2010): 466–481.

Holt, T. J. "Lone Hacks or Group Cracks: Examining the Social Organization of Computer Hackers." In *Crimes of the Internet*, edited by F. Schmalleger & M. Pittaro, 336–355. Upper Saddle River, NJ: Pearson Prentice Hall, 2009.

Holt, T. J., and D. C. Graves. "A Qualitative Analysis of Advanced Fee Fraud Schemes." *The International Journal of Cyber-Criminology*, 1 (2007): 137–154.

Holt, T., and M. Kilger. "Techcrafters and Makecrafters: A Comparison of Two Populations of Hackers." *2008 WOMBAT Workshop on Information Security Threats Data Collection and Sharing* (2008): 67–78.

Holt, T. J., M. Kilger, D. Strumsky, and O. Smirnova. *Identifying, Exploring, and Predicting Threats in the Russian Hacker Community*. Presented at the DefCon 17 Convention, Las Vegas, NV, 2009.

Holt, T. J., J. Soles, and L. Leslie. *Characterizing Malware Writers and Computer Attackers in Their Own Words*. Paper presented at the 3rd International Conference on

Information Warfare and Security, Omaha, NE, April 24–25, 2008.

Hopkins, N. "Computer Virus Targeting Iran 'the Most Sophisticated Threat' Decoders Have Seen." *The Globe and Mail*, May 29, 2012, p. A16.

Houpt, S. "News International Pays up for Phone Hacking." *The Globe and Mail*, January 20, 2012, p. A 15.

Ianelli, Nicholas, and Aaron Hackworth. *Botnets as a Vehicle for Online Crime*. Pittsburgh, PA: CERT Coordination Center, 2005.

Information Warfare Monitor. "Tracking GhostNet: Investigating a Cyber Espionage Network." 2009. http://www.f-secure.com/weblog/archives/ghostnet.pdf. Accessed February 14, 2010.

Jaffe, G. "Gates Urges NATO Ministers to Defend against Cyber Attacks." *The Wall Street Journal On-line*, 2006. http://online.ws.com/article/SB118190166163536578.html?mod=googlenews_wsj. Accessed April 24, 2009.

Jordan, T., and P. Taylor. *Hacktivism and Cyber Wars*. London: Routledge, 2004.

Jordan, T., and P. Taylor. "A Sociology of Hackers." *Sociological Review* 46 (1998): 757–780.

Keller, G. "Police Sweep Nets 25 Alleged Anonymous Hackers." *The Globe and Mail*, February 29, 2012, p. A14.

King, A., and J. Thomas. "You can't cheat an honest man: Making ($$$s and) sense of the Nigerian e-mail scams." In *Crimes of the Internet*, edited by F. Schmalleger & M. Pittaro, (206–224). Upper Saddle River, NJ: Pearson Prentice Hall, (2009).

Kirk, J. "Estonia Recovers from Massive Denial-of-Service Attack." *Infoworld*, IDG, News Service, 2007. http://www.infoworld.com/d/security-central/estonia-recovers-massive-denial-service-attack-188. Accessed April 6, 2012.

Ladurantaye, S. "A Country of Clickers: Canada Tops in Web Usage." *The Globe and Mail*, March 2, 2012, pp. B1, B5.

Landler, M., and J. Markoff. "Digital Fears Emerge after Data Siege in Estonia." *The New York Times*, May 24, 2007. http://www.nytimes.com/2007/05/29/technology/ 29estonia.html. Accessed July 15, 2009.

Leggatt, H. "Number of Adults Using Social Networks Quadrupled since 2005." *BizReport*, 2009. http://www .bizreport.com/2009/01/number_of_adults_using_social _networks_quadrupled_since_2005.html. Accessed March 30, 2012.

Lenhart, A. *Is the age at which teens get cell phones getting younger.* Pew Internet and American Life Project. 2010. http:// pewinternet.org/Commentary/2010/December/Is-the-age -at-which-kids-get-cell-phones-getting-younger.aspx. Accessed March 20, 2011.

Lenhart, A., M. Madden, and P. Hitlin. *Teens and Technology.* Pew Internet and American Life Project, 2005. http://www .pewinternet.org/~/media/Files/Reports/2005/PIP_Teens _Tech_July2005web.pdf.pdf Accessed March 20, 2010.

Lenhart, A., and M. Madden. *Teens, Privacy, and Online Social Networks.* Pew Internet and American Life Project, 2007. http://www.pewinternet.org/Reports/2007/Teens-Privacy -and-Online-Social-Networks.aspx Accessed March 21, 2010.

Markoff, J. "Vast Spy System Loots Computers in 103 Countries." *The New York Times,* 2009. http://www .nytimes.com/2009/03/29/technology/29spy.html?_r=1. Accessed December 15, 2011.

Meyer, G. R. *The Social Organization of the Computer Underground.* Master's thesis, Northern Illinois University, 1989.

Mitnick, K. D., and W. L. Simon. *The Art of Deception: Controlling the Human Element of Security.* New York: Wiley, 2002.

Nolan, S. "Torture Spurs India-Bangladesh Hacker War." *The Globe and Mail*, March 2, 2012, p. A11.

Raghavan, T. "In Fear of Cyberterrorism: An Analysis of the Congressional Response." J.D. University of Illinois College of Law, 2003.

Sanger, David E. *Confront and Conceal: Obama's Secret Wars and Surprising Use of American Power*. New York: Crown Publishing, 2012.

Schell, B. *Contemporary World Issues: The Internet and Society*. Santa Barbara: ABC-CLIO, 2007.

Schell, B., and J. Dodge, with S. Moutsatsos. *The Hacking of America: Who's Doing It, Why, and How*. Westport: Quorum Books, 2002.

Schell, B., and C. Martin. *Contemporary World Issues: Cybercrime*. Santa Barbara: ABC-CLIO, 2004.

Schell, B., and C. Martin. *Webster's New World Hacker Dictionary*. Indiana: Wiley, 2006.

Schell, B., and J. Melnychuk. "Female and Male Hacker Conferences Attendees: Their Autism-Spectrum Quotient (AQ) Scores and Self-Reported Adult Experiences." In *Corporate Hacking and Technology-Driven Crime: Social Dynamics and Implications*, edited by T. Holt and B. Schell (144–169). Hershey, PA: IGI Global, 2011.

Shane, S. "Hackers Group Anonymous Intercepts FBI Call." *The Globe and Mail*, February 4, 2012, p. A15.

SHARCNEC. "FAQ." https://www.sharcnet.ca/my/help/faq. Accessed March 29, 2012.

Shaw, E. D., J. M. Post, and K. G. Ruby. "Inside the Mind of the Insider." December 1999, pp. 1–11. www.securitymanagement.com.

Sockel, H., and L. Falk. "Online Privacy, Vulnerabilities, and Threats: A Manager's Perspective." In *Online Consumer Protection: Theories of Human Relativism*, edited by K. Chen and A. Fadlalla (1086-1092). Hershey, PA: IGI Global, 2009.

Sophos. *Female virus-writer, Gigabyte, arrested in Belgium, Sophos comments.* http://sophos.com/en-us/press-office/press-releases/2004/02/va_gigabyte.aspx. Accessed June 5, 2010.

Steele, G., Jr., D. R. Woods, R. A. Finkel, M. R. Crispin, R. M. Stallman, and G. S. Goodfellow. *The Hacker's Dictionary.* New York: Harper and Row, 1983.

Strickland, J. "Wide Angle: Top 10 Social Networking Sites." Howstuffworks.com. http://dsc.discovery.com/technology/tech-10/social-networking-sites-top-10-06.html. Accessed March 30, 2012.

Symantec Corporation. *Symantec Internet security threat report, Volume 17,* 2012. http://www.symantec.com/threatreport/. Accessed June 2, 2012.

Taylor, P. *Hackers: Crime in the Digital Sublime.* London: Routledge, 1999.

Tossell, I. "The ABCs of Cyber-security." *The Globe and Mail Report on Business* 28 (May 10, 2012): 55–60.

Tsuruoka, D. "Apple Said Using Baidu as Search Option in China." *Investor's Business Daily.* http://news.investors.com/articleprint/605708/201203271250/aapl-reportedly-adds-bidu-search.aspx. Accessed March 27, 2012.

Wall, D. S. "Cybercrimes and the Internet." In *Crime and the Internet,* edited by D. S. Wall, 1–17. New York: Routledge, 2001.

Wolak, J., K. Mitchell, and D. Finkelhor. *Online victimization of youth: Five years later.* Washington, DC: National Center for Missing & Exploited Children, 2006.

As we've said many times, and the President and [Defence] Secretary made clear, [the] cyber domain is a domain that we need to constantly evaluate and constantly assess and try to improve the range of capabilities that we have in cyberspace.
—Captain John Kirby, Pentagon (Agence France-Presse, 2012)

This chapter delves deeper into how hacks are perpetrated as well as how frequently these attacks have been reported by business and government network administrators in recent years. It also looks at the problems created by these intrusions and the controversies surrounding reported cases. Also, countermeasures—both technically and legally—for curbing these exploits are explored.

This chapter also gives an overview of the kinds of solutions that are associated with IT security, operating system and database security, and computer networking and networked applications. A special section is devoted to modern-day concerns regarding web services and cloud computing.

A masked hacker, part of the Anonymous group, hacks the French presidential palace website on January 20, 2012 near the eastern city of Lyon. Anonymous is a shadowy group of international hackers with no central hierarchy. (Jean-Philippe KsiazekAFP/Getty Images)

Fundamentals of Hack Attacks and Patches as a Countermeasure

The Basics of Hack Attacks

To facilitate a hack, one of two things must occur. First, a Black Hat typically needs to use social engineering to make a computer system think that he or she is a system administrator or a legitimate user. Then, the intruder needs to communicate with a computer system. To do this, he or she must key into a computer special identifying strings, or passwords, and an authorized username. This two-step process is known as logging in.

Black Hats determined to infiltrate systems often get legitimate user passwords using a variety of online or offline techniques (Mitnick and Simon 2002; Schell and Martin 2004):

- Glancing over an authorized user's shoulder when the user is logging in—which is why financial institutions, for example, warn banking customers at the automated teller machine (ATM) to protect their personal identification numbers (PINs)
- Recording authorized users' login keystrokes on video
- Searching for notes on or in authorized users' desks
- Calling system operators and claiming to be an employee who forgot the password
- "Trashing" (i.e., searching through actual garbage bins) and collecting scraps of paper with passwords written on them
- Searching for authorized users' passwords by reading email messages stored on company computers
- Guessing different combinations of personally meaningful birth dates or children's names of authorized users

These somewhat simple strategies can be used to engage in basic attacks, but there is another, more sophisticated process involving the use of various methods to bypass the entire security system by exploiting gaps, or vulnerabilities, in the systems. Such vulnerabilities are present in most any program running on the computer system, including the operating system and the web browser, and through communications protocols on the network.

In fact, many common commands and protocols are often exploited (Schell and Martin 2004):

- FTP (File Transfer Protocol), used to transfer files between systems over a network
- TFTP (Trivial File Transfer Protocol), allowing the unauthenticated transfer of files
- Telnet and SSH, two commands used to remotely log into a computer
- Finger, a command providing information about users that can be used to retrieve the .plan and .project files from a user's home directory; these text files are used to store information about the user's location, near-future plans, and the projects he or she is working on
- NFS (Network File System), a method of sharing files across a local area network (LAN) or through the Internet
- Email subsystem
- The UUCP (an acronym for UNIX-to-UNIX copy) protocol, used for the store-and-forward exchange of email

These vulnerabilities can be exploited, or compromised, by an attacker to gain deep access to a computer or network. Exploits are programs that take advantage of the weakness in a vulnerability to compromise the system. Myriad exploits are available online that can be either acquired for free in hacker websites or purchased from vendors in online black markets (Chu, Holt, and Ahn 2010; Furnell 2002; Taylor 1999). The use of an exploit enables attackers to install "code" directly into the network for various purposes. For instance, keylogging programs can be used to capture every keystroke entered by a user to acquire passwords, sensitive information, and various details about a network. Remote administration tools (RATs) also allow attackers to create backdoors for later entry into a system.

Other, somewhat more sophisticated crackers have used cellular modems to complete their exploits (Schell and Dodge, with Moutsatsos 2002). Setting up a wireless access point that appears to be part of a legitimate corporate network allows an attacker to capture all data moving through the connection. For corporate espionage purposes, it is quite an easy matter for a cracker to preposition such devices and then take advantage of security vulnerabilities to gain permanent entry into a targeted network. Other acts of espionage have been accomplished using electromagnetic (EM) signals, although this technique is far more costly than using cellular modems.

Patches: An Organizational Countermeasure for Hack Attacks

The nature of technology means that vulnerabilities are being constantly identified by security researchers and Black Hat hackers alike. Because many of these vulnerabilities are reported to the general public first through disclosure lists such as BugTraq, security professionals have difficulty in finding ways to secure these vulnerabilities before interested attackers create exploits. In some cases, however, vulnerabilities are made known to vendors before they are identified to the general public. Responsible software vendors go over incident reports with a fine-toothed comb and then make a serious attempt to close any security gaps in their products before distributing them into the marketplace. Furthermore, because new exploits are constantly being discovered, documented, and shared in the security system community, the sooner these vulnerabilities are addressed, the better. To prevent future network intrusions, system administrators need to regularly install updates for their systems' software called "fixes" or "patches."

The sad reality is that far too many systems officers fail to completely update their system programs, so that a number of gaps remain open needlessly. A number of reasons for delay are cited, such as that the job is too time-consuming, it may be too complex, or it may be given a low priority by the organization. Also, within some enterprises and government agencies, an important security patch might not be scheduled for installation until sometime after the patches are made available by the vendor because the company or agency fails to enforce its security policy, the security function is under-resourced, or the patch disrupts the system when it is installed—causing the system administrator to spend an inordinate amount of time fixing the configuration so that it can receive the new patch.

Moreover, some systems officers have been known to delay making much-needed security repairs because they do not want to inconvenience users. For example, although system administrators should ensure that authorized users change their passwords on a regular basis, some companies are lax in doing so as a means of keeping employees happy. Often individuals report difficulty in remembering multiple passwords or remembering passwords that are overly long or incorporate numbers and letters (necessary to create a truly strong password). As a result, there may be a range of weaknesses in system security that could be easily fixed but remain open to ensure a more satisfying user experience. The longer that vulnerabilities remain unpatched, the more likely that the system will be compromised by old or well-known exploits. In fact, 286 million malware variants were alive and active as of 2011 that could be used against both new and legacy systems. Many of these tools have the potential to expose data to undesirables in the virtual world, so it is vital that basic security measures be implemented to better protect computer networks (Tossell 2012).

As a case in point, in 2008, Microsoft became overwhelmed when attackers found a vulnerability in Internet Explorer that had been kept a well-hidden company secret for almost 10 years. When the vulnerability was eventually discovered by hackers, they exploited it as a means of stealing legitimate users' passwords. Microsoft scurried to release a patch to fix a huge percentage of the world's computers utilizing Internet Explorer (Tossell 2012). More recently, Stuxnet used multiple zero-day, or unknown, vulnerabilities to cause harm to targeted Supervisory Control and Data Acquisition (SCADA) industrial control systems and targeted nuclear facilities in Iran in June 2010.

Without doubt, staying ahead of the cybercriminal curve remains a daily challenge in cyberspace. As malware such as Flame becomes more sophisticated, the amount of damage to property and persons is bound to climb, because the attacks are becoming increasingly more malign. The translation of this reality? More money is lost when these attacks are successful, because more records in the network are breached.

The Evolving Structure of the Internet: The Good News and the Bad

The Good News: A New and Exciting Information Era

Consumers around the world seem to have a growing love affair with mobile devices. In Canada alone, the growing uptake of mobile devices suggests that by 2015, the wireless penetration rate will exceed 100 percent, because most consumers will own more than one mobile gadget. Similar, but slower adoption rates have been noted in the United States, where more than 80 percent of adults own a cell phone, and approximately one third of those adults own a smart phone that can be used to check their email or connect to the Internet (Smith 2011). It is further estimated that the average smart phone uses 35 times the bandwidth of a regular cell phone, while a tablet uses up to 120 times the bandwidth. Globally, the wireless industry has already surpassed one zettabyte of mobile data, with the expectation that this number will double every two years. To put this in context, only a few years ago, the entire Internet was believed to represent half of a zettabyte (Trichur 2012).

Here is another sobering thought: almost 40 percent of smart phone users around the world use the Internet before they even get out of bed in the morning. First, they shut off the device's alarm. Then, they start reading their tweets, Facebook, and the weather network to get a sense of how to dress for the day. Afterward, they visit the washroom. According to experts who monitor Internet usage rates, the only time in the day when usage dips significantly on a global scale is at dinner time (Trichur 2012).

Meanwhile, the infrastructure of the Internet is evolving radically because of the dawning of a new era. According to International Business Machines (IBM) Corporation, growing evidence suggests that we are, indeed, entering a new information era. The change that is driving the new era is the rise of big data—the estimated 2.5 quintillion bytes of data being produced each day, representing the collective output of every individual, every company or government agency, and everything instrumented. Because this massive amount of data contains patterns that, when analyzed, can help solve some of society's most pressing issues, IBM has invested heavily in research and development (R&D) in a field that the company calls "smarter analytics." In a world creating and being defined by big data, the need for analytics is overwhelming, affirms the company. In a 2011 study jointly funded by IBM and *MIT Sloan Management Review*, a major finding was that organizations embracing analytics were 2.2 times more likely to substantially outperform their industry peers that were less likely to be early adopters of smarter analytics (IBM, June 4, 2012).

One of the research studies funded by IBM involves the research team of Dr. Carolyn McGregor at the University of Ontario's Institute of Technology (UOIT) in Oshawa, Ontario, Canada. Her research team is developing streaming analytics to help neonatal care hospitals figure out which newborn babies are at risk for illness before the symptoms appear; by analyzing 43 million streaming data points per patient per day, the research team is trying to help find solutions for keeping "at risk" newborns alive. That is all good news (IBM, June 4, 2012).

The Bad News: The Evolution of the Internet Creates a New Playing Field for Network Attackers

The bad news is that the expanding information field and the evolution of the Internet are also moving to the attacker's advantage. One major concern among IT security experts is that the move to more sophisticated web applications exposes more of an organization's internal processes to the Internet. Unfortunately, many of the firms building these applications do not have an organized secure development approach, and they fail to conduct adequate "penetration tests" that might uncover flaws or vulnerabilities that could be repaired before they are exploited by hackers (Richardson 2012).

Penetration testing is the process of probing for and identifying security vulnerabilities; it is a critical tool for assessing the security state of an organization's IT systems, including computers, network components, and applications. White Hat hackers are often hired by companies to conduct penetration testing, making these investments money well spent (Schell and Martin 2006; Taylor 1999).

A second major concern is that the Internet is undergoing three radical shifts, which raise further IT security concerns (Richardson 2012):

1. Virtualization blurs the boundaries between servers and redraws network typologies, often without clear boundaries where "firewalls" would have traditionally helped keep the network safe.

2. "Cloud computing" has recently rolled in as an enormous wave of change, but because it blurs the locality of data and running processes, there are, understandably, IT security concerns.

3. There is a massive expansion of the number of things in the world needing IP addresses; consequently, if one of the goals of IT security professionals is to have better visibility into the security status of their networks, this explosion of endpoints is a key reason why IT security professionals will not likely achieve this visibility in the near future.

We will examine items 1 and 2 in greater detail in the following subsections.

A Further Look at the Purpose and Function of Firewalls

By definition, firewalls are computer programs or hardware devices that provide additional security on networks by blocking access from the public network to certain services in the private network. They contain rule sets that either grant or deny traffic flowing into or out of a network. Simply stated, firewalls are to the perimeter of a network what a moat and a wall are to a castle. Because system administrators need to grant access from the outside world to some services within the perimeter—such as email or a web server—they need to drill holes for these services in the firewalls. Unfortunately, these holes can be exploited by Black Hats. For example, control of outgoing traffic is often an area of neglect; thus there is a real risk that users might introduce malicious code into the networking by opening an infected email attachment or by surfing to a website with malicious content that installs a "backdoor" program on an internal system. These backdoors may initiate connections to a network attacker that, from the firewall's perspective, seems to be coming from the "inside" and, therefore, is allowed. The harsh reality facing system administrators is that backdoors can allow attackers to take control of an internal system, creating considerable harm (Schell and Martin 2006; Symantec 2012.

The Pros and Cons of Moving to "the Cloud"

An area of recent concern to IT security experts is the growing buy-in for "cloud computing"—which means moving more information online to servers hosted by other external organizations ("the cloud"). These security concerns are rooted in the fact that cloud computing blurs the locality of data and running processes. Currently, cloud computing is somewhat of a mystery, and without question, it is one of the latest hot ideas for business that makes many CEOs nervous because of the many pros and cons of its early adoption.

To assist CEOs in making the decision about whether to move more of their companies' information to servers hosted by other organizations, Dr. Andrew McAfee, principal research scientist at MIT's Center for Digital Business, shares these key points for consideration (Schachter 2011):

- *Budgetary Quandary.* In theory, anything "the cloud" provides can be matched by on-premise approaches with known network IT security features. However, according to a recent Microsoft report, IT budgets are being stretched to the limit, with only about 11 percent of the IT-earmarked funds being allocated to new applications. The balance of funding goes to network maintenance and infrastructure, leaving few resources to ensure that employees have access to all the information they want and need, regardless of where they are or which devices—mobile or otherwise—they are using. For this reason, more CEOs are turning to "the cloud" as a means of dealing with the budgetary quandary.

- *Capitalizing on Collaboration.* Just as ARPAnet allowed for secure sharing of information among distributed agents in earlier years, so cloud computing now allows companies to capitalize on collaboration by allowing groups to work together in ways not formerly possible. As a case in point, a U.S. consulting firm named Jive (a creator of cloud-based collaboration software) revealed that more than 25,000 individuals registered for its software, paving the way for 2,100 groups to collaborate. Despite the IT security concerns about cloud computing, a cloud-based feature certainly would be seen as being a cost-effective one from CEOs' vantage point.

- *The Growing Need for Better Analytics.* Businesses wanting and needing better analytics to help them understand, predict, and understand patterns in huge data sets represent another audience that is keen on adopting cloud computing. We have already discussed how IBM's and Dr. McGregor's cloud-gathered data are helping to predict which newborn babies might be at increased risk for health problems. As another case in point, U.S.-based Radiant Systems has used analyzed cloud-gathered data to better understand employee theft.

- *Increased Opportunities for Developing and Hosting New Applications.* Before the advent of cloud computing, software developers had to purchase, configure, and maintain their own servers—a venture that distracted them from their main business of writing code. Cloud computing lets companies increase the scale and power of their IT services and the speed with which they can be deployed. As a case in point, when U.S.-based 3M Company moved to the Windows Azure cloud platform, the company was able to make the visual tools available to its graphic designers, thereby increasing the designers' productivity without making a heavy financial investment.

- *Administrative Barriers, Costs, and Reliability Concerns.* Moving to "the cloud" brings with it the decision to simplify companies' notoriously hodgepodge collection of legacy systems gathered over the years. Along with the need to face this major cost factor, there is an ongoing controversy about whether buying into "the cloud" actually saves companies money. To this point, Dr. McAfee maintains that over the longer term, the economies associated with building and maintaining a state-of-the-art IT infrastructure favors "the cloud" because of healthy economies of scale. Finally, there remains a question about how reliable "the cloud" is for maintaining fully functional web services 24 hours a day, 7 days a week, 365 days of the year. Moreover, uncertainty persists about who is responsible for breaches "in the cloud" when they occur—the hosting company or the company that owns the data? This certainly is a question that will surely be put to the legal test.

Network Hacks: Recent Surveys on the Frequency and the Types of Harm Caused

At the close of Chapter 1, we discussed Flame, which is likely the most sophisticated piece of malware ever designed—a stealth digital surveillance device so complex that it ran on sensitive government computer networks for years without detection. Even more frightening, Flame is apparently modular in design, meaning that it has the capacity to be updated and to become more sophisticated "on the fly." The malware, it seems, was created as a "snoop device" that could record keystrokes, operate a computer's built-in camera, or infect other devices through Bluetooth (El Akkad 2012).

In May 2012, the computer security company Kapersky Lab reported that 189 customer machines were infected with Flame in Iran, 98 machines were infected in Israel and the Palestinian territories, and 64 machines were infected in Sudan and Syria combined. Interestingly, during this period of infection, none of the 43 tested antivirus programs could detect any malicious components of Flame—which likely took years and millions of dollars to create. For this reason, IT security experts believe that Flame is not the work of a "basement hacker." Flame, it seems, is less of a virus and more of an "attack toolkit" with source code written in it for the authors to expand the modules in the future as a means of more effectively snooping targeted machines. What is particularly worrisome is that although the tool was very likely developed for state-sanctioned cyberwarfare, now that word is out "on the street" about Flame's unique capabilities, experts believe that Flame's source code will soon make its way into the hands of the Black Hats hired by the criminal arm. As TomKellermann of the Trend Micro IT Security company remarked, "[Y]ou don't need to know how to build a gun in order to pull the trigger in cyberspace" (El Akkad 2012, A3).

Moreover, on June 1, 2012, *The New York Times* reported that U.S. President Barack Obama accelerated cyberattacks on Iran's nuclear program and expanded the assault after the Stuxnet virus *accidentally* escaped in 2010. Codenamed "Olympic Games," the operation allegedly began under former president George W. Bush, and is the first publicly leaked U.S. cyberattack ever launched on another country—in this case, Iran. It utilized malicious code aimed at preventing Iran from developing nuclear weapons and Israel from launching a military strike. Within a week of Stuxnet's escape, a newer variant temporarily brought to a halt 1,000 of Iran's 5,000 nuclear centrifuges. It is interesting to note, according to this media piece, that top U.S. administration officials considered suspending "Olympic Games" after Stuxnet "escaped" the nuclear facility and started showing up in the networks of other countries (Agence France-Presse 2012).

It is also interesting to note that on June 11, 2012, the Obama administration was reported to be facing intense pressure to identify and make examples of any officials who helped bring to light a series of recent disclosures, including new information about the Obama administration's drone strikes and a joint effort by the United States and Israel to damage Iranian nuclear equipment with Stuxnet. Although citizens might be somewhat shocked to learn that there is no U.S. law against disclosing classified information, the classification system was created for the executive branch by presidential order, not by statute, to control access to information and the means by which it must be treated. While government officials who break those rules may be reprimanded or fired, the system covers far more information than it is a crime to leak. According to the media, Obama denied that the White House had sanctioned any leaking (Savage 2012).

With the appearance of Stuxnet and Flame, questions have arisen about which other network hacks have created concerns for governments' and industry's IT security experts and how much harm has been incurred. To gain insight into these questions, in the United States, Canada, and elsewhere, surveys are distributed to system administrators inquiring about network intrusions, the suspected identity of the perpetrator(s), the methods the attackers employed, the frequency of system intrusions for various industry sectors, and the estimated losses (dollar amounts) as a result of these incidents. These survey findings are often used as a basis for determining organizations' system risk management strategies. When system administrators try to estimate the appropriate level of investment in computer security a company should make, they tend to assess their level of hack attacks or intrusion risk by evaluating the experiences of other organizations with similar systems and business characteristics. Caution should be exercised when interpreting such data, however, as it is impossible for survey respondents to give completely reliable answers to the questions asked about network intrusions for a number of reasons. First, an unknown number of network intrusions go undetected and, therefore, cannot be reported; a recent case in point is Flame. Second, even if hack attacks occur and are detected, they may go unreported as a means of protecting the organization's credibility in the marketplace (Schell and Martin 2004). Third, in some jurisdictions such as in Canada, there is no statutory requirement for private firms to report breaches of user data, but there could be soon. Although a digital privacy law was introduced in the Canadian Parliament, as of April, 2013, it had not been enacted (Tossell 2012).

The results of the 15th Annual Computer Crime and Security Survey conducted in the United States and the 2011

TELUS-Rotman Joint Study on Canadian IT Security Practices will be discussed here. Typically, surveys such as these ask government and industry leaders in the IT security domain to discuss the kinds of network breaches, or "incidents," that have occurred over a stipulated time period. Although an "incident" may involve one site, hundreds of sites, or thousands of sites, a common definition for an "incident" is "the act of violating an explicit or implied IT security policy." As noted in Chapter 1, these acts are wide ranging and commonly include attempts to gain unauthorized access to systems or data, disrupt website service to legitimate online users, and change system hardware and software characteristics without the owner's knowledge, instruction, or consent. It is possible to accomplish these steps in as little as 45 seconds, and with enhanced automation each passing year, the time to accomplish these steps decreases even further.

Besides these broad-based surveys, other kinds of system intrusions reports are compiled. For example, Verizon Business's *Data Breach Investigations Report* (DBIR) identifies the number of data breach investigations from the 2004 time period to the present. In recent years, the DBIR has also included a case database from the U.S. Secret Service. Unlike other, more broad-based surveys, the DBIR's entire sample consists of organizations that have suffered large data breaches. Accepting that banks are a favorite target of Black Hats, it seems logical that the cases detailed in the 2010 DBIR would be heavily financial institution oriented, followed by the hospitality industry. Also, some of the cases detailed in the DBIR have occurred outside the United States (Richardson 2012).

15th Annual Computer Crime and Security Survey (2010/2011)

There is a general consensus among those in the IT security field that cyberthreats know no boundaries, and that in the heavily networked world that we live in, the networks of governments and industry can be under attack by cyberin-truders 24 hours a day, 7 days a week, 365 days a year. Although the CSI Computer Crime and Security Survey of security professionals has been undertaken for 15 years, it has continued to evolve in an attempt to adequately capture the evolving landscape of cybercrime—including the emergence of stealth toolkits like Flame.

The 2010/2011 survey covered a midyear-to-midyear period from July 2009 through June 2010. The survey was sent to about 5,400 security practitioners in the United States both by snail mail and by email, with a total of 351 completed surveys being returned. This yielded a 6.4 percent response rate, which the author felt was good enough for generalization of the findings to the larger field of enterprises in the United States. Assuming that the respondent pool was representative of the larger pool of information of security professionals in the United States and that the forms were, in turn, a random selection of the larger group, the author of the report believes that the number of returns would give readers a 95 percent confidence level in the study findings, with about a 5 percent margin of error.

Of course, as with any survey, some study limitations must be recognized. First, there is a skewing of respondents to those individuals and organizations having a demonstrated interest in IT security. Second, potentially only those individuals with intrusion data at hand might be motivated to complete the survey. Third, because all responses are submitted anonymously to increase respondent participation rates, it is impossible to track down those professionals who have self-selected not to complete the form. Fourth, guaranteeing anonymity makes it nearly impossible to compare data on a year-by-year basis, because entirely different practitioners may be responding from year to year. Accepting these limitations, the director of Computer Security Institute (CSI) maintains that it seems reasonable to assume that the results do represent an important view of what engaged IT security professionals are seeing and responding to in the field (Richardson 2012).

Respondent Sample

For the 2010/2011 survey, the respondent sample by industry sector was as follows: consulting (21.5%), information technology (10.9%), financial services (10.6%), education (8.9%), federal government (7.4%), health services (6.6%), manufacturing (6%), local government (3.2%), retail (3.2%), and all other responses (21.8%). The respondent sample by job title was as follows: security officer (20%), chief executive officer (12.6%), system administrator (10.9%), chief information security officer (10.6%), chief information officer (5.9%), chief security officer (2.9%), chief privacy officer (0.3%), and other (38%).

The respondents' firms and government agencies had the following reported annual revenues: less than $10 million (38.2%), more than $1 billion (28.1%), $10 million to $99 million (20.4%), and $100 million to $1 billion (13.3%). The respondents firms by number of employees were as follows: 1–99 employees (31.3%), 100–499 employees (13.2%), 500–1,499 employees (10.3%), 1,500–9,999 employees (22.4%), 10,000–49,999 employees (12.1%), and 50,000 or more employees (10.6%).

Finally, the percentage of respondents described their organization's need to comply with the following laws and industry regulations (which are described more fully later in this chapter): the Health Insurance Portability and Accountability Act (HIPAA) (51.5%); the U.S. state data breach notification law (47.4%); the Sarbanes-Oxley Act (SOX) (42.3%); the Payment Card Industry Data Security Standard (PCI-DSS) (42.3%); international privacy or security laws (32.5%); Federal Information Security Management Act (FISMA) (32%); the Gramm-Leach Bliley Act (GLBA) (28.9%); the Health Information Technology for Economic and Clinical Health Act (HITECH Act) (23.2%); the Payment Card Industry Payment Application Standard (16%); and other (13.9%).

Key Study Findings

According to Richardson (2012), the key findings of the survey analysis were as follows:

- Malware infections continued to be the most commonly experienced hack attack, with 67.1 percent of the respondents reporting such attacks.
- Fewer financial fraud incidents were experienced as compared to previous years, with only 8.7 percent of the respondents saying that they experienced such during the reporting period.
- While about half of the respondents said that their firm experienced at least one security incident during the reporting period, a worrisome 45.6 percent of the respondents said that their networks had been the victim of at least one targeted attack.
- Fewer respondents were willing to disclose particulars of the dollar losses their firms experienced as a result of the hack attacks, but it seems that the average losses are likely down from previous survey years.
- Respondents said that regulatory compliance requirements and their firms' efforts to be compliant had a positive effect on their IT security programs.
- Contrary to survey results from earlier years and especially around the year 2000, the majority of respondents (59.1%) did not believe that the hack attacks were caused by "insiders"; 39.5 percent of the respondents said that none of the incidents were caused by "insiders."
- Slightly more than half (51.1%) of the respondents said that their firms do not use cloud computing because of IT security concerns; however, 10 percent of the respondents maintained that not only do their firms use cloud computing, but that they deployed cloud-specific security tools.

Concluding Remarks

Richardson (2012) concluded the report by making the following points:

- Although IT security measures have improved gradually over the years, the effectiveness of these measures may be challenged by wholesale changes to the Internet that are currently under consideration—likely forcing a regression in the progress made to date.

- There is both good news and bad news in terms of hack attacks. The good news is that the percentage of respondents who report network breaches has been decreasing over time, with more than half of the respondents for the current survey saying that their firms have not experienced any security incidents. The bad news is that among current hack attacks, a growing number of highly sophisticated attacks are targeting particular businesses or government offices; because these attacks are more malign than earlier exploits, more money is lost when an attack is successful, and more records are breached.

- More bad news is that the field is changing to the attackers' advantage, as the move to more sophisticated web applications and the adoption of cloud computing expose more of a firm's internal processes to the Internet and the possibility of hack attacks.

2011 TELUS-Rotman Joint Study on Canadian IT Security Practices

The 2011 study on Canadian IT security practices is the fourth in a series of annual studies undertaken jointly by the Rotman School of Management at the University of Toronto and TELUS Security Labs. The study began in 2008, because at that time, such IT security trend studies were U.S. or globally focused—and not Canadian. As a result, Canadian IT security managers had to make critical decisions based on trends and insights outside of a Canadian environment; that is, they had to assume implicitly that Canada's risk profile and IT prepared-ness and governance structures were the same as, say, those in the United States. In 2008, there were noted differences between the U.S. and Canadian enterprises; for example, the private sector's role in health care is much larger in the United States relative to Canada's strongly publicly funded health care system. Moreover, the United States has thousands of banks, whereas Canada is dominated by only six big banks (Etges and Hejazi 2011).

Besides documenting trends in the IT security environment in Canada, each year the TELUS-Rotman study format adds a new dimension to deal with emerging threats. For 2011, the 52-question study, administered in the summer of 2011, not only continued to focus on the legacy resulting from the recent economic financial crisis, but also addressed security issues caused by social networking and mobile security. In addition, Canadian organizational participants were asked to rate the importance of three key pillars of a balanced security strategy: people, process, and technology. These ratings were then corre-lated with risk posture, breaches, satisfaction with technologies, and security performance. By the end of the data collection phase, respondents from 649 organizations had participated in the study (Etges and Hejazi 2011).

Respondent Sample

The authors (Etges and Hejazi 2011) cite the following respon-dent sample characteristics. For 2011, the respondents tended to come from private companies (65.02%), of which about 14 percent were publicly traded. About 15 percent of the respondents affirmed that they came from the public sector. The respondents by industry sector were represented as follows: information technology and related services (26.68%), finance services and insurance (8.25%), retail and wholesale trade

(6.91%), government (6.72%), educational services or scientific or manufacturing (each 6.14%), construction or real estate (5.57%), and health care and social assistance (4.8%). The balance of respondents were found in smaller numbers in the information publishing and broadcasting industry (4.41%), utilities (2.47%), transportation and warehousing (2.30%), and mining or agriculture (1.92%). About 11 percent of the respondents were from industry sectors other than those just mentioned.

The job titles of the respondents were distributed as follows: managers (21.61%); security analyst, consultant, or auditor (13.56%); director (12.87%); system administrator (11.26%); chief executive officer (10.34%); chief technology officer (2.76%); vice president of IT or security or risk management (2.53%); chief information officer or chief security officer (each 0.92%); and chief information security officer (0.69%). The balance of respondents (22.53%) had various other job titles.

The respondents by their firms' annual revenues for the past year were distributed as follows: less than $1 million (33.53%), $1 million to $24 million (20.23%), $25 million to $99 million (8.09%), $100 million to $499 million (7.13%), $500 million to $999 million (4.24%), $1 billion to $1.99 billion (3.47%), $2 billion to $10 billion (5.59%), and more than $10 billion (2.70%). About 15 percent of the respondents did not provide this information. Finally, almost half of the respondents came from smaller firms having 1–49 employees (44.88%); about 12 percent had 50–249 employees; about 7 percent had 1,000–2,499 employees; and the balance maintained that they came from firms with 2,500 or more employees.

Key Study Findings

The key study findings were summarized as follows (Etges and Hejazi 2011):

- Over the four years addressed by the study, network breach numbers generally continued to rise, with slight variations for government and public organizations. The breach types indicate an emerging interest by Black Hat hackers in targeting specific individuals with the intent of financial gain.

• Over the last year covered by the survey, the network breach numbers for government and private companies decreased, but the breaches for publicly traded organizations continued to climb, with the latter reporting six times the number of breaches experienced in 2008—due, in large part, to the 2008 financial crisis that caused a surge of network breaches across Canada.

• The costs associated directly with these breaches—which increased significantly in 2008 and 2009—have fallen for all organization types year over year moving into 2011. For 2011, the average number of breaches for government networks, public networks, and private networks were 17.3, 18, and 4.6, respectively.

• As in previous years, the government's IT security budgets continued to lag behind the budgets assigned for IT security in the private sector, making it difficult for government offices to attract and retain top IT security talent.

• In general, the organizational respondents who were most satisfied with their IT security postures allocated a significant portion of the budget to IT. More than 90 percent of the respondents reported satisfaction levels of "neutral" and "better" once the IT security budget reached 5 to 6 percent of the total IT budget. The most satisfied respondents had an IT security budget of 10 percent or higher of the total IT budget.

• In 2011, respondents were asked to consider the fundamental question of whether the three pillars of their security system—people, process, and technology—could be viewed as strengths or as weaknesses in their organizations. The researchers then gauged the degree to which these responses were related to the effectiveness of the firm's overall security posture. Respondents whose organizations viewed the three pillars as strengths and as critical to their security approach showed a high level of satisfaction with their IT security programs. Moreover, respondents whose firms indicated that any of the three pillars were strengths were more than 80 percent more likely to be "satisfied" or "very satisfied" with their overall IT security posture—with slight advantages being noted with process and people strengths relative to technology strength.

- The study asked respondents to assess the complexity of their IT security environments, allowing the researchers to analyze how complexity relates to network breaches, satisfaction, and outsourcing. Government respondents reported higher complexity in their IT security environments than respondents from private-sector organizations, which likely relates to the greater number of breaches occurring in government networks. Again, privately owned companies in Canada seem to be doing a good job of managing the complexity of their IT environments, with an average of 6 percent of the IT budget dedicated to IT security.

- For 2011, there was an increase in sophisticated and targeted attacks on individuals. These attacks tend to be reported less frequently, because they are more difficult to detect and require a longer time frame to be noticed. Increasingly, besides financial gain intentions, the network intruders seem to be trying to capitalize on political or ideological issues.

- For 2011, the most common cyberbreach types included viruses, worm, spyware, malware, and spam—representing 47 percent of the private-sector breaches, 43 percent of the public-sector breaches, and 42 percent of the government-sector breaches. Phishing and pharming exploits, in which the organization was described fraudulently as the sender of emails, represented 24 percent of the government-sector breaches, 22 percent of the public-sector breaches, and 18 percent of the private-sector breaches.

- Bots within the organizations' networks and denial-of-service attacks represented about 10 percent of the breaches for all three sectors. Also, for all three sectors, financial and online banking fraud represented about 5 percent of the breaches, and sabotage of data or networks represented about 3 percent of the breaches.

- In both the public and private sectors, the number of insider hacker breaches was down in 2011. While the government offices suggested that about 42 percent of the breaches were caused by insiders, the numbers were, comparatively, 27 percent for the public sector and 16 percent for the private sector.

- The loss of mobile devices with proprietary business information contained within them was the primary security concern for 2011, followed by a number of integration and data leakage concerns.

Laws Created to Keep Abreast of the Evolving Internet

As noted earlier in this chapter, respondents to the recent Computer Crime and Security Survey described their organization's need to comply with a number of U.S. laws and industry regulations regarding network breaches. Specifically, many of these laws outline the responsibilities of organizations and government agencies for appropriately dealing with breaches, their prevention, and the timely disclosure to potential victims once a breach has occurred.

As an example, in mid-January 2007, U.S. retailer TJX (with 2,000 retail stores such as Marshall's and T.J. Maxx), because of existing laws, released the news that it had suffered a massive computer breach on a portion of its network that handled credit card, debit card, check, and merchandise transactions in the United States and elsewhere. At the time of the press release, the company did not know the extent of the breach, which was first discovered in December 2006. Nevertheless, the system administrator at TJX feared that one or more of the network intruders may have had access to credit and debit information from transactions in the United States, Canada, and Puerto Rico in 2003, as well as from transactions completed between May and December 2006. TJX worked with IBM and General Dynamics to deal with the breach's aftermath (Roberts 2007).

In 2010–2011, the culprit in the TJX breach, Albert Gonzalez, was charged by authorities. Gonzalez pleaded guilty to the combined theft of and subsequent reselling of more than 170 million credit and ATM cards' information from 2005 through 2007, obtained as a result of network breaches he conducted at TJX and Heartland Payment Systems. For these exploits, he was sentenced to two concurrent 20-year terms in prison. As a point of interest, Gonzalez performed his hack attacks via SQL injection, one of the simplest sorts of application-layer attacks known to hackers—and one approach to cracking networks that continues to be a major source of problems for companies across all sectors. [SQL injection is a security vulnerability occurring in an application's database layer that is caused by the incorrect delimiting of variables embedded in SQL statements. It is an example of a broader class of vulnerabilities occurring whenever one programming or scripting language is embedded inside another (Schell and Martin 2006).]

To put this sentencing in context, if caught for network breaches in the United States, crackers are often charged with "intentionally causing damage without authorization to a protected computer." Since 2000, a first offender has typically faced up to 5 years in prison and fines of up to $250,000 per count, or twice the loss suffered by the victim—with the courts selecting the punishments in part based on the ranges provided in legislation, and in part based on the evidence provided in the courtroom. In the United States, the victim can also seek civil penalties (Richardson 2012; Schell and Martin 2004).

In the CSI survey report, Richardson (2012) noted, in passing, that although hack attacks like the case just described can hurt a company's public image and result in excessive harm to property and persons, it is rather surprising to learn that not all system managers are aware of certain compliance laws and regulations for their industry sectors. Even worse, they simply do not acknowledge that they are beholden to these laws. Given that the 2010/2011 CSI survey applied exclusively to the United States and that at the time of the report's writing 46 of the states had breach notification requirements, it is difficult to fathom why most businesses would not fall within the scope of these laws. Nevertheless, only 47.4 percent of the respondents maintained that they were affected by the laws.

Moreover, noted Richardson (2012), there may be confusion in some industry sectors about whether the compliance rules apply to them. For example, although only 6.6 percent of the respondents to the survey were in the health care sector, the Health Insurance Portability and Accountability Act applies not only to this sector but also to any organization that interacts with data that previously had been identified as HIPAA protected. Thus insurance companies storing information about medical policy claims would need to comply with HIPAA, as would the accounting companies to which they outsource customer billing data. Relative to most pieces of legislative acts applicable to networks and online data protection, HIPPA likely has the widest range of accountability across U.S. industry sectors.

Let us turn now to a fuller discussion of the key U.S. laws and regulations meant to safeguard networks and the information contained within them.

Health Insurance Portability and Accountability Act of 1996

The focus of HIPAA is ensuring health protection for U.S. employees in a number of ways, and the Center for Medicare and Medicated Services (CMS) has the responsibility to implement various unrelated provisions of HIPAA. Title I of HIPAA maintains that health insurance coverage for individuals and their family members must continue when they transfer to another employer or lose their employment. Title II speaks to the importance of security and privacy to health data. The developers of HIPAA felt that standards like those defined in this legislative act would improve the efficiency and effectiveness of the U.S. health care system by encouraging secure and private handling of electronic data. For information security purposes, in particular, HIPAA requires a double entry or double check of data entered by personnel. By April 2005, all U.S. health care organizations had to meet the new HIPAA Security Rule regulations by taking extra precautions to secure protected health information (Schell and Martin 2006).

U.S. State Data Breach Notification Law

Since 2002, a number of U.S. states, as noted by Richardson (2012), have passed data breach notification laws as a positive response to the escalating number of breaches in organizations' and government offices' networks that contain consumer databases with personally identifiable information. The first state data breach notification law was enacted in California in 2002 and became effective the following summer. The goal of state data breach notification laws is to compel state agencies and businesses to disclose in specified ways and in a timely fashion any breach of the security of the data held on the citizens of that state. Thus a network breach that releases personal information of state citizens or is reasonably believed to have been acquired by an unauthorized person would need to be disclosed. The exception to the timely notification of the breach rule is when a law enforcement agency determines that such disclosure would impede an ongoing criminal investigation. There is little variation in the wording of the data breach notification laws from state to state. Moreover, California has since broadened its state data breach notification law to include compromised medical and health insurance information.

The website of the National Conference of State Legislatures (http://www.ncsl.org/) has updates on new pieces of legislation dealing with state and local cybersecurity issues. According to this website, six key values serve as the 47 states' and federal government's priorities:

1. State and local governments must be viewed as critical stakeholders in national cybersecurity efforts, because they operate and manage networks necessary for basic homeland security and for emergency management functions. It is expected that the federal government will work with state and local governments to share threat information and to assist in providing the technical support to protect networks and other related critical infrastructure.

2. The federal government must assist in the funding of the cybersecurity efforts at the state and local levels, because stopping breaches in the network requires a coordinated effort at all levels of government.

3. It is very important that federal, state, and local governments collaborate to invest in cybersecurity awareness, education, and training for public-sector employees, contractors, and private citizens.

4. The civil liberties and privacy of all citizens must be maintained while establishing the safety and stability of the Internet and electronic communications. Also, safeguarding public-sector databases holding personal information on citizens requires cooperation and collaboration on data standards and cybersecurity methodologies at all levels of government.

5. If privacy and security requirements are preconditions of federal programs and funding, they must be uniformly interpreted and implemented across all agencies and all levels of government—local, state, and federal.

6. The combined capacity of federal, state, and local governments to adequately safeguard the United States' critical infrastructure systems remains essential to ensuring

effective operations across the full spectrum of threats that businesses, government agencies, and citizens face daily. In addition, for communities to effectively manage emergency situations, cybersystems must be resilient to acts of terrorism, attacks, and natural disasters.

Sarbanes-Oxley Act

The Sarbanes-Oxley Act, also known as the Public Company Accounting Reform and Investor Protection Act in the U.S. Senate, and as the Corporate and Auditing Accountability and Responsibility Act in the U.S. House of Representatives, was enacted in the summer of 2002 as a reaction to major corporate and accounting scandals at Enron, Tyco International, and WorldCom. The SOX legislation includes 11 sections, with compliance rules covering topics ranging from additional corporate board responsibilities to criminal penalties for infringements of the act. The act also created the Public Company Accounting Oversight Board to oversee, regulate, inspect, and discipline accounting firms in their role as auditors of public companies.

SOX also had fraud implications. Simply put, given the vast amounts of personal information stored on company computers, fraud opportunities abound for cybercriminals. A major problem prompting the passage of SOX was that companies storing huge amounts of information have tended to give little thought to precisely what is being stored in company or institutional networks or how securely it is being stored. Consequently, occasional occurrences of fraud or alterations of data by crackers have often gone undetected (Schell 2007).

A number of IT security experts have argued that, rather than spend lots of money to store data in accordance with SOX requirements, companies should allocate adequate funding to determine exactly which kinds of information should be stored and for how long. Many companies at the time of SOX's passage had policies, for example, dictating that data should be stored for periods lasting from six to nine months, but that timeline may not be realistic. Such confusion over this important information storage issue generated heated debate in the United States, especially over Section 404 of SOX, which outlined the requirement for companies to archive information by July 15, 2005 (Schell 2007).

Payment Card Industry Data Security Standard

The PCI-DSS was developed in the United States by the PCI Security Standards Council. The payment card issuers enforce the standard, which is designed to protect consumers and businesses in the short term and to encourage a worldwide adoption of consistent data security measures over the longer term. There are 12 broad requirements with which organizations must comply. Exactly which requirements must be submitted to confirm compliance varies by merchant level, as determined primarily by the number of payment card transactions that are completed annually.

In short, the PCI-DSS requires that any organization that accepts, acquires, transmits, processes, or stores data that contains payment card information—including retailers, financial institutions, hospitals, restaurants, hotels, and so on—must protect the privacy and confidentiality of those payment card data. Organizations or institutions found to be noncompliant must pay substantial fines and may even have their payment card privileges revoked. However, it must be emphasized that PCI-DSS compliance does not equal IT security, so the reality is that merchants continue to experience data breaches. As a result, companies with severe data breaches may spend millions of dollars in fines plus remediation costs. Moreover, there is often the loss of consumer trust and a tarnishing of the brand if a major breach occurs (Dell 2012).

Intellectual Property Rights and Copyright Infringement

Protecting intellectual property rights (IPR) from abuse is as important for companies today as protecting computer networks from crackers. Infringement of IPR and copyright can cost millions of dollars in lost revenues to entertainment companies and computer companies alike. For this reason, the Digital Millennium Copyright Act (DMCA) was passed in the United States in October 1998. Its purpose was to implement global copyright laws for dealing with IPR challenges caused by present-day technologies. In particular, the DMCA gave protections against technical measures that could be utilized to disable, or bypass, the encryption devices used to protect copyright, thereby encouraging the creators of copyrighted material to put their work on the Internet in a digitalized format. The DMCA penalties were intended to be applied to anyone attempting to or succeeding in disabling an encryption device that protects copyrighted material. In other words, IPR infringement is theft—taking something that does not belong to the perpetrator, thereby depriving the copyright owners of the royalties from the sale of their creative or technological products (Schell and Martin 2006).

An interesting case of alleged violation of IPR occurred in December 2006. At that time, John Wiley & Sons, Inc., sent a legal notification to Google, Inc., informing the search engine company that there appeared to be unauthorized copies of content from 11 Wiley company e-books available on the Internet, including the following: *Clinical Interviewing* by John Sommers-Flanagan, *Handbook of Psychological Assessment* by Gary Groth Maruat, *HDTV for Dummies* by Danny Briere, *Kepler's Conjecture* by George Szpiro, *Modern Banking* by Shelagh Heffeman, *Multimedia Content and the Semantic Web* by Giorgos Stamou, *OpenOffice.org for Dummies* by Gurdy Leete, *Physics for Dummies* by Steve Holzner, *Understanding Headaches and Migraines* by Mark Forshaw, *Webster's New World Hacker Dictionary* by Bernadette Schell and Clemens Martin, and *Windows XP Digital Music for Dummies* by Ryan Williams. The company claimed serious infringement of its copyrights. Wiley said that it would withhold further legal action against Google under the DMCA if the latter removed or blocked access to the infringing material within 48 hours of the time and date of the email, and that Google must provide reasonably requested assistance to help Wiley find and prosecute the party or parties responsible for making the copyrighted material available. This request included sending any information to Wiley that Google had on file regarding the owner of the offending website (Chilling Effects Clearinghouse 2012). Some of this content was subsequently removed after multiple filings on each side, though there is still some contest over Google's right to post intellectual property such as books in a publicly accessible format.

Copyright claimants can also file complaints under the Digital Millennium Copyright Act, Section 512(c) m, which offers a safe harbor for hosts of "Information Residing on Systems or Networks at the Direction of Users." Simply put, "safe harbors" give online providers such as Google immunity from liability for users' possible copyright infringement, provided that the online providers expeditiously remove material when they get complaints like the one received from Wiley. To avoid being held liable for copyright infringement by materials its users have posted on its servers, online providers will usually try to avoid the possibility of a lawsuit by following the DMCA's "takedown" procedure when they receive complaints. In turn, the online user whose information was removed can file a counter-notification if he or she believes that the complaint was filed in error (Chilling Effects Clearinghouse 2012).

International Privacy and Security Laws

Privacy Laws

On a global basis, privacy laws are enacted in countries interested in safeguarding their citizens while they engage in online activities. Thus privacy laws worldwide deal with the right of individual privacy, which is critical to maintaining the quality of life that citizens in a free society expect.

Privacy laws generally maintain that an individual's privacy shall not be violated unless the government can show some compelling reason to do so—such as by providing evidence that the safety of the nation is at risk. This tenet forms the basis of privacy laws in the United States, Canada, and elsewhere (Schell and Martin 2006).

Hardly a day goes by without news of some security breach adversely impacting citizens' personal information making media headlines. A recent case occurred on June 7, 2012, when computer security experts in the United States and Europe warned that they had uncovered evidence that the social networking site LinkedIn had suffered a data breach that exposed the passwords of millions of online users. The day before the media release, Sophos computer security experts found files with some 6.4 million scrambled passwords. When the experts searched more deeply into their find, they concluded that at least part of the list belonged to Sophos employees who used passwords to secure their LinkedIn accounts. The data were discovered on underground websites where criminal crackers often exchange stolen information such as scrambled passwords. The files seemed to include only stolen passwords, but IT security analysts now believe that it is likely the cyberthieves also have the corresponding email addresses and, therefore, could access these accounts. Marcus Carey, an IT security expert at the Rapid7 company in Boston, believes that the crackers may have been inside the network for days, based on the type of information stolen and the large quantity of data released to the criminal underground (Finkle and Saba 2012).

Security Laws in the United States

Like privacy laws, security laws of varying sorts are enacted in the United States and elsewhere to protect citizens' and governments' confidential information that is stored on government and industry networks. Security laws also detail what is considered to be "unauthorized access to networks" and the penalties incurred if crackers are caught and convicted of network intrusion.

For example, U.S. cases are generally prosecuted under the computer crime statute identified in 18 U.S.C. Section 1030. The primary U.S. federal statute criminalizing cracking was originally the Computer Fraud and Abuse Act (CFAA). In 1996, the CFAA was modified by the National Infrastructure Protection Act and codified at 18 U.S.C. Section 1030, Fraud and Related Activity in Connection with Computers. As noted earlier, a first-time hacking intruder whose activities fall under this statute, and who is charged with intentionally causing damage to a protected computer and found guilty of the charge, typically faces a prison sentence of up to five years in jail and fines up to $250,000 per count, or twice the loss suffered by victims (Schell and Martin 2004).

After the September 11, 2001, terrorist attacks, the U.S. government passed a series of laws aimed at halting computer criminals and terrorists having the intent of causing harm to persons. These laws are generally passed as an attempt to stay one step ahead of the criminal curve, but often such legislation represents a response to an event rather than a preemptive strike. For example, the 2001 USA PATRIOT Act (Uniting and Strengthening America by Providing Appropriate Tools Required to Intercept and Obstruct Terrorism) was aimed at terrorists, in particular. Moreover, in 2002, the Homeland Security Act was passed, containing Section 225, the Cyber Security Enhancement Act of 2002; this act detailed the mission and functions of the Department of Homeland Security (DHS).

Furthermore, when spam became an online nuisance around 2003, the U.S. Senate passed the CAN-SPAM Act, with the purpose of doing exactly what its name implies: Controlling the Assault of Non-Solicited Pornography and Marketing. The aim of this legislation was to target spammers and massive emailers whose objectives—according to the email's headers—appeared to be legitimate but were not. The alarming statistic that drove this piece of legislation in 2003 was publication of the fact that unsolicited commercial email was estimated to account for more than half of all email traffic, a rise from just 7 percent just two years earlier. Spammers were identified in the CAN-SPAM Act to be individuals gaining access to a protected computer without authorization and intentionally initiating the sending of multiple commercial email messages from or through the computer and an Internet connection. Criminals who violate the CAN-SPAM Act can receive punishment in the form of a fine, imprisonment for not more than five years, or both (Schell 2007).

In April 2005, the House of Representatives' Homeland Security Subcommittee on Economic Security, Infrastructure Protection, and Cyber Security passed HR 285, the Cyber Security Enhancement Act of 2005. This act stated not only that the assistant secretary for cybersecurity would be the head of the Directorate's National Cyber Security Division, but also that the division would identify and reduce vulnerabilities and threats, as well as create cyberattack warning systems if critical infrastructures were at risk (Schell 2007).

Security Laws in Other Jurisdictions

Other jurisdictions around the world have also passed laws to keep their citizens, national information, and critical infrastructure safe from cybercriminals. For example, the European Union (EU) has a number of such laws, including the E-Privacy Directive, the E-Commerce Directive, and the Data Protection Directive. In the United Kingdom, for example, there is the U.K. Data Protection Act of 1984, the Copyright Design and Patents Act of 1988, the Criminal Damage Act of 1971, the Theft Act of 1968, the Telecommunications Act of 1984, the Police and Criminal Evidence Act of 1984, and the Computer Misuse Act of 1990 (Schell and Dodge, with Moutsatsos 2002).

Canada's anti-intrusion legislation involves Section 342.1 of the Canadian Criminal Code, aimed at several potential harms to property and persons, including stealing computer services, invading individuals' privacy, trading in stolen computer passwords, and cracking encrypted systems. Charges for such exploits are usually made under applicable sections of the Canadian Criminal Code—theft, fraud, computer abuse, information abuse, and the interception of communications. For example, Section 342.1 describes the crime of "unauthorized use of the computer," and Section 430 (.1) describes the crime of "mischief" as it relates to data (Schell 2007).

Despite these evolving laws to prevent and punish the harm caused by cybercriminals, citizens around the globe continue to call for a more concerted effort by their own government and other governments globally to collaborate to more effectively counter the increasingly sophisticated tribes of cyber perpetrators. For example, in June 2012, in internal documents obtained by Bloomberg News, a media release in the *Financial Post* indicated that cyberattacks pose a greater risk to Canada's economic prosperity than the Canadian government previously believed, and noted that Canada seems to lack the tools to fight these sophisticated cybercriminals. In fact, poor protection against cyberattacks puts at risk not just Canadian national security, but also public safety, economic prosperity, and a critical loss of intellectual property. According to the authors of this media release, the Canadian government's ability to respond effectively to these cyberexploits is hindered by the lack of a national emergency policy like the one the United States has established for cyberattacks, as well as aging facilities and difficulty in recruiting IT specialists eligible for "top secret" security status. In short, present-day cyberattacks are a mutating threat that will require cooperation among governments, industry, and online citizens if real progress is to be made on the IT security front (Mayeda and Miller 2012)

Federal Information Security Management Act

On March 5, 2002, U.S. Representative Tom Davis, Republican-Virginia, introduced the Federal Information Security Management Act (FISMA) as a means to improve the United States'

A U.S. Air Force employee gains computer access with a card in a demonstration of the Personal Identify Verification (PIV) software developed by the National Institute of Standards and Technology (NIST). As part of a Homeland Security directive, NIST's program is intended to provide and authenticate credentials of anyone who has access to sensitive government buildings, data, and computer networks. (Department of Defense)

information security and to develop information security risk management standards so as to protect the nation's critical information infrastructure. In 2002, this legislation was enacted, giving the Office of Management and Budget (OMB) the mandate to coordinate information security standards and guidelines produced by civilian-based federal agencies (Schell and Martin 2006).

In general, FISMA was aimed at promoting key security standards and guidelines for business and government agencies to support the implementation of and compliance with the act. There was interest in developing standards for categorizing information and information systems by mission impact, developing standards for minimum security requirements for information and information systems, and giving guidance for selecting appropriate security controls for information systems.

In addition, the government sought means for assessing security controls in information systems, determining security control effectiveness, authorizing secure information systems, and monitoring the security controls and security authorization of information systems (National Institute of Standards and Technology 2012).

The long-term goals of FISMA included (1) implementing cost-effective, risk-based information security programs in the United States; (2) establishing a suitable level of security "due diligence" for federal agencies and contractors working for the government; (3) having a more consistent and cost-effective application of security control across the federal information technology infrastructure; and (4) in the end, having more secure information systems within the federal government, including the critical infrastructure of the United States (National Institute of Standards and Technology 2012).

Gramm-Leach-Bliley Act

Although it may be difficult to believe, personal information that most citizens would consider to be personal and private—such as bank account numbers and bank account balances—is routinely exchanged for a price by banks and credit card companies. For this reason, the GLBA, which is also known as the Financial Services Modernization Act of 1999, established some privacy protections against the sale of citizens' private information, particularly that of a financial nature. Also, the GLBA codified protections against "pre-texting," defined as the act of obtaining someone else's personal data through false means. Another purpose of the GLBA was to remove regulations that did not allow banks, insurance firms, and stock brokerage firms to merge. Critics argued that if such regulations were eliminated, merged financial institutions would have little or no restrictions on how such personal information could be used. For example, before the passage of the GLBA, an insurance company with data on citizens' health records would be considered to be distinct from a bank that had personal financial information on clients wanting a home mortgage. With the passage of the GLBA, following the merger of two such firms, the new merged entity was not permitted to either pool the information it had on all of its clients or to sell the pooled information to interested third parties (Schell and Martin 2006).

Because of such risks to citizens' personal information, the GLBA included three key requirements for protecting the personal information of clients: (1) the information had to be securely stored; (2) the merged institutions had to advise clients about the policy of sharing personal information—particularly of a financial nature—with others; and (3) the institutions had to give consumers the right to opt out of the information-sharing schemes if they desired. It is interesting to note that on July 26, 2001, just two years after this act's passage, the Electronic Privacy Information Center (EPIC) filed a petition requesting an amendment to the GLBA to ensure that clients were given improved notice and a better way of conveniently opting out of information-sharing schemes. Moreover, because of a number of court cases arising from alleged violations of the GLBA, an increasing number of financial institutions and insurance companies have begun purchasing cybersecurity insurance for protection against hack attacks such as denial of service, crack attacks by insiders and outsiders, malware, and electronic theft of personal financial information. Breaches of the GLBA have over the past decade resulted in lawsuits that resulted in damages totaling $1 million or more per case (Schell and Martin 2006).

It is a bit of a secret that a catalogue for Victoria's Secret—an Internet website and online retail store for women's lingerie—was one of the main reasons that U.S. Congress included privacy protections for financial information when passing the GLBA. The debate apparently started when Representative Joe Barton discussed his concerns that his credit union had sold his address to Victoria's Secret, after which, he claimed, he started getting the catalogues at his residence in Washington, D.C. He claimed further that he became stressed when the catalogues started arriving, because he did not want his wife to wrongly think that he was buying lingerie for other women or that he was using the lingerie model pictures for his personal enjoyment. Barton went on to state that because he spent so little money in Washington, D.C., he knew that his credit union was the only business that had his personal address. He suggested that with the passage of the GLBA, there would be better controls on financial institutions selling personal information to third parties. The passage of the GLBA is the reason that individuals now have the right to direct financial institutions to not sell their personal information to third parties (Schell 2007).

Health Information Technology for Economic and Clinical Health Act

On February 17, 2009, President Obama signed into law the Health Information Technology for Economic and Clinical Health Act, as a means of stimulating in the United States the adoption of electronic health records (EHRs) rather than continued reliance on paper records. Besides supporting the development and application of secure emerging technologies, the HITECH Act was considered to be part of the economic stimulus bill known as the American Recovery and Reinvestment Act of 2009 (ARRA). The HITECH Act stipulated that, starting in 2011, health care providers in the United States would be offered incentives for demonstrating the meaningful use of EHRs, with incentives for usage being given out until 2015. After this date, penalties will be levied to government agencies and businesses not demonstrating such uses. The HITECH Act also established grants to train the personnel required to support a health IT infrastructure (Rouse 2009).

Payment Card Industry Payment Application Standard

A number of businesses have complained that their obligations under the Payment Card Industry Data Security Standard (PCI-DSS) and the Payment Card Industry Payment Applicant

Standard (PA-DSS) are somewhat difficult to ascertain. Experts, however, warn that businesses that fail to understand or avoid understanding their obligations might face steep costs if a data breach occurs, because of staggering fines, recovery-related costs, and damage to the business brand. Consider these recent facts. In 2011, 96 percent of the merchants that experienced a data breach did not comply with the PCI-DSS or the PA-DSS; when found not to be compliant, the breached merchant was often subject to fines from the payment card brand or the acquiring bank. On average, a merchant's direct cost associated with recovering from an exploit is about $194 per stolen record; given that a typical breach involves tens of thousands of records (or more), the total recovery costs can be staggering. Finally, if the fines and costs related to recovery are not motivation enough for businesses to comply with the PCI-DSS and the PA-DSS, the potential loss of consumer trust and the blow to the business's brand could be an ever more potent catalyst for compliance (Herbig 2012).

According to Verizon's *2012 Data Breach Investigations Report*, when 855 recent network intrusion incidents were studied, 174 million compromised records were found. The report concluded that 96 percent of these attacks were not highly difficult to achieve, and 97 percent of the attacks were avoidable through simple or intermediate controls. Small-business owners' systems are the most vulnerable to hack attacks, warn IT security experts at Verizon, because target selection is based more on opportunity than on choice. (For more information on this topic, go to http://www.verizonbusiness.com/resources/reports/rp_data-breach-investigations-report-2012_en_xg.pdf?CMP=DMC-SMB_Z_ZZ_ZZ_Z_TV_N_Z037 for an executive summary of the *2012 Data Brach Investigations Report*.)

The PA-DSS is maintained by the PDI Security Standards Council. It was originally known as PABP—that is, Visa's "Payment Application Best Practices." Although Visa started the program, it has since transitioned to the PCI Security Standards Council (PCI SSC). In 2005, Visa created the PABP to ensure that vendors would provide products supporting merchants and to eliminate the storage of sensitive cardholder data. The PCI SSC not only maintains the PA-DSS but administers a program to validate applications' compliance with this standard. The PCI SCC has published a list of PA-DSS validated applications, which can be found at https://www.pcisecuritystandards.org/security_standards/pa_dss .shtml (ControlScan 2012).

The Militarization of Cyberspace

The continuous and varied threats posed by cyberattacks from hackers acting either because of their own ideologies or on behalf of a nation-state have led governments to substantially retool their policies toward cyberspace and cybersecurity in general. For instance, successive U.S. presidential administrations have established roadmaps to improve the governmental response to cybercrime and prospective attacks over the last two decades (Brenner 2008). Their efforts have led to modest policy changes, and served mostly as barometers of the importance of cyberattacks and cybersecurity issues at any given time. This situation changed with the dissemination of the Department of Defense's policies in July 2011, which detailed that organization's view of cyberspace as a protected domain in much the same way as the physical environments of sea, air, and land (Department of Defense 2011). The document recognized that the defensive measures currently used to protect America's critical infrastructure and its defense industrial base were ineffective and required significant expansion. Without a change, there will be no way to truly begin to secure this domain from the increasing criminal and nation-state attacks. In particular, the Department of Defense (2011) placed a specific emphasis on the need for careful responses to theft of data, destructive attacks to degrade network functionality, and denial-of-service attacks. These forms of hacking attacks pose a direct threat to the communications capabilities of the nation, and the maintenance of secrecy and intellectual property.

To reduce the risks posed by malicious actors and attacks, the Defense Department's report calls on five specific strategies to improve the military and governmental response to attacks:

1. Treat cyberspace as an operational domain for the military to utilize its potential for both attack and defense.
2. Employ new defensive strategies to protect defensive systems.
3. Create strategic partnerships between the government and the private sector to develop a "whole-of-government" security strategy that minimizes the piecemeal approach.
4. Create relationships with U.S. allies that create a more collective cybersecurity strategy.
5. Expand the cybersecurity workforce and improve the innovative application of technology to secure the nation.

These techniques will help to improve defense of the nation, although the Department of Defense's report does not simply discuss security. Indeed, there is also some detail given on the nature of cyberattacks relative to traditional warfare, and the fact that cyberspace is largely ignored in existing rules of armed conflict on an international scope. Thus the Department of Defense (2011) will attempt to collaborate with partnering nations to determine the appropriate response to certain forms of attack. An effort will be made to develop policies regarding which forms of cyberattack may lead to physical responses (such as those that cause death in the real world), and which will lead to cyber-based military responses (including data theft or destruction).

Similar policies and strategic plans are emerging in developed nations around the world, from Canada to the United Kingdom. As more nations determine the way in which their military forces will respond to cyberattacks, there will be a substantive increase in the policy implications for hackers and for the way that combatants engage one another (Brenner 2008). For instance, the use of Stuxnet by the U.S. government could be viewed as an act of war, as it directly attempted to cause physical harm in much the same way as a bomb or physical incursion. The small size of the Iranian military and its distance relative to the United States do not, however, allow for a measured physical response. Thus it is possible that Iranian actors may engage in cyberattacks out of revenge or spite. It is unclear how these policies may play out over time or in the real world in the event of actual attacks, but it is critical to recognize that the involvement of military response capabilities will dramatically affect cyberspace and the actions of hackers generally.

Industry "Best Practices" for Preventing Hack Attacks and Recovering from Them

While a number of excellent strategies for protecting networks have been created to assist system administrators in small, medium, and large enterprises, some practical and up-to-date pointers are found in the *Sophos Security Threat Report 2012* (Eschelbeck 2012). The recommendations for various hacker-related activities that have caused harm to property or persons in recent years are summarized here.

Protection Strategies

For Hacktivism

There is little question that 2011–2012 was a busy year for hacktivist groups such as LulzSec and Anonymous. LulzSec launched cyberattacks on Sony, the U.S. Senate, and the U.S. Central Intelligence Agency (CIA). Anonymous was suspected of bringing down various websites in El Salvador, Israel, and Toronto, Canada, through distributed denial-of-service (DDoS) attacks. As a manifestation of not respecting citizens' privacy, hackers affiliated with Anonymous released 90,000 email addresses of U.S. military personnel, apparently in an attack on Booz Allen Hamilton. The range of targets seems to illustrate that almost any institution of any size is at risk for hacktivist attacks on its organizational website. According to IT security experts, encryption is the best way to protect against hacktivists' harm and their unauthorized access to sensitive data (Eschelbeck 2012).

Encryption, or encipher, is the mathematical conversion of information into a form using algorithms from which the original information cannot be restored without using a special "key." However, even encryption is not without its flaws.

In January 2005, for example, at an encryption conference held in Toronto, Canada, about 60 encryption systems integrators and middleware vendors from around the world met to discuss their concerns. According to these experts, the toughest job facing their companies is being able to fix the security holes in their products to meet the encryption requirements of the United States' Federal Information Processing Standard 140-2 (FIPS 140-2). In fact, according to the experts at the conference, about 30 percent of the new cryptographic modules failed to pass the FIPS 140-2 standardized tests approved by the National Institute of Standards and Technology (NIST). What is even more concerning, they affirmed, is that about 20 percent of returning modules continue to have security bugs. Although many middleware developers want to extend their applications to a wireless environment, no real standard seems to have replaced the broken Wired Equivalent Privacy algorithm.

Middleware, by definition, is an application connecting two separate applications. Thus middleware systems generally provide functionality such as distribution of components, deployment, and transaction services that developers can integrate into their own applications without having to worry about the implementation details. Back in 2006, as a case in point, Microsoft's .NET architecture as well as various implementations of Sun Microsystems' J2EE Standard were popular forms of middleware (Schell and Martin 2006).

The Wired Equivalency Protocol (WEP) is a protocol adding security to wireless LANs, based on the IEEE 802.11 Wi-Fi standard, an OSI Data Link layer technology that can be turned "off" and "on." Without getting too deep into the technical details, WEP was developed to give wireless networks the same level of privacy protection as a wired network. WEP is formulated on a security notion called RC4, which uses a combination of system-generated values and secret user keys. The initial implementation of the protocol supported only 40-bit encryption and had a key length of 40 bits and 24 additional bits of system-generated data, resulting in a 64-bit total. However, since WEP's "birth," scientists have determined that 40-bit WEP encryption is too weak—meaning that it can be easy to hack. For this reason, product vendors generally use 128-bit encryption with key lengths of 104 bits or greater. Wireless network devices such as mobile phones use WEP keys to encrypt the data stream for communications over the wire (Schell and Martin 2006).

For Malware

Data breaches caused by malware—software designed to infiltrate or damage a computer system without the owner's informed consent and including such cyberdestroyers as viruses, worms, spyware, adware, and Trojan horses—often are extraordinarily costly. In 2010, for example, the Ponemon Institute claimed that the costs of a data breach reached $214 per compromised record and averaged $7.2 million per data breach event, including the direct costs of the data breach (i.e., notification to clients and legal defense costs) and indirect costs such as consumer loss of trust and lost business (Eschelbeck 2012).

What is more, since 2005, security breaches have compromised more than 500 million records, not including data losses attributable to human error or negligence—which have been another major problem. To reduce the risk of malware infection, IT security experts advise screening web use on the network with quality protection technologies that can detect malware on hacked websites and respond quickly to emerging malware URLs. To counter the malware threat, the Sophos security firm, as a case in point, has used proactive detection technologies designed to detect not just the millions of existing malware, but also future malware before it is even created. Their tools can proactively scan networked computers to reduce the likelihood of infections. To that end, Sophos, suggests that in the last six months of 2011, 80 percent of the malware seen by their clients (more than 5.5 million unique files) were detected and mitigated by 93 individual scans (Eschelbeck 2012).

For Drive-by Downloads and Blackholes

According to experts at Sophos Labs, more than 30,000 websites are infected by cyberinvaders daily, and 80 percent of those infected sites are legitimate. In 2011–2012, drive-by downloads became a top web threat, with one drive-by malware known as Blackhole rising to number one. Drive-by attacks generally exploit multiple unpatched vulnerabilities in the user's browser, browser plugin, application, or operating system. Hackers either lure users to malicious sites they have embedded with malicious code, or else hack legitimate sites as a means of hosting the malware. Because legitimate sites are trusted by online users, they can be highly successful means of distributing malware through the browser to unsuspecting visitors.

Blackhole, in particular, is sold to cybercriminals as a professional "crimeware kit" that provides web administration capabilities. Because Blackhole offers sophisticated techniques for generating malicious code, it is very insidious, because its heavily obfuscated scripts tend to cleverly evade antivirus detection. Another dark side of crimeware kits such as the clever Blackhole is that they are continuously updated as new vulnerabilities are found. Probably the best protection strategy against

Blackhole, note the experts at Sophos Labs, is to track detections with data provided by clients and industry partners. Such tracking will give system administrators good visibility as to where the exploit sites are being hosted. Also, because Blackhole is a continually moving target (the code is polymorphic and the exploit sites frequently move to new URLs), multiple layers of protection are needed. At Sophos, experts not only detect the malware payload but also provide detection for Blackhole exploit sites at all possible levels (Eschelbeck 2012).

For Software Vulnerabilities

At any hacker convention aimed at finding solutions for software vulnerabilities, there is a consistent and ongoing "joke" year after year about Windows—because it is the most attacked operating system, with the primary vectors for cracking Windows being through PDF or Flash. Despite this reputation and Microsoft's ongoing updates to patch Windows operating system vulnerabilities, the content delivery systems remain the weakest link on any operating system. In turn, favorite targets of hackers have been Microsoft Office and Internet Explorer because of their popularity.

Consequently, IT security experts have urged software company developers and vendors to integrate security into their product development life cycles—including scanning for common coding error from the initial steps of development—and not wait to include such features until the end of this process, when the product is ready to go to market. Although NIST recently expanded its database of software flaws to help software developers avoid putting "bugs" or "glitches" into their code, unfortunately basic vulnerabilities such as SQL injection (defined earlier in the chapter) and cross-site scripting still account for the major security flaws existing in web applications. [Cross-site scripting (XSS) is a security exploit in which an attacker inserts malicious coding into a link that appears to be from a trustworthy source. When someone clicks on the link, the embedded programming is submitted as part of the client's web request and can execute on the user's computer, typically allowing the attacker to steal information.]

Knowing about this weak link, Anonymous was able to breach a number of high-profile websites in 2011. According to experts at the Sophos Labs, the best protection strategy for software is to keep the updates turned on, to install the patches regularly, and to run antivirus programs. Also, companies should use application control technologies to retain control over what the users install on the enterprise network, thereby reducing "the threat surfaces." Put simply, fewer programs and plugins means lower risk for the network (Eschelbeck 2012).

For USB Drives and Other Mobile Devices Such as Tablets

Given that a considerable amount of proprietary information owned by companies and government agencies is "misplaced" into competitors' hands through lost or stolen USB flash drives, thumb drives, CDs, or DVDs, companies should insist that computer users encrypt all business data before storing such data on USB drives. Then, if the devices are lost or stolen, the data cannot be accessed. Moreover, companies may want to issue a policy stipulating how or where USB flash drives and other removable devices are to be used; to this end, there may be a restriction placed on bringing removable devices from home into the office. Finally, companies should regularly scan corporate removable devices for malware and sensitive data (Eschelbeck 2012).

The same principle applies to mobile devices such as tablets, an increasingly popular choice among employees encouraged to bring their own devices to work. For example, at the Canadian public relations firm Hill & Knowlton, employees are encouraged to use mobile devices, because they are a necessity for serving clients. According to estimates from the intelligence firm IDC Canada, two thirds of all Canadian workers are mobile in their work in a huge capacity—with this share expected to reach three fourths of all Canadian workers by 2015.

According to a poll of Canadian businesses conducted in the fall of 2011, the number one driver of the bring-your-own-device (BYOD) movement was senior executives bringing their own mobile devices into the workplace, followed by employees buying into the "going mobile" era because of its combined assets of flexibility and optimization of work-life balance.

However, firms espousing the BYOD principle may face serious organizational IT security concerns. When employees bring a tablet, for example, into the office, suddenly it is very easy to move information back and forth from home to organization, and to combine personal and business information. This movement to and fro has profound implications for IT security and device management. Gartner, Inc., predicts that about 80 percent of businesses will have deployed tablets by 2013. Therefore, it is a "must" that businesses start now to develop a strategy regarding BYOD. Publishing clear usage rules and being open to use of multiple devices is likely the wave forward for businesses and governments (Rockel 2012).

For Cloud "Insecurity"

Earlier in this chapter, we talked about the growing popularity of moving computation, software, data access, and storage delivered as a service over the Internet to another host— collectively known as "cloud computing." But, warn the IT security experts at Sophos, putting data "in the cloud" raises a set of unique security, compliance, and privacy risks. In a recent Ernst & Young *Global Information Security Survey*, about 61 percent of the survey respondents said that they would be evaluating moving to cloud services over the next 12 months, but another survey undertaken by Sophos found that only a few of the organizations that were considering the move had cloud security policies in place. At a minimum, note the experts at Sophos, companies contemplating or engaged in cloud services need to ask pertinent questions about where their data are stored, who has access to the data, and whether the data are stored on shared servers. Companies considering this move must also assess cloud computing's impact on privacy, governance, risk management and assurance, and regulatory compliance (Eschelbeck 2012).

A number of well-publicized incidents in 2011–2012 demonstrated that storing data "in the cloud" poses security and compliance risks. In addition, the fact that companies and individuals may not know if their data are accessed under the USA PATRIOT Act is worrisome, as this law allows U.S. authorities to intercept and inspect any data "housed, stored, or processed by a U.S.-based or wholly owned company." As a case in point, in June 2011, Microsoft said that it could be required to give data to U.S. authorities without informing customers, even when the data were stored in the European Union, where the EU 1995 Data Protection Directive requires companies to notify customers when sharing their personal information. What is more, while Anonymous and LulzSec dominated the data breach media headlines in 2011–2012, what became painfully obvious is that more organizations are collecting data about their customers and doing a lousy job of protecting that information. Thus, as protection strategies for cloud computing, companies should encrypt data before storing it "in the cloud." Moreover, companies should select a cloud services provider that is transparent about security measures, backup, and failures. Standard security processes such as access control and other data protection techniques should be part of the "cloud services" package (Eschelbeck 2012).

For Social Networks

Earlier in this chapter, we mentioned the June 2012 LinkedIn hack attack. Other social network hack attacks targeted Facebook, Twitter, and YouTube in 2011. Perhaps not surprisingly, considering the popularity of social networking websites for individuals globally, companies have started to jump onto the social networking bandwagon. They have established Facebook pages, LinkedIn and YouTube profiles, and Twitter accounts, as they clearly see the potential to hone in on new prospects via the social networking venue.

The harsh reality, as illustrated in the 2012 LinkedIn exploit, in which more than 6 million user records were lost, is that social networking sites—like other websites—can be compromised. Sometimes the results can be ugly. For example, in 2011, hackers replaced the innocent Sesame Street's YouTube channel with hardcore pornographic movie content. Similarly, a small group of malware writers created a program called Koobface that targeted multiple social networking platforms to infect user systems (Dromer and Kollberg 2012). These compromised computers were then used to create a botnet that would hijack browser queries and spread secondary malware infections.

How can one protect these hugely popular social networks? Without question, sloppy password security is a major reason why social networks are hacking targets. These social networks need to consider themselves to be legitimate businesses, offering clients a higher level of security for accounts. One of the leaders in this respect appears to be the Google Plus social network, introduced by Google in 2011.

The major problem is that social networking sites seem less interested in protecting their accounts than in supporting revenue-generating advertising. Therefore, they tend to be more interested in increasing the number of users and advertisers than in establishing sensible security defaults. To this end, in 2011, Sophos published an open letter to Facebook, calling on the company to better protect its users by (1) including privacy by default, (2) doing a better job of vetting its application developers, and (3) doing a better job of vetting its HTTPS for anything suspicious. The bottom line is that IT managers should educate their users about choosing hard-to-crack passwords using a string of numbers and letters (Eschelbeck 2012).

The Need for Security Policies and Security Policy Checklists in Businesses and Government Agencies

As a general means of protecting their networks, government agencies and businesses need to develop security policy checklists that are developed by security experts and that use questions dealing with a number of security-related issues. Before detailing these questions, it needs to be emphasized that one major question needs answering first: Are all of the items on the checklist (below) to be distributed to all employees and fully understood by them? If so, the following set of questions needs to be discussed and set as a form of organizational policy (Schell and Martin 2006):

- *Administrator rights and responsibilities:* Under which conditions may a system administrator examine an employee's online account or his or her email, and which parts of the system should the system administrator not examine (e.g., Netscape bookmarks)? Can the system administrator monitor network traffic, and if so, which boundaries exist?

- *Backups:* Which systems are backed up and how often? How are backups secured and verified?

- *Connections to and from the Internet:* Which computers should be seen from the outside? If computers are outside the firewall (i.e., bastion hosts), how securely are they separated from computers inside the firewall? Are connections from the Internet to the internal network allowed, and if so, how are they authenticated and encrypted? Which traffic is allowed to go outside the internal network? If there is traffic across the Internet, how is it secured, and what protection is in place against various forms of malware?

- *Dial-up connections:* Are dial-up connections allowed, and if so, how are they authenticated, and which access level to the internal network do dial-up connections provide? How are modems distributed within the company, and can employees set up modem connections to their home or desktop computers?

- *Documentation:* Does a map of the network topology exist, and is it clearly stated where each computer fits on that map? Along these same lines, is there an inventory of all hardware and software, and does a document exist detailing the preferred security configuration of every system?

- *Emergency procedures:* Which kinds of procedures exist for installing security "patches" or handling exploits? In cases of system intrusion by hackers, is it company policy to shut down the network immediately, or does the company intend to monitor the system intruder for a while? How and when are employees notified of system exploits, and at which stage and at what time are law enforcement agencies called in to investigate?

- *Logs:* Which information is logged, how, and where? Are the information logs secure from tampering, and if so, are they regularly examined—and by whom?

- *Physical security:* Are systems physically protected from outsider hackers and adequately secured, where needed, from insider hackers? Are reusable passwords used internally or externally, and are employees told through company policy to change their passwords routinely?

- *Sensitive information:* How is sensitive and proprietary company information protected online, and how are the backup tapes protected?

- *User rights and responsibilities:* What degree of freedom do employees have in terms of selecting their own operating system, software, and, say, games for their computers? Can employees in the enterprise send and receive personal email or do personal work on company computers, such as booking trips online? Which policies exist within the enterprise for resource consumption (i.e., disk or central processing unit quotas? [The central processing unit (CPU) is the "brains" of the computer where most calculations occur.] Which policies exist within the enterprise regarding insider abuse (accidental and intentional) of IT services? Which penalties are applied, when, say, an employee brings down a server?

The Importance of Intrusion Prevention, Intrusion Detection, and Intrusion Recovery

Intrusion Prevention Is Important

As has been noted in various IT security and system administration survey reports in this chapter, because targeted attacks on company and government agency networks have been increasing in recent years, intrusion prevention has become a priority for companies of any size. Therefore, companies are moving away from the very time-consuming process of detecting intrusions whereby system administrators react to them manually, and are moving toward implementing automated mechanisms found in marketed intrusion-prevention systems (IPS).

According to IT experts at Gartner, Inc., there are three key criteria for providing a useful network and host-based IPS application (Pescatore and Stiennon 2004):

1. *The IPS must not disrupt normal operations*, meaning that when it is put online, an IPS must not place unacceptable or unpredictable latency into a network. Moreover, a host-based IPS should not use more than 10 percent of a system's resources, so that network traffic and normal processes on the servers can continue to run. Blocking actions should take place in real time or almost real time, with latencies in the tens of milliseconds rather than in seconds.

2. *The IPS must block exploits using more than one algorithm* to operate at both the application level and the firewall-processing level.

3. *The IPS must have the capability to ascertain "attack events" from "normal events."*

Automated intrusion-prevention systems continue to evolve and their capacities continue to improve, but they still are not totally effective. For this reason, trained analysts will continue to flag and more thoroughly investigate suspicious traffic activity.

Intrusion Detection Is Important

An intrusion-detection system (IDS) is a security appliance or software running on a device that tries to detect and warn of ongoing computer system cracks or attempted cracks in real time or near real time. IDSs tend to come in three varieties: anomaly based, pattern based, and specification based. According to surveys conducted among system administrators, the first two are more popular choices than the latter.

Anomaly-based IDSs treat all exposed behavior of systems on the network that is unknown to them as a potential attack; thus these systems require extensive training of the IDS so that "good traffic" can be distinguished from "bad traffic." Pattern-based IDSs, by comparison, assume that attack patterns are known and, therefore, can be detected in the current network; however, because these IDSs cannot detect new attack types, they require constant maintenance to incorporate new attack patterns as they are discovered. Finally, specification-based IDSs look for states of the system known to be undesirable; upon detecting such a state, they report that there has been a network intrusion (Schell and Martin 2006).

All three types of IDSs generate logs and other network information—traffic patterns, unusual open ports, or unexpected running processes—which are then routinely reviewed by security analysts to search for suspected or real intrusions. Consequently, the log and network information review process is time-consuming, which is why companies have increasingly invested in automated systems such as Hewlett-Packard's "Virus Throttler" software, which not only identifies and alerts system analysts of suspicious network traffic but also causes some of the network's functions to slow down so that the malware is impeded (In Brief 2004; Schell and Martin 2006).

Intrusion Recovery Is Important

All three IT security hack attack reports discussed in this chapter alluded to the fact that small, medium, and large enterprises absolutely need to recover from system intrusions as quickly as possible to maintain consumer trust and to save money. However, the harsh reality is that regardless of the range of products available to help protect networks, not all companies are making these kinds of investments, because their IT budgets just cannot accommodate a reliable suite of prevention or detection measures. As noted, the initial step in preventing unauthorized access is the deployment of intrusion-prevention systems that actively and automatically limit illegal access to systems. Attacks that cannot be blocked by the prevention systems would typically be detected by intrusion-detection systems— applications monitoring operating system software and network traffic for real or probable security breaches. If these systems fail and an attack is successful, other steps need to be put into place. For this reason, government agencies and companies need to have an appropriate disaster recovery plan.

Disaster recovery plans are defined as strategies outlining both the technical and the organizational factors related to network security. Such plans generally begin with a comprehensive assessment of the network to determine "acceptable risk" levels for the system. These results can then be used to produce a set of IT security policies and procedures for assisting employees and work groups within the enterprise to cope effectively if a network becomes disrupted or stops altogether. Furthermore, appropriate decisions can be made by system administrators as to which methods and systems will be required by the enterprise so that it can implement its security policies and procedures quickly and effectively—which is, of course, the primary goal of intrusion recovery (Schell and Martin 2006).

How Well Enterprises Are Coping with Network Prevention, Intrusions, and Recovery

In the *2010/2011 CSI Computer Crime and Security Survey* findings, Richardson (2012) provides some insights into how well enterprises seem to be doing in terms of staying ahead of the cybercriminals or appropriately and rapidly recovering from exploits if they could not be prevented. Richardson discusses the effectiveness of fighting and recovering from hack attacks by looking at a three-axis model: Basic Attacks, Malware Attacks, and Attacks 2.0. Here are his key discoveries, given the survey respondents' views:

1. *Basic Attacks.* The basic core of unelaborated attack vectors accounts for the bulk of basic attacks on networks— phishing, rudimentary port scans, brute-force attacks on password-protected accounts (a trial-and-error exhaustive effort used by application programs to decrypt encrypted data such as passwords), and the more conventional viruses. Though these attacks are rather basic, they can still cause considerable damage. They are very much like smash-and-grab attacks on retail storefronts during riots. According to the study findings, IT security respondents believe that their organizations are able to protect their networks from these basic attacks, because they have taken the appropriate protection measures. Overall, system administrators tend to view basic attacks as a nuisance more than anything else.

2. *Malware Attacks.* The middle core of the three-axis model represents a layer of extended versions of previous attacks. This realm includes malware created from generational and customized toolkits, phishing attacks using real company or government agency names known to online victims to capitalize on the scam, and tools scanning for unpatched systems with known vulnerabilities. This realm, it seems, is where insider hackers tend to focus, because that is where they have access. According to the study findings and

virus-scanning tests conducted by NSS Labs (particularly after the attack of the Aurora virus), enterprises are less successful in preventing these kinds of attacks—not because of their sophistication, but because existing tools are not keeping up with the threats.

3. *Attack 2.0 Layer.* The outermost axis, the Attack 2.0 layer, includes the "advanced persistent threats" (APTs), as many IT security experts are now labeling them. It is at this level that the threats with the highest sophistication are found— malware that is customized to be more effective in targeted attacks. According to Verizon, of the more sophisticated network breaches that its IT experts were brought in to investigate, a significant 59 percent of the attacks causing considerable downtime and damage involved highly customized malware. In the *CSI Computer Crime and Security Survey*, 22 percent of the respondents said that at least some of their security incidents involved targeted attacks, and about 3 percent of them said that their networks experienced more than 10 targeted attacks. This layer remains a major problem.

The bottom line, affirms Richardson (2012), is that companies and government agencies are in a "cyber arms race" against cybercriminals. At the core or basic layer, the news is good: attacks persist, but they are largely rebuked with a suite of protections put in place. At the extended level in the middle, companies are in an arms race where they are "holding their own" but struggling against the inventiveness of cybercriminals and their funding sponsors (often nations or nation-states). At the Attack 2.0 level, things become really blurry regarding whether organizations can effectively compete in the cyber arms race. Web applications and cloud computing seem to be fruitful targets for attacks that migrate from the middle level out to the Attack 2.0 layer. Considering the evolving state of web development and presenting vulnerabilities, the news seems to be quite discouraging rather than uplifting. Clearly, governments and businesses need to consider this reality and be prepared to increase funding for more research and development directed toward the creation of preventive measures that will really work.

Crystal Ball Gazing: What Might the Future Bring?

We now come to an intriguing question and some crystal ball gazing. Here's an important question that we will attempt to answer now and continue to explore in Chapter 3: regarding IT security preparedness and the resolve of cybercriminals to invent more sophisticated and harm-producing types of malware, what might the future bring in terms of trends and concerns for IT security administrators?

In traditional crimes such as assault and bank robbery, we have learned from past cases to more effectively prepare for future "street" crimes. This same notion can be applied to the virtual world. Accepting that we are always trying to stay ahead of the next generation of cyberthreats, it might be wise to look at trends that are likely to occur with greater frequency in 2013 and beyond and to hear from the experts about new trends that may be on the horizon. The experts at the Sophos company have these insights to share (Eschelbeck 2012):

- Cybercriminals will likely continue to focus on social media to launch emerging forms of malware because of their massive user base and their integrated applications, which can be easily exploited.
- Cybercriminals recognize changes in the market for computer technology, as attacks have been identified on the Mac Operating System X, Adobe, Java, and various Microsoft products. Thus Black Hats will likely launch more targeted attacks on non-Windows platforms as they gain an increasingly large proportion of the market share.

- Over the 2011–2012 period, IT security experts noticed an increase in malicious hack attacks on mobile device platforms such as Android. This increase is due to the rapidly expanding smart phone market, the lack of regulatory controls on applications within the Android marketplace, and the increasing volume of financial and personal information stored on cellular phones. Experts expect that mobile devices will become new targets of malware in the near future.

- Web technologies continue to evolve, with a move from HTML5 to IPv6. The good news is that these emerging technologies will pave the way for some exciting new capabilities, such as web pages listed in languages such as Chinese and Russian. The bad news is that they will produce new attack vectors that will be of keen interest to the Black Hats.

- Employees will continue to bring their own mobile devices into the workplace without adequate security controls, thereby increasing the IT security concerns for small, medium, and large enterprises.

- Hacktivism is bound to continue. with known Black Hat activities including stealing data, intelligence gathering, and producing some novel but potentially very destructive politically motivated exploits. Additionally, hacktivists may be increasingly integrated into cyberattacks between nation-states to hide the origin of such attacks.

- Governments will continue to enact more laws with suitable penalties as a means of curbing cybercrime. In the United States, for example, there is a law proposed called the U.S. Stop Online Piracy Act (SOPA), and in Europe there is the proposed European Union's Data Protection Directive.

- Cyberspace will be increasingly militarized by governments as they attempt to distinguish attacks that constitute cybercrime from acts of war. This will help to ensure the identification and management of attackers and provide clarity to policymakers regarding the proper response, whether military, economic, or legal.

- Cloud computing will continue to be of keen interest to CEOs because of the web service cost savings that it can provide. As more companies use these services, there will need to be an increased focus on encrypting data wherever they flow rather than just on protecting a device or the network.

- Human error and lags in implementing effective patching and password management will continue into the future. This issue will remain a significant challenge for system administrators. So, one more time: companies need to keep devices in healthy working order by identifying missing patches in areas frequently targeted by the Black Hats and implementing the required patches in a timely manner. This strategy will go a long way toward improving network security. Moreover, emerging technologies such as file and folder encryption will help safeguard new devices and the adoption of more services "in the cloud."

Conclusion

This chapter provided an overview of the problems, challenges, and controversies facing organizations and government agencies around hack attack trends. Much of the chapter focused on findings from three reports with views from network and system administrators: the 15th annual U.S.-based *2010/2011 Computer Crime and Security Survey*, the fourth annual Canadian-based *2011 TELUS-Rotman Joint Study on Canadian IT Security Practices*, and the globally based *Sophos Security Threat Report 2012*.

The second part of this chapter looked at legal and technological solutions for preventing, detecting, and recovering from hack attacks on government and business networks. The chapter closed with a more detailed look at the effectiveness of these solutions and the concerns about emerging kinds of attacks that system administrators can anticipate in 2013 and beyond.

The next chapter will provide position essays by experts in the IT, business, social science, and legal fields on important questions related to the new types of hacking that may be looming on the horizon as well as the proposed means for curbing the adverse impact of increasingly sophisticated hacking and malware directed against various targets. Essays will include both original arguments made by academics actively researching hackers and their exploits, as well as personal stakeholders in the debate—including IT security industry leaders and anti-hacking legislators.

References

Agence France-Presse. "Obama Expanded Cyberassault on Iran: Report." *The Globe and Mail*, June 2, 2012, p. A16.

Brenner, S. W. *Cyberthreats: The Emerging Fault Lines of the Nation State.* New York: Oxford University Press, 2008.

Chilling Effects Clearinghouse. "Wiley Complains of Copied E-Books." ChillingEffects.com, 2012. http://www.chillingeffects.org/dmca512/notice.cgi?NoticeID=5970. Accessed June 11, 2012.

Chu, B., T. J. Holt, and G. J. Ahn. *Examining the Creation, Distribution, and Function of Malware On-Line.* Washington, DC: National Institute of Justice, 2010. www.ncjrs.gov./pdffiles1/nij/grants/230112.pdf. Accessed June 10, 2012.

ControlScan. "PCI Compliance FAQs." 2012. https://www.controlscan.com/support_resources_qa.php#18. Accessed June 8, 2012.

Dell. "PCI Security and PCI Compliance." DellSecureWorks, 2012. http://www.secureworks.com/compliance/pci/?_kk=27e5105c-9880-4410-9b40-bcf5fec8164e&_kt=68 98954847&gclid=CNaFhpKXvLACFcIUKgod5Fd-qg

Department of Defense. *Department of Defense Strategy for Operating in Cyberspace.* Washington, DC: 2011.

http://www.defense.gov/news/d20110714cyber.pdf. Accessed June 11, 2011.

Dromer, J, and D. Kollberg. "The Koobface malware gang – exposed!" Sophos, 2012. http://nakedsecurity.sophos.com/koobface-7/ Accessed June 20, 2012.

El Akkad, O. "Flame Set to Spread like Wildfire." *The Globe and Mail*, May 30, 2012, p. A3.

Eschelbeck, G. *Sophos Security Threat Report 2012.* Sophos Ltd., 2012. http://www.sophos.com/en-us/medialibrary/PDFs/other/SophosSecurityThreatReport2012.pdf. Accessed June 9, 2012.

Etges, R., and W. Hejazi. *2011 Executive Summary TELUS-Rotman Joint Study on Canadian IT Security Practices.* Toronto: TELUS Security Labs.

http://business.telus.com/en_CA/content/pdf/whyTELUS/Security_Thought_Leadership/TELUS_Rotman_2011 _Results.pdf. Accessed April 4, 2012

Finkle, J., and J. Saba. "LinkedIn Confirms It Had Security Breach. *National Post*, June 7, 2012, p. FP2.

Furnell, S. *Cybercrime: Vandalizing the Information Society.* London: Addison- Wesley, 2002.

Herbig, J. "PCI Compliance and Small Merchants: Whose Concern Is It Anyway?" PCIComplianceGuide.org, 2012. http://www.pcicomplianceguide.org/merchants-pci -compliance-whose-concern-is-it.php. Accessed June 8, 2012.

IBM. "A Smarter Planet Is Built on Smarter Analytics." *The Globe and Mail*, June 4, 2012, p. B5.

In Brief. "HP Strikes at Worms." *The Globe and Mail*, December 2, 2004, p. B11.

Mayeda, A., and H. Miller. "Cyber-attack Security 'Poor.' " *National Post*, June 7, 2012, p. FP3.

Mitnick, K. D., and W. L. Simon. *The Art of Deception: Controlling the Human Element of Security.* New York: Wiley, 2002.

National Institute of Standards and Technology (NIST). "Federal Information Security Management Act (FISMA) Implementation Project." NIST.gov. May 16, 2012. http://csrc.nist .gov/groups/SMA/fisma/index.html. Accessed June 8, 2012.

Pescatore, J., and R. Stiennon. *Key Considerations When Evaluating Intrusion Prevention Products.* Gartner, Inc., 2004. http://www.midsizeenterprise.com/midmarket/404/ IT_article_1_404.html.

Richardson, R. "2010/2011 CSI Computer Crime and Security Survey." GoCSI.com, 2012. http://reports. informationweek.com/abstract/21/7377/Security/research -2010-2011-csi-survey.html. Accessed June 1, 2012.

Roberts, P. F. "Retailer TJX Reports Massive Data Breach." Infoworld.com, 2007. http://www.infoworld.com/d/ security-central/retailer-tjx-reports-massive-data-breach-953. Accessed June 5, 2012.

Rockel, N. " 'Bring Your Own Device to Work' Is More Than a Trend." *The Globe and Mail,* February 8, 2012, p. B7.

Rouse, M. "HITECH Act (Health Information Technology for Economic and Clinical Health Act." TechTarget.com, 2009. http://searchhealthit.techtarget.com/definition/ HITECH-Act. Accessed June 8, 2012.

Savage, C. "U.S. Security Leaks Difficult to Find, Harder to Prosecute." *The Globe and Mail,* June 11, 2012.

Schachter, H. "Cloud Gazing: What to Consider with Online IT." *The Globe and Mail,* November 14, 2011, p. B6.

Schell, B. *Contemporary World Issues: The Internet and Society.* Santa Barbara: ABC-CLIO, 2007.

Schell, B., and J. Dodge, with S. Moutsatsos. *The Hacking of America: Who's Doing It, Why, and How.* Westport, CT: Quorum Books, 2002.

Schell, B., and C. Martin. *Contemporary World Issues: Cybercrime.* Santa Barbara: ABC-CLIO, 2004.

Schell, B., and C. Martin. *Webster's New World Hacker Dictionary.* Indiana: Wiley, 2006.

Smith, A. "Smartphone Adoption and Useage." Pew Internet and American Life Project. 2011. http://pewinternet.org/Reports/2011/Smartphones.aspx Accessed July 23, 2012.

Taylor, P. *Hackers: Crime in the Digital Sublime.* London: Routledge, 1999.

Tossell, I. "The ABCs of Cyber-security." *The Globe and Mail Report on Business* 28 (May 10, 2012): 55–60.

Trichur, R. "Canada on Track to 100% Wireless Penetration Rate." *The Globe and Mail,* June 5, 2012, p. B4.

3   Perspectives

This chapter explores a range of pertinent issues related to the problem of malicious computer hacking. Both the technical and social sciences are included to demonstrate the value of both perspectives in finding ways to reduce the efficacy of attacks in various contexts. This chapter explores malicious activities affecting end-user systems, video-game environments, and critical infrastructure systems. The authors consider ways that these systems could be secured from attacks as well as social policies that could be used to redirect hackers or affect the likelihood of data breaches and botnet attacks. In turn, these essays give substantive insights into the phenomenon of hacking and cybercrimes generally.

Protecting Critical Infrastructures

Bob Radvanosky

Critical infrastructure systems today are reaching a convergence of architectures. What was once an isolated set of environments contained from the rest of the outside world is becoming increasingly a set of environments more interconnected with

A supporter of controversial website WikiLeaks demonstrates in support of founder Julian Assange in Hong Kong in December 2010. Skirmishes raged across cyberspace between WikiLeaks supporters and the companies they accuse of trying to stifle the group. (AP Photo/Kin Cheung)

the world through unsecured networks such as the Internet. These systems play an important role in our daily lives by providing automated capabilities to processes considered too repetitive. In most configurations, these systems also allow extremely complex processes to operate safely and efficiently. Such interconnected critical infrastructure systems include transportation and utilities.

Slowly, over the past decade, individuals ranging from the curious to those with negative intent have been taking notice of these interconnected systems and their environments and have pieced together how these systems play an important and vital role in our modern society. Individuals with negative intent commonly have motives of either profiting from the capitalization of these environments or causing their ineffective functioning or even their destruction. While we may not know all of the risks that our society is exposed to today, there are a few experts who can estimate, to some extent, the probabilities of what could happen if these environments were shut down, or worse yet, destroyed. Our society as we know it today would crumble or be reduced to an unsustainable condition.

For the negative motives outlined previously to effectively take place, some basic requirements need to happen— including individuals having the use of the necessary tools and the intelligence gathered to make sense of these interconnected systems and their environments. Although the organizations utilizing these systems may have implemented precautionary efforts to protect and safeguard these systems from prying eyes, these efforts still cannot prevent hack attacks from, say, insiders who have discovered the technical specifics about these systems from the vendors and the manufacturers supporting them.

One threat or attack vector that is emerging is the growing threat of economic terrorism by nation-states. As economic resources become increasingly expensive (such as energy, oil, water, and food), some countries could consider utilizing malware and cyberwarfare tactics to benefit from the disruption of and, in some circumstances, the destruction of critical infrastructures and the systems supporting them. The problem with this statement is that for now it is somewhat speculative, as hard-core proof—"finding the smoking gun"—is difficult to obtain because of a lack of conclusive evidence of nation-state cyberinterference being used for economic gain.

That said, enumeration tactics that are commonly, openly, freely, and publicly available via the Internet can be used by anyone wishing to identify specific critical infrastructure targets. Essentially, if a device is connected to the Internet, and if it can be ascertained, it can be exploited and used for nefarious purposes.

One tool used for such purposes has gained much attention in the media because of its invasiveness. Available through the Internet for a small fee, this tool can be incorporated as part of an application or an entire application suite to interrogate its database for a user-specified search string. In short, this tool can provide some very useful information to a perpetrator intent on causing harm to a network, because it has the capability to triangulate the purpose, function, and activity of a targeted infrastructure sector. "SHODANHQ" is the tool named after a fictional artificial intelligence encountered in a video game. SHODANHQ offers both good and bad guys an affordable and simplified ease-of-use tool to execute targeted interrogative attacks against a specific system, a suite of systems controlled by a single organization, or a suite of systems being used by a country's nation-state infrastructure.

Though the type of information being returned to the perpetrator is limited (e.g., searched output returned is based by country, host name, network IP address or address range, and port numbers), this type of intelligence provides anyone wanting to target a specific location or infrastructure with adequate information that would otherwise be difficult to acquire. In recent years, the amount of activity aimed at critical infrastructures worldwide—and specifically cyber-related systems supporting these infrastructures—has increased enough that corporations and policymakers are now seriously discussing how to address some of the issues of concern that could present with the exposure of these systems (Federal Computer Week 2012; ISC-CERT 2011).

Part of the dilemma that our society is facing today relates to the fact that significantly older legacy systems that were never intended to be used for public accessibility or that were not properly designed for such are now being exposed at rapid rates of discovery. At one point in time, these systems were interconnected on privately owned and controlled networks using framed-relay networks. They were generally not switched, adding even greater protection against eavesdropping and man-in-the-middle hack attacks against such network traffic. However, over the years, starting as early as 1996, communications providers began consolidating and standardizing their communications networks, often substituting the older framed-relay networks with present-day faster network communications capabilities (such as DSL). Many organizations have been aware of this reality and have carefully coordinated upgrades to faster, always-connected networked communications links so as to keep critical infrastructures functional.

Some other forms of communications, such as dial-up telephony communications via modems or terminal adapters, have also been consolidated and standardized using similar network communications that the former framed-relay networks now reside on. The infrastructure systems that were serial only and were accessed via dial-up telephony communication networks now have serial-to-Ethernet converters tied into an always-connected communications network.

Despite these upgrades to communications networks, the problem remains that anyone with the know-how can figure out that many small to medium-sized infrastructure organizations make up tens to hundreds of thousands of single-user devices and applications—representing the majority of critical infrastructure systems throughout the world. In fact, this phenomenon is not limited to just one country but to several countries, as they increasingly became part of a more global effort to standardize and streamline the costs associated with supporting critical infrastructure networks. To further exacerbate the problem, many of these organizations remain unaware that the very systems that they support are connected in such a way that they could completely lose control of their critical infrastructure with nothing more than a simple keystroke from a hacker.

A recent report from the U.S. Department of Homeland Security indicated that the amount of exploitable vulnerabilities discovered, researched, and analyzed over the past three years has significantly increased (ISC-CERT 2011). What is worrisome is that this trend does not appear to be abating in rate and frequency. Clearly, those with nefarious intent will have a large selection of networked targets to choose from, depending on their motives, the intended message that they want to convey, and the end success factors that they wish to accomplish.

Through the use of readily available online tools such as SHODANHQ, combined with other online tools such as NMAP and Metasploit, tech-savvy individuals with nefarious intent can discover, enumerate, research, and penetrate the systems that control, regulate, and maintain the operation of critical functions that our society depends on for basic survival and healthy functioning. However, despite this somewhat gloomy outlook, there are defensive measures that can be taken. It is important to note that these measures must be applied one at a time, depending on the type of system, the severity of the impact, and the mitigation strategy.

One of the key issues faced by most IT professionals today is that IT cannot apply defensive measures unilaterally. Years ago, when the majority of the communications networks were isolated, there was hardly any need for specifying "security" as part of the design and operation of these systems. Today, however, there is a need to do so. Simple measures such as valve actuator rate limiters pump restart timers, and hard-wired interlocks can be effective measures previously done by software only. For the automation operations that cannot economically be

hard-wired, the introduction of newer communications protocols utilizing secured authentication, along with industrialized
firewalls with virtual private network (VPN) capabilities and
stronger versions of control management, are making a huge
difference in securing critical infrastructures.

The remaining problem is not so much the implementation
of these protections but rather the understanding and awareness of security measures and countermeasures that are now
so very necessary. Put another way, the most difficult part
of securing critical infrastructure networks from hack attacks
is educating both IT and engineering professionals where,
when, and why the use of these measures and countermeasure
tactics are necessary. Consequently, many IT professionals are
becoming increasingly more often tasked with roles that were
previously maintained and administered by engineering professionals. Given this present-day reality, IT professionals have
to deal with different forms of logic diagramming, such as
relay ladder logic and function block diagrams. Again, with
many of the issues outlined previously, the greatest challenge
to keeping critical infrastructures secure is awareness and
education.

By far, the largest and most complex of the challenges that
remain today involves cross-training, as engineering professionals now need to have a fundamental understanding and
knowledge of the IT implications should breaches occur. In
turn, IT professionals need to have a fundamental understanding and knowledge of the impact on operations, based
on their increasingly administrative roles in automation systems' operations. The reason for this two-sided cross-training
is that the real-time environments that engineers have developed over the past several decades are largely outside the experience of most IT professionals. In fact, many IT personnel
simply have no concept of what controllers do, what they
are used for, and what the typical failure modes are.
Conversely, the majority of engineering professionals have
no idea what sort of harm is possible on networks these days.

The transport medium and the operating systems that run and control the plethora of automation systems remain practically a "black box" to the bulk of IT personnel. Thus the effort to build bridges and properly educate both sides of this professional equation must begin.

IT needs to forget whatever habits have been ingrained within the business enterprise, and engineers need to start paying attention to where their data are going, what those data ride on, and how the data must eventually get to the IT side of the enterprise environment. Both sets of professionals need to consider which failure modes may exist, and both sets need to consider the likely sources of attack from within the firewall as well as from outside it. Clearly, this cultural change will not happen overnight; there will continue to be legacy issues. The only hope is that we learn from the mistakes that were made in the past instead of repeating the same old failures as we continue to move into the forever-evolving cyberfuture.

References

Federal Computer Week. "Cyber Incident Reports Skyrocket over Three-Year Period." July 2, 2012. http://fcw.com/articles/2012/07/02/ics-cert-report-cyber-attacks-skyrocket.aspx. Accessed July 4, 2012.

U.S. Department of Homeland Security, Control Systems Security Program, Industrial Control Systems Computer Emergency Response Team (ICS-CERT). "ICS-CERT Incident Response Summary Report: 2009–2011." http://www.us-cert.gov/control_systems/pdf/ICS-CERT_Incident-Response_Summary_Report_09_11.pdf. Accessed October 1, 2012.

Bob Radvanosky is an expert in Critical Infrastructure Protection (CIP)/homeland security industries and is a part time advisor for Infracritical.

Examining Social Dynamics and Malware Secrets to Mitigate Net-centric Attacks

Ziming Zhao and G.-J. Ahn

It was estimated that more than a quarter of all networked computers have been compromised by one or more malicious programs (Sturgeon 2007). With sophisticated social engineering, signature-evading technologies, and code obfuscation methods, adversaries are capable of circumventing anti-malware systems and can then eventually contaminate production computers. Malware-infected computers are deliberately organized into large-scale destructive botnets to steal information and disrupt, deny access to, degrade or destroy critical Net-centric information systems (Stone-Gross et al. 2009; Thomas 2010). The power of botnets relies on their coordination and the volume of the responses from the bot nodes. In a typical botnet, hundreds to thousands of bot nodes respond to a botmaster's commands. When these nodes are instructed to connect to one web page at the same time, the aggregated volume of the network traffic would be tremendous for most companies to handle, causing denial of service to the targeted servers. When these nodes are instructed to download banking credentials, for example, the botmaster receives credentials from each bot, which can number in the thousands or even millions in some botnets. Another critical problem caused by botnets is email spamming. Nowadays spam not only causes a network-clogging problem, but also can serve as a means for adversaries to distribute additional malware.

How botnets can be used as adversarial platforms depends on how the bot-herders configure and manipulate the controlled network of computers. For example, Lethic and Rustock were two dominant spamming botnets detected in 2010 (Anselmi and Kuo 2010). However, due to their highly modularized design and runtime functionality, they can be easily reshaped for launching denial-of-service attacks or stealing financially sensitive information from consumers (Stone-Gross et al. 2009). The situation keeps getting more complicated when botnets make use of legitimate web services for their malicious command and control (C&C) communications. We even recently observed that well-known social networks, such as Facebook and Twitter, could be used as a platform from which to launch botnet attacks (Thomas 2010). Given the significance of this problem, huge research efforts have been invested in capturing, understanding, and analyzing the malware and its C&C communications in the wild (Porras, Saidi, and Yegneswaran 2009; Rajab et al. 2007; Stone-Gross et al. 2009). Honeypots— the isolated and monitored nonproduction systems—are deployed as traps to capture malware and collect its host-based behaviors as well as network-based communications in a proactive manner (Bacher et al. 2005). As countermeasures to recent widely adopted code obfuscation techniques such as packing (Guo, Ferrie, and Chiueh 2008) and emulation (VMProtect), both static (Coogan et al. 2009) and dynamic (Guo et al. 2008), approaches have been proposed to automatically unpack and analyze malware.

Figure 3.1 shows a typical workflow of cybercrime. In step 1, malware programmers develop crafted attack tools. The most prevalent and destructive tool developed to carry out various attacks is a set of bots. Malware programmers turn bots over to bot-herders through online black markets or offline channels.

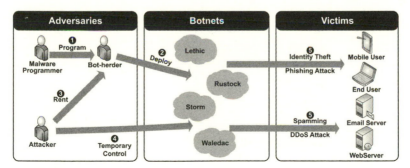

Figure 3.1   Cybercrime Workflow

In step 2, bot-herders deploy a botnet through social engineering, drive-by download, or other possible vectors. In step 3, bot-herders rent a botnet out to other adversaries, from which bot-herders and malware programmers profit; the latter tend to have targets in mind but do not have the technological expertise to design or administer the botnet. In step 4, attackers, such as spammers, take control of the botnet. A rented botnet may result in a variety of attacks launched by multiple adversaries who might have different intents. In step 5, attackers coordinate bot nodes to perform multiple attacks such as spamming, identity theft, distributed denial-of-service attacks, and phishing attacks.

Most research in the area of botnets focuses on finding bots and associated C&C channels, and shutting the botnets down in a timely manner (Gu et al. 2010). Although promising results have been obtained from defeating botnets, and preventive solutions against thousands of known malware programs have been deployed on networked systems, the loss of production systems from Net-centric attacks and cybercrime has been growing faster than ever (Internet Crime Complaint Center 2009). The reason is at least twofold. First, little research has explored the ways in which how bots and other unwanted programs are created and distributed by adversaries. The majority of adversaries who have engineered these tools and coordinated attacks remain at large. They keep threatening the Internet by developing more sophisticated penetration tools and launching more Net-centric attacks, even if previous malware approaches are blocked by deployed countermeasures. Second, malware authors attempt to disguise their motives by making use of other protection approaches apart from code obfuscation, which is normally used to protect data rather than code (Caballero et al. 2007), from malicious code analysts.

As a consequence, prior code extraction techniques have proved ineffective in accommodating the new trend of malware evolution. Moreover, significant botnets today constantly change and evolve by adding bots, deleting bots, changing to new channels, and being upgraded. Attempting to discover their C&C servers may bring immediate benefits but stimulate the evolution of botnets. Park and Reeves (2009) claim that it is also important to monitor botnets for an extended time to learn the purpose of the botnets and to develop more effective countermeasures. In other words, existing approaches concentrate on steps 2, 4, and 5 in Figure 3.1, but largely overlook steps 1 and 3. Furthermore, because malware authors have adopted protection approaches to hide malware-related data from analysis, research results on steps 2, 4, and 5 that may work smoothly for prior malware may be unable to accommodate the new trend of malware evolution.

To cope with the aforementioned two challenges, it is critical to identify the linkage between the rogue programs and adversaries and to automatically extract secrets from malware for mitigating and combating rogue program attacks. As a clue to address these challenges, recent research efforts indicate that adversaries are using online social networks (OSNs) to build interest groups for vulnerability analysis, malicious code and tool development, botnet trade and rent, and attack coordination (Chu, Holt, and Ahn 2010). Therefore, investigation of the organizational structures and examination of adversarial conversations in the online underground social networks could help discover and mine adversarial evidence. In addition, automatic extraction of interesting binary code pieces and reuse of such code for security analysis have been recently proposed (Caballero et al. 2010; Kolbitsch et al. 2010). One application of these binary code reuse techniques is to reveal external malware-related data, such as C&C messages. However, these techniques are not designed to extract malware-embedded secrets directly, and existing extraction methods are highly manual. A major drawback of these attempts is that human knowledge of the binary code location and behavior is required to identify interesting code pieces.

We argue that a novel cybercrime analysis model combining analysis of social dynamics and malware secrets, as shown in Figure 3.2, is necessary. This model is visualized as a process

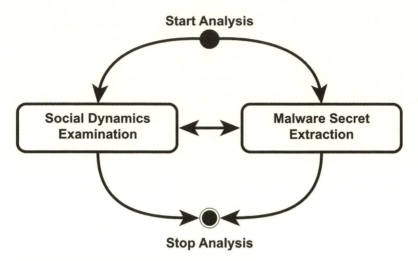

Figure 3.2 Cybercrime Analysis Workflow

passing through some iterations with two activities: (1) examine adversarial online relationships and conversations for knowledge of creation, distribution, and trend of malware that is being circulated online; and (2) examine captured and archived malware for evidence and knowledge extraction. Examination of social dynamics to bridge the gap of research efforts directed toward steps 1 and 3 and automatic extraction of internal cipher text data from malware are necessary to complement existing efforts focusing on steps 2, 4, and 5. Such an approach would help bridge the gap between malware analysis and adversaries' identification.

As shown in Figure 3.3, the suggested approach for examining adversarial social dynamics consists of two stages. First, it formulates an online underground social network by considering its social relationships and user-generated contents. Second, a systematic ranking analysis mechanism is built by introducing several indices indicating the influence of adversaries, the relevance of adversaries to certain events, and the ongoing trend of underground society.

In summary, such a novel approach to identify adversaries through social dynamics and secret extraction from malware is

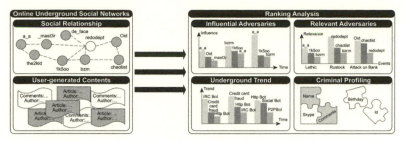

Figure 3.3   Examining Adversarial Social Dynamics

desperately needed. We believe it would not only complement existing malware, bots, and C&C analysis, but also help experts to better understand and mitigate cybercrime while identifying new trends of malware evolution.

References

Anselmi, N. S. D., and J. Kuo. *Microsoft Security Intelligence Report: Volume 9.* Redmond, WA: Microsoft, 2010.

Bacher, P., T. Holz, M. Kotter, and G. Wicherski. *Know Your Enemy: Tracking Botnets—Using Honeynets to Learn More about Bots*, 2005.

Caballero, J., N. M. Johnson, S, McCamant, and D. Song. "Binary Code Extraction and Interface Identification for Security Applications." In *Proceedings of the 17th Annual Network and Distributed System Security Symposium (NDSS).* Berkley, CA: Citeseer, 2010.

Caballero, J., H. Yin, Z. Liang, and D. Song. "Polyglot: Automatic Extraction of Protocol Message Format Using Dynamic Binary Analysis." In *Proceedings of the 14th ACM Conference on Computer and Communications Security*, 317–329. New York: ACM, 2007.

Chu, B., T. J. Holt, and G. J. Ahn. *Examining the Creation, Distribution, and Function of Malware On-Line.* Washington, DC: National Institute of Justice, 2010. www.ncjrs.gov./pdffiles1/nij/grants/230112.pdf. Accessed June 10, 2012.

Coogan, K., S. Debray, T. Kaochar, and G. Townsend. "Automatic Static Unpacking of Malware Binaries." In *Proceedings of the 16th Working Conference on Reverse Engineering (WCRE)*, 167–176. New York: IEEE, 2009.

Gu, G., V. Yegneswaran, P. Porras, J. Stoll, and W. Lee. "Active Botnet Probing to Identify Obscure Command and Control Channels." In *Proceedings of the 26th Annual Computer Security Applications Conference (ACSAC)*, 241–253. New York: IEEE, 2010.

Guo, F., P. Ferrie, and T. Chiueh,. "A Study of the Packer Problem and Its Solutions." In *Proceedings of the Recent Advances in Intrusion Detection (RAID)*, 98–115. New York: Springer, 2008.

Internet Crime Complaint Center. "2009 Annual Report." 2009. http://www.ic3.gov/media/annualreport/2009 -ic3report.pdf. Accessed January 29, 2010.

Kolbitsch, C., T. Holz, C. Kruegel, and E. Kirda. "Inspector Gadget: Automated Extraction of Proprietary Gadgets from Malware Binaries." In *Proceedings of the 31th IEEE Symposium on Security and Privacy (S&P)*, 29–44. New York: IEEE, 2010.

Park, Y., and D. Reeves. "Identification of Bot Commands by Run-Time Execution Monitoring. In *Proceedings of the 25th Annual Computer Security Applications Conference (ACSAC)*, 321–330. New York: IEEE, 2009.

Porras, P., H. Saidi, and V. Yegneswaran. "A Foray into Conficker Logic and Rendezvous Points." In *Proceedings of the 2nd USENIX Workshop on Large-Scale Exploits and Emergent Threats (LEET)*.Berkley, CA: USENIX Association, 2009.

Rajab, M., Zarfoss, J., Monrose, F., & Terzis, A. "My Botnet Is Bigger Than Yours (Maybe Better Than Yours): Why Size Estimates Remain Challenging." In *Proceedings of the 1st*

Usenix Workshop on Hot Topics in Understanding Botnets (HotBots), 5-5. Berkley, CA: USENIX Association, 2007.

Stone-Gross, B., M. Cova, L. Cavallaro, B. Gilbert, M. Szydlowski, R. Kem-merer, C. Kruegel, and G. Vigna. "Your Botnet Is My Botnet: Analysis of a Botnet Takeover." In *Proceedings of the 16th ACM Conference on Computer and Communications Security (CCS)*, 635–647. New York: ACM, 2009.

Sturgeon. W. "Internet Guru Warns of Botnet Pandemic." ZDNet, January 29, 2007. http://www.zdnet.co.uk/news/networking/2007/01/29/internet-guru-warns-of-botnet pandemic-39285665/. Accessed November 4, 2011.

Thomas, K. "The Koobface Botnet and the Rise of Social Malware." In *Proceedings of the 5th IEEE International Conference on Malicious and Unwanted Software (MALWARE)*, 1–8. New York: IEEE 2010.

VMProtect. http://www.vmprotect.ru.

Ziming Zhao is a PhD student in the Department of Computer Science at Arizona State University.

Gail-Joon Ahn is an Associate Professor of Computer Science and Engineering in the School of Computing, Informatics, and Decision Systems Engineering at Arizona State University.

The Role of Nation-States in Cyberattacks

Max Kilger

There is, in some respects, what appears to be an emerging consensus within the information security and intelligence communities of an approaching turning point with respect to the role of nation-states in cyberattacks. Not only is there increased activity in cyberattacks by nation-states, but the nature of the roles, the relationships, and the level of collaboration between nation-states and individuals involved in these cyberattacks also appear to be rapidly evolving and increasing in complexity to the point where they are becoming increasingly more difficult to unravel.

The research community, in response to this threat, in the past several years has produced a plethora of research articles and scholarly examinations of the current and future risks, vulnerabilities, mechanisms, motivations, defenses, potential responses, and legal authorities relevant to the phenomenon of cyberattacks. In addition, the research community has examined the roles that nation-states, organizations, loosely formed groups, and individuals may play in those attacks.[1] Some of this work involves setting forth drafts of policies and rules for cyberconflict (for example, see Rauscher and Korotlov 2011), some work involves defining cyberconflicts in the legal arena (Hathaway et al.2012), and other work endeavors to place cyberattacks into the milieu of military doctrine (Hughes 2010).

Historically, the attribution of cyberattacks and cyberreconnaissance to specific parties has been a difficult task, given the technical challenges in uncovering what are often multiple layers of technical obfuscation constructed by perpetrators to obscure and mislead efforts to make deterministic attribution of specific cyberattacks. Attribution not only is an important component in the process chain of "pursue and prosecute," but is also inherently linked to deterrence (Glaser 2011). Without plausible links to be able to identify the actual perpetrators of a cyberattack, it is somewhat difficult to imagine that deterrence can operate as an effective force in inhibiting cyberattacks.

At the same time, the nature of this lack of attribution is such that Libicki (2011) suggests that cyberspace is "tailor-made" for ambiguity and that this property of ambiguity might not always be such a bad thing, especially when examined at the nation-state level. When compared to kinetic attacks, Libicki (2011) states, "The working hypothesis is that a cyber attack used in lieu of kinetic methods creates more ambiguity in terms of effects, sources, and motives. Thus, if cyber attacks

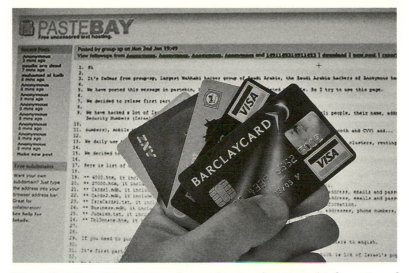

View of credit cards against a webpage showing the personal information of thousands of Israelis on January 2, 2012. Anonymous Saudi hackers claimed to have leaked files containing credit card numbers of 400,000 Israelis, the first strike in what became a Saudi-Israeli cyberwar, with targets including the Israeli and Saudi Arabian stock exchanges. (Lucidwaters/Dreamstime)

work—and this is a tremendous if—they change the risk profile of certain actions, and usually in ways that make them more attractive options."

Libicki goes on to suggest that a cyberattack response in retaliation to an initial kinetic attack might pose less risk than a tit-for-tat kinetic attack. Further, he says, this situation is complicated by the fact that part of this ambiguity involves the question of whether the cyberattacker is an actor or actors associated with a nation-state.

In the world of cyberattack attribution, deciding whether the attacker is a nation-state, is associated with a nation-state, or is acting without any state-sponsored connections may, indeed, have important implications. In what Kilger (in press) calls the rise of the civilian cyberwarrior, this author suggests that the ability of a single individual to attack a component of another nation's critical infrastructure might possibly change the nature of the power relationship between the state and the individual. For the first time, a single individual can effectively attack a nation-state.[2] This implies that the number of potential actors in the threat matrix, especially for critical infrastructure targets, may increase exponentially. Thus, as the incidence of cyberattacks likely increases significantly, being able to discriminate whether the attack has any nation-state component to it is likely to be a critical part of any analytical examination of the attack. This line of thought also suggests that the opportunities for collaboration between individuals and nation-states in mounting cyberattacks on the infrastructures of other countries are also likely to increase.

Closer examination of this attribution challenge suggests that the determination of nation-state involvement in a cyberattack is far from a black-and-white issue. Healy (2012) advances a useful, 10-point ordinal taxonomy of the level of collaboration/acquiescence of the nation-state with individuals or groups who deploy cyberattacks. The endpoints of the scale start with scale point 1 denoting *"state prohibited; the national government will help stop the third-party attack"* and the far end at scale point 10 indicating *"state integrated; the national government attacks using integrated third-party proxies and government cyberforces."* In-between categories of individual/nation-state collaboration on this scale include, but are not limited to, *state ignored, state encouraged,* and *state coordinated.*

It is clear from Healy's arguments that there is a dynamic range of potential collaborations between nation-states and individual actors in the planning and execution of cyberattacks. This spectrum of attribution may prove useful in helping to determine the actions that are taken by the victimized party as well as who might be assist in those actions. In the end, Healy argues, "the international security community must focus on the needs of policymakers, which is best served by looking to the responsibility of nations. Too much time has been wasted obsessing over which particular villain pressed the 'ENTER' key."

Similarly, a recent workshop focused on the role that norms in the international community might play in "reducing threats and conflict in cyberspace" (Massachusetts Institute of Technology [MIT] 2011). Among the topics examined in the workshop were the effectiveness and feasibility of internationally constructed cybernorms such as states' responsibility for cyberattacks originating within their physical borders and the prospects of internationally accepted cybernorms curtailing the rising tide of cybercrime.

While international cooperation and the establishment of cooperative policies, regulations, and, perhaps, even cybernorms among nation-states are actions that are likely to have some positive impact on the state of global information security, it is probable that for some time to come the most effective solutions are likely to take shape in the form of a two-pronged tactical approach to the problem. On the technical side, the continued investment in defensive measures in their various forms (e.g., firewalls, intrusion detection systems, heuristic engines for malware) as well as surveillance systems such as honeynets will continue to serve as somewhat effective first-line defenses against cyberattack.

The second prong of the approach is to obtain a better understanding of the social dynamics of the actors involved in cyberattacks—whether they are individual actors, loosely formed groups, or nation-states. Understanding the personality traits, motivations, social relationships, cultural and ethnic traditions, and world perspectives of these malicious online actors will help defenders prioritize the defense of potential targets, determine specific vectors within the threat matrix that are most salient to their enterprise, and identify specific individuals and actors engaging in these malicious acts.

Finally, the ability to better understand the nature and magnitude of evolving relationships between individual actors, loosely formed groups, and nation-states will assist defenders in pursuing actions and policies that are the most appropriate and effective measures in reducing the level of threat and magnitude of damage resulting from cyberattacks. Given the fact that the U.S. Department of Defense (2011) has issued a recent report that details the possibility of using traditional kinetic military force in response to some types of instances of cyberattacks, developing a comprehensive understanding of the nature of the relationship between individual malicious online actors and nation-state entities and their roles in cyberattacks may become a critical element in keeping the peace.

Notes

1. The difficulties in sometimes discriminating the general origins of the cyberattacker in terms of nation-state or unaffiliated individual/group was originally labeled by the author as the "nation-state or kids that skate" dilemma.

2. By "effectively attack," we mean here that the material resources needed for the attack are nominal, the probability of a successful attack is reasonably high, the consequences of the attack are large in magnitude, and the probability that the attacker will be caught is low.

References

Glaser, C. *Deterrence of Cyberattacks and U.S. National Security.* Report GW-CSPRI-2011-5. George Washington University Elliot School of International Affairs, 2011.

Hathaway, O., Oona A., Crootof, R., Levitz, P., Nix, H., Nowlan, A., Perdue, W. & J. Spiegel. "The law of cyber-attack." *California Law Review* (100, 4): 817–886 (2012).

Healy, J. *Beyond Attribution: Seeking National Responsibility for Cyber Attacks.* Washington, DC: Atlantic Council, 2012.

Hughes, R. "A Treaty for Cyberspace." *International Affairs* 86, no. 2 (2010): 523–541.

Kilger, M. "The Emergence of the Civilian Cyber Warrior." In *Cyber Infrastructure Protection.* Carlyle, PA: Strategic Studies Institute, U.S. Army War College, in press.

Libicki, M. "The Strategic Uses of Ambiguity in Cyberspace." *Military and Strategic Affairs* 3 (2011): 3.

Massachusetts Institute of Technology (MIT). *Notes from the 2011 Cyber Norms Workshop,* 2011. http://www.citizenlab .org/cybernorms/index.html#desc. Accessed October 14, 2012.

Rauscher, K., and A. Korotlov. *Working for Rules Governing Cyber Conflict.* New York: East West Institute, 2011.

U.S. Department of Defense. *Department of Defense Cyber Policy Report.* November 15, 2011.

Max Kilger is currently the chief membership officer for the Honeynet Project and has served as a profiler with the Project for the past 11 years. He is a leading expert in the social and behavioral aspects of computer hackers and cybercrime.

The Case for Strong Data Breach Notification Legislation

Douglas E. Salane

Data Breach Notification Legislation

In 2003, California enacted the first comprehensive data breach notification legislation, the California Security Breach Notification Act (Cal. Civil Code). Prompted at the time by a major breach at a California state agency that compromised the names, addresses, and Social Security numbers of state employees, including legislators, the California Senate modified a proposed data protection law to require notification of California residents when sensitive personal information was breached. Under the original statute, information triggering breach notification included a first and last name, along with any of the following items: (1) Social Security number; (2) driver's license number or California state ID card number; or (3) an account, debit, or credit card number in combination with any security information that could be used to authorize a transaction—for example, the security code on a credit card. The legislation received almost unanimous support in the legislature.

The California breach law was landmark legislation. It was one of the first attempts to codify sensitive personal information whose unauthorized use could cause harm to consumers. The law recognized that organizations that collect and store sensitive consumer information have an obligation to safeguard that information and inform consumers when it is compromised so that they can protect themselves. The law provided the basic structure for similar breach notification legislation, which as of August 2012 was available in 46 states, the District of Columbia, Guam, Puerto Rico and the Virgin Islands (National Conference 2012).

Many states are in the process of updating existing data breach laws, generally to strengthen and broaden them. For example, California updated its statute in 2008 to include medical records and health insurance information. More recently, it updated its law to include notice to the attorney general. In addition, the new California law requires notifications to include a general description of the incident, the type of information breached, and the time of the breach. Connecticut recently updated its law to include a notification requirement whenever there is unauthorized acquisition of sensitive personal information (Wong 2012). State laws are evolving to address new risks to consumers, and most state legislatures come down strongly on the side of consumer protection when it comes to data breaches.

The Need for Strong, Broad-Based Consumer Protections

Data breach notification legislation is a form of broad-based consumer protection. Strong consumer protection laws provide incentives for organizations that hold sensitive personal information to put in place secure systems. Data breach notification imposes a penalty for data loss, not only in the cost of notification, but also because the breach cannot remain a secret. For the most part, consumers do not know who holds their data or how they will use it. With so many parties holding and sharing sensitive personal data, broad-based consumer protections that cut across industries and technologies are needed to ensure organizations secure sensitive personal data.

Notification laws foster at least some level of transparency. Privacy Rights Clearinghouse, a nonprofit privacy advocacy and education organization, has maintained a list of data breach incidents since 2005. Since that year, data breaches have resulted in the loss of at least 563 million records, and Privacy Rights maintains that the true number is probably far larger. Most of the information that Privacy Rights obtains comes from reports to state attorney generals, which are mandated by most state laws when the number of breached records exceeds a significant threshold.

Even without breach notification laws, security analysts eventually would learn about most major breaches, such as the major breaches in the card payment industry (CardSystems Solutions, 2005; Heartland Payment Systems, 2009; Global Payments, 2012). It might have been quite some time, however, before anyone outside the breached companies learned the magnitude of the breaches or any details surrounding the breaches. Breached organizations usually release as little information as possible, even if the information would advance security at other organizations within their own industry. A recent report by the Federal Reserve Banks of Philadelphia and Chicago identified "rapid and detailed information sharing by breached parties across industry sectors" as a key factor in mitigating and limiting the impact of a data breach. Breach notification requirements ensure organizations include consumers in the information sharing and provide incentives to share breach information in a timely fashion.

Consumers and organizations cannot rely on security technologies alone to guarantee information security. Security experts concede that they are losing the security battle at the information technology level (Garfinkle 2012). Policy and legal experts argue that information security requires incentives that are rooted in law and policy (Cate 2009). For example, many new payment systems, which are often developed for mobile platforms, remain largely unregulated. Although consumers are conditioned to rely on service providers to ensure the security of payment systems, cost advantages in these new systems might be achieved by avoiding the extensive security infrastructures of established payment systems (Anderson 2012). Broad-based consumer protections are needed to ensure security costs are factored in when such new systems are offered to the public.

With strong consumer protections in place, developers have added incentives to give security high priority from the start. The following comment by a developer at a recent ACM roundtable discussion of mobile system developers (Creeger 2011) illustrates the point: "Data loss requires notifying each client of the breach and potential access by anyone, including a competitor. Loss of a mobile device means data notification requirements are triggered if data security is not provable to some level of technical certainty. Being able to prove that guarantee drove us to ensure that proper screen locks and encryption were in place." No data breach notification legislation mentions mobile phones, but this legislation is most assuredly influencing security decisions in the area of mobile payment system development.

Data Breach Costs

Data breaches can be expensive, but consumer notification mandated by breach legislation is not the main cost. A Poneman Institute survey of major corporations across various industry sectors found the average cost per breached record in 2011 was about $194, down from $214 per record in 2010.

An earlier survey of chief security officers (CSOs) at 14 different organizations pegged the cost at roughly $64 per lost record (Samuelson Law 2007). In addition, the CSO survey found that notification costs, which include call centers, costs of legal counsel, defense services, and victim compensation (such as reissuing cards or payment discounts), account for about 29 percent of breach costs. The Poneman study revealed that only 35 percent of breach costs are due to consumer notification.

Data breaches expose organizations to liabilities for damages. Typically, breach notification legislation does not enable consumers to sue for damages. In several states, however, notification laws do allow individuals to bring a private right of action to recover damages if breach notification was not expeditious (Winn 2009).

The most significant costs of a breach are often lost customers, damaged reputation, and even lowered stock valuations. The extent of these types of losses will depend largely on whether the company can show it acted responsibly in trying to protect consumer data and on how it responds to the breach. Normally, company stock valuations recover, especially for companies that take a proactive approach in their breach response, as was the case in the Heartland breach. Even though there is great incentive to lower the bar for breach reporting to avoid publicizing breaches, lack of transparency in breach response undermines the confidence of both customers and business partners.

Why Attempts at Federal Legislation Fall Short

There have been eight attempts to implement federal data breach legislation that would preempt state laws. The latest is Data Security and Breach Notification Act of 2012, Senate bill S.3333. Although similar to the California breach law, many believe the federal versions of breach notification legislation raise the bar that triggers reporting. Basically most proposed federal laws would require notification only if there is evidence of harm to consumers, with this determination being made by the data handler.

Making reporting requirements subject to the definition of "consumer harm" is tricky. Harm is very difficult to predict or monitor, as is the extent of losses to consumers as the result of a breach. What level of harm should trigger breach notification? Moreover, letting data holders decide when harm is evident raises serious concerns. There is little incentive for a data holder to error on the side of notification. Also, different organizations in a given industry are likely to employ different standards. Thus organizations that elect to put customer protection first might be penalized.

Many who advocate for a uniform national standard for data breach notification cite the complex task that businesses face in complying with a "haphazard patchwork" of breach notification laws (Roggenbaum 2006). As Roggenbaum notes, businesses have generally taken the conservative approach of complying with the most stringent of requirements across all states, thereby establishing a de facto standard. Also, as already discussed, consumer notification is not the major cost of a data breach.

Establishing uniform national standards is not a simple matter in the federal arena. A uniform standard for reporting must specify triggers for breach disclosure, parties to be notified, timing for notification, the form and the type of personal information affected, possible ways notices can be delivered, notice exceptions, and penalties for noncompliance. States have been in a better position to determine these factors for their residents than the federal government, which has been unable to produce passable legislation.

The key concern should be obviating the need for reporting by protecting consumer data. The first step is to store sensitive personal information in encrypted form whenever feasible, because compromised protected data does not trigger a notification requirement. Too often organizations try to protect data by relying on the security of their private networks, which is now almost impossible because a boundary between the Internet and a private network can seldom be maintained. The second step is to store sensitive consumer data only when required. Finally, organizations must ensure that third parties with which consumer data are shared take all appropriate measures to safeguard those data.

Concluding Remarks

Strong data breach notification laws are a form of broad-based consumer protection that makes organizations responsible for consumer data, regardless of the industry, service, or technology involved. Such protections are needed in a world where the information systems we use are inherently insecure, yet integral to our social and economic well-being. Most important, breach notification laws give both consumers and businesses the information that they need to factor security into purchase decisions and to mitigate risks when breaches occur.

References

Anderson, R. *Risk and Privacy Implications of Consumer Payment Innovation.* Presentation at Consumer Payment Innovation in the Connected Age, Federal Reserve Bank of Kansas City, Kansas City, MO, March 29–30, 2012. http://www.kc.frb.org/publicat/pscp/2012/anderson.pdf. Accessed May 10, 2012.

Cal. Civil Code §1798.29, 1798.80-1789.84.

Cate, F. H. "Security, Privacy, and the Role of Law." *IEEE Security and Privacy* 7, no. 5 (2009): 60–63. http://www.philadelphia.org/payment-card-center/publications/discussion-papers. Accessed October 31, 2012.

Creeger, M. "ACM CTO Roundtable on Mobile Devices in the Enterprise." *Communications of the ACM* 54, no. 9 (2011): 45–53.

Garfinkle, S. "The Cybersecurity Risk." *Communications of the ACM* 5, no. 6 (2012): 26–32.

National Conference of State Legislatures. "State Security Breach Notification Laws." August 2012. http://www.ncsl .org/issues-research/telecom/security-breach-notification -laws.aspx.

Poneman Institute LLC. "2011 Cost of a Data Breach Study." March 2012. http://www.symantec.com/about/news/ resources/press_kits/detail.jsp?pkid=ponemon-cost-of-a -data-breach-2011. Accessed October 1, 2012.

Privacy Rights Clearinghouse. "Chronology of Data Breaches." http://www.privacyrights.org/data-breach/print. Accessed October 1, 2012.

Roggenbaum, F. R. "Data Breach Notification Another 'Haphazard Patchwork' of State-by-State Requirements." *Journal of the Federal Regulatory Counsel* 17, no. 4 (2006). http://www.forc.org/public/journals/4. Accessed September 1, 2009.

Samuelson Law, Technology and Public Policy Clinic. *Security Breach Notification Laws: Views from Chief Security Officers.* University of California-Berkeley School of Law, 2007.

Winn, J. K. "Are 'Better' Security Breach Notification Laws Possible?" *Berkley Technology Law Journal* 24 (2009). http:// ssrn.com/abstract=1416222. Accessed December 10, 2010.

Wong, K. "Connecticut to Require Notice to Attorney General Following a Breach." *Data Privacy Monitor,* June 2012. http://www.dataprivacymonitor.com/data-breach -notification-laws/changes-to connecticuits-data-breach -notification-statute/. Accessed August 21, 2012.

Douglas E. Salane is an associate professor in the Department of Mathematics and Computer Science and is the director of the Center for Cybercrime Studies at the John Jay College of Criminal Justice.

A Criminologist's Perspective on the Implications of Criminological Research for Policies and Practices Aimed at Addressing Hacking and Malware Infection

Adam M. Bossler

For decades, most research on hackers has focused on the evolution and composition of the hacker subculture. Recently, scholars have started examining traditional criminological theories, such as Michael Gottfredson and Travis Hirschi's (1990) general theory of crime, Ron Akers' (1998) social learning theory, and Lawrence Cohen and Marcus Felson's (1979) routine activity theory to gain insight into computer hacking. The findings from these studies support two basic propositions: (1) there are multiple types of hackers separated by skill level, dedication, and self-control levels (Bossler and Burruss 2011; Furnell 2002; Holt and Kilger 2012; Jordan and Taylor 1998); and (2) peers substantively impact the development of hackers (Bossler and Burruss 2011; Holt and Kilger 2012). There are several implications for policy and practice that can be derived from the criminological literature to reduce hacking and malware infection by improving formal (e.g., law enforcement) and informal (e.g., parents, teachers) mechanisms.

Implications for Parental and School Practices

1. *Monitor with whom youth associate.* The literature on hacking is similar to that focusing on "traditional" offenses, in that the greatest predictor of whether someone hacks is his or her association with individuals who hack (Bossler and Burruss 2011). In these relationships, youth are more likely to imitate hacking behaviors they witness and be exposed to values that support such behavior. Hacking will then continue as long as the behavior is positively reinforced in some fashion (e.g., praise from peers) (Skinner and Fream 1997).

2. *Provide guidance to youth who show curiosity in computers.*
    Youth are curious individuals who are surrounded by tech-
    nology. If parents and teachers do not engage with youth
    about developing technologies, youth will go to other sour-
    ces to get answers (see point 1). Adults, however, believe
    that many youths are not prone to committing unethical
    computer acts, because they normally do not get into trou-
    ble. In a recent study, Bossler and Burruss (2011) found
    that most hackers in a college sample got involved in hack-
    ing because of their low levels of self-control, which
    increased their likelihood of associating with hackers.
    They also found a group of young adults who committed
    hacking activities even though they were not part of a
    hacker social learning process. Instead, these students had
    higher levels of self-control and patience, enjoyed chal-
    lenges, had the ability to resist instant gratification, and
    could learn the necessary skills and techniques over time.
    Instead of curtailing this curiosity, parents and schools need
    to develop positive outlets, such as computer clubs, in
    which youth can express their curiosity, creativity, and skill.
    The clubs could allow for the exploration of technology and
    give information about legal professions where computer
    expertise is a requirement.

3. *Provide social reinforcement for legal innovative uses of tech-
    nology.* The hacker subculture provides social reinforcement
    (e.g., praise, status) for successful hacks, even if many asso-
    ciations in this subculture are not strong or deep (Holt
    2009; Holt et al. 2012). Thus it is important for parents
    and teachers to praise youth for innovative legal uses of
    technology to decrease the need for social reinforcement
    from other sources. The assignment of computer-savvy
    mentors in schools, libraries, computer camps, or nonprofit
    organizations to students interested in computers could be
    an effective way to learn more about technology, while at
    the same time receive social encouragement from someone
    with expertise.

4. *Provide computer ethics training in schools.* Research has illustrated that the current hacker subculture incorporates values that support unethical uses of computer technology (Rogers, Smoak, and Liu 2006). Thus it is vital that parents and schools include training that focuses on ethical use of a variety of technologies. Because many schools already have some form of ethical and leadership development, the key would be to evaluate whether there is enough focus on ethics involving technology and cyberspace. In addition, these courses could stress how innovative technological adaptations can be used to solve economic, medical, and social problems.

5. *Focus on altering behavior as much as target hardening.* Most information security research focuses on the technical aspects of malicious software, with an emphasis on creating software applications (such as antivirus software) to mitigate malware. However, criminologists are just as interested in understanding how human behavior patterns influence victimization risk. Bossler and Holt (2009), in their analysis of data loss to malware infection in a college sample, found that personal (e.g., computer skills and using better passwords) and physical guardianship (e.g., antivirus software, firewalls) did not significantly reduce malware infection. Similar to other forms of victimization (Schwartz et al. 2001), safety precautions are not as effective when victimization is caused intentionally or unintentionally by family, friends, and acquaintances. Instead, youth need to be cognizant of the potential consequences of their own and their friends' risky and sometimes illegal computer activities to stop this short-sighted behavior.

6. *Educational campaigns about the risks of hacking.* Much of our efforts directed toward reducing various forms of cybercrime focus on advertising the punishments associated with cybercrime convictions (i.e., deterrence). A more effective strategy might be antihacking and piracy campaigns that illustrate how hacking and similar related behaviors increase

the odds of victimization for the youth or young adult and his or her family and friends (Bossler and Holt 2009).

Policy Implications for Law Enforcement

1. *Focus on top tier hackers.* The literature illustrates that hackers can be categorized into different groups based on skill level and ability to use technology (Holt and Kilger 2012). Law enforcement's primary focus must be the top-tier hackers who are able to identify new vulnerabilities, create original tools, and modify existing tools in an innovative way. Attempting to target networks that facilitate malware and hacking may prove more valuable than seeking out low-level or petty hackers who would not have the ability to perform many activities without the tools provided by more advanced hackers.

2. *Monitor online forums for the accessibility of tools.* Recent research has shown that high-skill hackers sell their skills, services, and tools on forums and Internet Relay Chat channels (Chu, Holt, and Ahn 2010). This practice allows a larger group of hackers to commit more effective attacks at low costs and exponentially increases the number of actors with the ability to accomplish attacks against critical infrastructure. Thus law enforcement needs to cautiously observe these trends and assess to what degree the capacity of top-tier hackers is spreading to lower levels because of this practice.

In sum, criminological research supports the role that criminology can play in developing a comprehensive framework to understand hacking and create effective and innovative policies and practices at informal (e.g., parenting) and formal (e.g., law enforcement) levels. The most effective policies and procedures will not have a singular focus but will instead use evidence gathered by both computer security professionals and criminologists.

References

Akers, R. L. 1998. *Social Learning and Social Structure: A General Theory of Crime and Deviance.* Boston, MA: Northeastern University Press.

Bossler, A., and G. Burruss. "The General Theory of Crime and Computer Hacking: Low Self-Control Hackers?" In *Corporate Hacking and Technology-Driven Crime: Social Dynamics and Implications,* edited by T. Holt and B. Schell. (38-67) Hershey, PA: IGI Global, 2011.

Bossler, A. M., and T. J. Holt. "On-line Activities, Guardianship, and Malware Infection: An Examination of Routine Activities Theory." *International Journal of Cyber Criminology* 3 (2009): 400–420.

Chu, B., T. J. Holt, and G. J. Ahn. *Examining the Creation, Distribution, and Function of Malware On-Line.* Washington, DC: National Institute of Justice, 2010. www.ncjrs.gov./pdffiles1/nij/grants/230112.pdf. Accessed June 10, 2012.

Cohen, L. E., and M. Felson. "Social Change and Crime Rate Trends: A Routine Activity Approach." *American Sociological Review* 44 (1979): 588–608.

Furnell, S. *Cybercrime: Vandalizing the Information Society.* London: Addison-Wesley, 2002.

Gottfredson, M. R., and T. Hirschi. *A General Theory of Crime.* Stanford, CA: Stanford University Press, 1990.

Holt, T. J. "Lone Hacks or Group Cracks: Examining the Social Organization of Computer Hackers." In *Crimes of the Internet,* edited by F. Schmalleger and M. Pittaro, 336–355. Upper Saddle River, NJ: Pearson Prentice Hall, 2009.

Holt, Thomas J., and Max Kilger. "The Social Dynamics of Hacking." *Know Your Enemy* Series. Honeynet Project, 2012. https://honeynet.org/papers/socialdynamics.

Holt, T. J., D. Strumsky, O. Smirnova, and M. Kilger. "Examining the Social Networks of Malware Writers and Hackers." *International Journal of Cyber Criminology* 6 (2012): 891–903.

Jordan, T., and P. Taylor. "A Sociology of Hackers." *Sociological Review* 46 (1998): 757–780.

Rogers, M., N. D. Smoak, and J. Liu. "Self-reported Deviant Computer Behavior: A Big-5, Moral Choice, and Manipulative Exploitive Behavior Analysis." *Deviant Behavior* 27 (2006): 245–268.

Schwartz, M. D., W. S. DeKeseredy, D. Tait, and S. Alvi. "Male Peer Support and a Feminist Routine Activities Theory: Understanding Sexual Assault on the College Campus." *Justice Quarterly* 18 (2001): 623–649.

Skinner, W. F., and A. M. Fream. "A Social Learning Theory Analysis of Computer Crime among College Students." *Journal of Research in Crime and Delinquency* 34 (1997): 495–518.

Adam M. Bossler is an associate professor in the Department of Criminal Justice at Georgia Southern University specializing in criminological theory and cybercrimes. He received his PhD in criminology and criminal justice from the University of Missouri–Saint Louis in 2007.

Hacking and Criminality

Nathan Fisk

Today, the dominant narrative of hacking tends to involve a broad range of malicious computer use—digital trespassing, identity theft, doxxing (the act of identifying a person from one small bit of information such as an email address; typically, the "doxer" would then use this information to discover the address and phone number of the real person), and, more recently, cyberwarfare. The term "hacker" is inextricably tied to the risks and unknowns of everyday computer use, and with even the most minute of technical glitches, it is not uncommon to hear IT experts declare that a given technological system has been "hacked." Hinting at its complex history, the popularized term also retains an aura of mystery—a sense of folk heroism and technological wizardry, as demonstrated by the roles occupied by the "good" hackers who make frequent appearances in contemporary video games, movies, and television shows. This dominant narrative of hacking has by no means remained static over the past three decades. Following the original use of the term in the late 1950s to describe a ludic mode of engagement with technology, hacking has held meaning for and has been mobilized by various individuals and groups across a broad range of social contexts.

From the earliest uses of the term to describe technical practice, hacking has historically been tied to youth subculture. Originating with groups of engineering students at the Massachusetts Institute of Technology (MIT), the term described a form of playful resistance against the stresses of the university grounded in the performance of technical mastery (Williams 2002). Some adventurous students began to explore the locked underground tunnels on campus, while others began experimenting with the campus telephone network, describing their activities as "tunnel hacking" and "phone hacking" (which later became known simply as "phreaking"). While these types of activities were frequently in violation of university policies and were undertaken as a means by which to resist the authority of the university, they were largely tolerated as part of MIT's culture; eventually these perpetrators were punished with relatively small fines (Scott 1993). As such, hacking represented a mode of inquiry that emerged in opposition to the structures of traditional educational systems, and it remained largely outside of public view.

While the terms "hacking" and "hackers" took on a meaning much more closely aligned with computer users throughout the 1970s and early 1980s (Levy 2001), they remained relatively neutral. Indeed, Donn Parker's (1976) early work on computer criminals contains no mention of "hacking" or "hackers," and Stewart Brand's (1974) short book on hackers frames them as "computer bums." One public technical document on early ARPAnet protocols goes so far as to actively distinguish between malicious activity and "hacking" attempts (McKenzie 1973). Even phone phreaks—who were described as criminals themselves—referred to hackers as hobbyists and, more specifically, as soft targets for social engineering and weak account security (Jester 1982). During this period of time, the free software movement—the precursor to open-source software—began to emerge from hacker cultures, and to this day, open-source developers continue to label themselves as "hackers," despite shifting public understanding of the term.

Only later would the image of the criminal teenage hacker become firmly cemented in the American imagination, as a result of the exploits of a group of Milwaukee teenagers, coincidentally publicized during the theatrical release of the movie *War Games* (Krance, Murphy, and Elmer-Dewitt 1983). The actions of these teens, known as the "414 Gang," were minimally criminal with no physical harm resulting from their unauthorized access, though federal law enforcement and prosecutors persisted in their attempts to generate publicity around the event (Hollinger and Lanza-Kaduce 1988). Throughout the mid-1980s and 1990s, widespread acceptance of the personal computer (PC) into middle-class households across the United States gave youth the notion that hacking offered a route to power, social status, and financial independence within online spaces free from adult supervision and surveillance.

Simultaneously, large-scale law enforcement operations were mobilized against the newly perceived threat, generating continued news media coverage and fictionalized accounts of the hacker subculture. Despite the contested nature of the term in online social spaces frequented by those who described themselves as hackers, the dominant narrative of hacking became a frame through which to understand any form of malicious or criminal activity involving computers and the Internet.

Given the extent to which hacking had been equated with criminal acts, it is somewhat unsurprising that concepts of cyberwarfare began to rise to prominence amidst fears of terrorism and general threats to personal and national security throughout the 2000s. Similarly, concerns over identity theft and organized crime began to increase as a number of major breaches of customer databases required widespread public notification efforts (Vijayan 2007). This repositioning of hacking allowed other legal activities described as hacking, such as open-source and free-software development, to be collapsed into categories that were more broadly understood by the lay public. Hackers-as-criminals became simply hackers, while hackers-as-developers became simple geeks and software developers (Nissenbaum 2004). Where the term "hacker" once encompassed the performance of technological mastery and resistance, as per the "computer bum" in Brand's writing, this understanding became eclipsed by the image of the criminal hacker.

Today, however, much of the trend toward the criminal image within the dominant image of the hacker is beginning to change. Even in a time of highly publicized breaches by hacking "groups" such as Anonymous and LulzSec, popular practices such as jail-breaking various technologies under restrictive digital rights management schemes have brought a new public understanding of hackers and hacking. Similarly, the growing popularity of the maker movement, grounded in hacker culture and approaches to consumer technologies, has begun to bring back notions of the hacker as tinkerer. Perhaps those who describe themselves as hackers, makers, jail breakers, and tinkerers—those who are "reordering the technologies and infrastructures which have become part of the fabric of everyday life" (Coleman 2011, 515)—are finally beginning to reorder and rework the dominant narrative of hacking.

References

Brand, S. *II Cybernetic Frontiers*. New York: Random House, 1974.

Coleman, G. "Hacker Politics and Publics." *Public Culture* 23, no. 3 (2011): 511–516.

Hollinger, R., and L. Lanza-Kaduce. "The Process of Criminalization: The Case of Computer Crime Laws." *Criminology* 26, no. 1 (1988): 101–126

Jester, S. "Simon Jester Issue." *TAP* 71 (January 1, 1982). http://artofhacking.com/tap/tap3/live/aoh_tap71.htm. Accessed October 4, 2012.

Krance, M., J. Murphy, and P. Elmer-Dewitt. "The 414 Gang Strikes Again." *Time,* August 29, 1983. http://www.time .com/time/magazine/article/0,9171,949797,00.html. Accessed October 4, 2012.

Levy, S. *Hackers: Heroes of the Computer Revolution*. New York: Penguin, 2001.

McKenzie, A. M. *Restricted Use of IMP DDT* (No. RFC #521). Network Working Group, 1973. http://tools.ietf.org/html/ rfc521. Accessed October 4, 2012.

Nissenbaum, H. "Hackers and the Contested Ontology of Cyberspace." *New Media and Society* 6, no. 2 (2004): 195–218.

Parker, D. B. *Crime by Computer*. New York: Scribner, 1976.

Scott, M. "Wired 1.03: Hacking the Material World." *Wired,* August 1, 1993. http://www.wired.com/wired/archive/1.03/ tunnelers.html. Accessed March 14, 2012.

Vijayan, J. "TJX Data Breach: At 45.6M Card Numbers, It's the Biggest Ever." *Computerworld* (March 29, 2007). http:// www.computerworld.com/s/article/9014782/TJX_data _breach_At_45.6M_card_numbers_it_s_the_biggest_ever. Accessed July 20, 2011.

Williams, S. *Free as in Freedom*. Cambridge, MA: O'Reilly, 2002. http://oreilly.com/openbook/freedom/appb.html. Accessed June 20, 2011.

Nathan Fisk completed his PhD at Rensselaer Polytechnic Institute in 2011 and is interested in computer hacking, technology, and youth cybercrime.

The Life Cycle of a Botnet

Aditya K. Sood and Richard J. Enbody

Legend has it that when the 1930s bank robber Willie Sutton was asked why he robbed banks, he responded, "Because that's where the money is." Today, money is on the Internet, so that is where the criminals are, too. Sutton used guns; today's cyber-criminals use bots. Working through the Internet allows cyber-criminals to work anonymously from great distances, often from countries with weak cyberlaws. The resulting losses are in the billions of dollars and rising, and convictions are rare.

What is a bot? The word "bot" is short for "robot," so in general bots are automated tools on the Internet. Within the context of cybercrime, however, a bot is an automated tool for creating networks of infected computers: the botnet. The infected computers of a botnet are centrally controlled by a cybercriminal from a command and control (C&C) system. Botnets tend to be large, ranging from tens of thousands to millions of infected computers. A wide variety of malware can be installed on botnets, but the focus of this essay is on the malware that steals financial credentials, such as a user's bank account and password.

Botnets have existed for years, but have evolved from hacker exercise curiosities that did little damage to sophisticated tools for criminals. The current generation communicates over HTTP because it often is not feasible to simply turn off the Web so HTTP traffic is allowed. Also, using web technologies

From: Internal Revenue Service [mailto:admin@irs.gov]
Sent: Wednesday, March 01, 2006 12:45 PM
To: john.doe@jdoe.com
Subject: IRS Notification - Please Read This .

Internal Revenue Service
United States Department of the Treasury

After the last annual calculations
of your fiscal activity we have
determined that you are eligible
to receive a tax refund of **$63.80**.
Please submit the tax refund
request and allow us 6-9 days in
order to process it.

A refund can be delayed for a
variety of reasons. For example
submitting invalid records or
applying after the deadline.

To access the form for your tax
refund, please **click here**

Regards,
Internal Revenue Service

© Copyright 2006, Internal Revenue Service U.S.A. All rights reserved..

Figure 3.4   Phishing Email (http://www.irs.gov/pub/irs-utl/phishing_email.pdf)

and tools such as PHP, AJAX, and MySQL allows more complex management and improved interfaces.

The malware infection life cycle usually begins with phishing. In this context, a user is convinced to click on an illegitimate link embedded in an email by exploiting the trust of the user. Figure 3.4 is an example of a phishing email that exploits the trust of users by fooling them to believe that the email comes from the U.S. Internal Revenue Service (IRS).

This email looks authentic, but it has a malicious link embedded in it. A user needs to be fooled for only a moment—just enough time to click. After clicking the link, the malware infection life cycle starts, as shown in Figure 3.5.

When a user clicks the link embedded in the email, he or she is redirected by the browser to visit a website previously

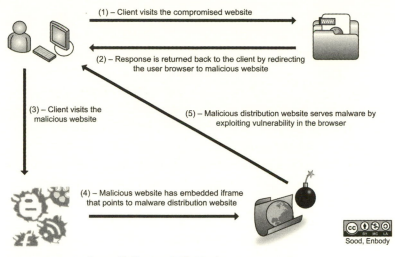

Figure 3.5   Malware Infection Life Cycle

compromised by the attacker. The compromised domain is used primarily to redirect incoming traffic, usually by means of an iframe that connects back to a malware distribution website. Why the double redirection? The first site is often a legitimate site, so a user is more likely to click on the link. Also, it is relatively easy to corrupt a web page with an illegitimate iframe; contrast that with the work needed to set up a malware distribution site. Also, multiple hops allow for more variations in paths to malware distribution sites, so that detection is more difficult and take-down is less likely.

The target malware distribution website hosts an automated browser-based exploit framework that examines the user's browser to detect vulnerabilities. When a vulnerable version of a browser is detected, the appropriate exploit is selected. On successful exploitation of the vulnerability, the framework serves malware that is surreptitiously installed on the user's system. From the point at which the user clicks the link in the phishing email, the entire infection process is automatic: one click and an infection results. If a user's browser is up-to-date, it likely is not vulnerable, and the infection will fail. The percentage of success for a known vulnerability is low (e.g., 5%), but the rate of visitation is high enough that tens of thousands of computers can become infected. If the malware distribution exploits a "zero-day" vulnerability (i.e., no defense exists), the rate of infection will be much higher. The art of downloading of malware on the users' machines by exploiting vulnerabilities in their browsers is known as a drive-by download attack—and it is difficult to detect.

How does browser-delivered malware embed itself in a user's computer? A user land rootkit hides itself in the operating system and subverts the integrity of running processes in the systems (Bustier, Elder, and Siebert 2011).These user land rootkits are powerful, because they have the ability to hijack the communication channel of various processes in the system using hooking (Bustier et al. 2011). The malware uses hooking to intercept communication among processes by forcing the system events to call the hooked (malicious) code before the actual function is called.

Let us now examine the process in the context of banking malware. Phishing directs a user to a malicious domain, where a drive-by download then installs malware on the user's machine. Sometime later, the user opens a bank webpage and enters his or her credentials in the web form. When the user clicks to send the credentials, a function is invoked to send the credentials to the banking server. The malware hooks the web browser's process to intercept that "send" function so that it can steal the user's credentials before they are actually sent to the banking server. After stealing a copy of the credentials, the hook is released so that the normal sending of credentials continues—it all happens without anyone realizing the momentary redirection for theft. This technique is called "form-grabbing"—the information in the web page's *form* is *grabbed* before it is sent (Sood and Enbody 2012).

Now consider that this one infected computer is part of a botnet along with tens of thousands to millions of other infected computers. The criminal controlling the botnet can automatically collect a large number of banking credentials. Alternatively, the botnet owner can rent large collections of infected computers to others. The C&C interfaces are sufficiently user friendly that relatively nontechnical criminals can rent and use the botnet.

What can a user do to defend against these attacks? First, a user should keep all software up-to-date, preferably enabling automatic updating. Most broad-based successful attacks exploit known vulnerabilities for which updates exist. Second, a user should be aware of phishing and resist the urge to click on links sent in emails. The most effective phishing attacks exploit a user's trust in friends, businesses, and legitimate websites. That cute-puppies video sent to a user may lead to a drive-by-download. Third, a user should install antivirus software and keep it up-to-date—an out-of-date virus checker is useless against new attacks. The first two pointers are more important than the third; in short, the best defense is preventing the infection rather than recognizing that one's machine is infected. It is difficult to completely remove malware from the world, but secure practices and countermeasures significantly help end users to reduce its adverse impact on computers and networks.

References

Bustier, A., F. Elder, and T. Siebert. "Bank Safe Information Stealer Detection Inside the Web Browser." In *Proceedings of the 14th International Conference on Recent Advances in Intrusion Detection* (RAID). New York: Springer 2011.

Sood, A. K., & R. J. Enbody. *Botnets Die Hard—Owned and Operated.* Presentation at DefCon 20, Las Vegas, NV, 2012. https://media.defcon.org/dc-20/presentations/Sood -Enbody/DEFCON-20-Sood-Enbody-Botnets-Die-Hard .PDF.pdf. Accessed October 1, 2012.

Aditya K. Sood is a senior security research, consultant, and PhD candidate at Michigan State University.

Richard J. Enbody is an associate professor in the Department of Computer Science and Engineering at Michigan State University.

Taking the Fun out of Playtime: Real Crime and Video Games

Rob D'Ovidio, Murugan Anandarajan, and Alex Jenkins

The video game industry—including the publishers and creators of traditional video games (e.g., first-person shooters, real-time strategy games, and arcade games), virtual worlds, massive multiplayer online role-playing games (MMORPGs), and gaming consoles—has grown into a multibillion-dollar industry that rivals the revenue generated by the motion picture industry (Chatfield 2009; Hines 2011; Smith 2011). With this growth, we have seen the video game evolve from a single-person experience that plays out solely on the screen directly in front of the player, to an experience that can involve multiple people playing together from anywhere across the globe, with remote servers interacting with local gaming devices (e.g., laptop computers, video game consoles, handheld gaming devices, and smart phones) to deliver a graphically rich interactive gaming experience.

The modern game play experience is enhanced by text, audio, and video chat features that allow players to interact in real time and is supported by complex economic engines that facilitate the purchase, trade, and sale of in-game goods and currencies (e.g., weapons and clothing for avatars). The value of these in-game transactions ranges from fractions of a penny to millions of U.S. dollars. For example, a space station, a space resort, and virtual land in the MMORPG Entropia Universe recently sold for $330,000, $635,000 and $2.5 million, respectively (Reahard 2012; Tassi 2010; Westaway 2010). It is the interactive capabilities within video games and the stored economic value in the digital goods, virtual currencies, and accounts amassed by players that make many video games attractive targets for crime. This has particular salience for computer hackers who may attempt to compromise users in some way, shape, or form. This essay discusses crimes involving video games and uses routine activities theory to explain the attractiveness of these technologies for criminals.

Looking at Crime in Video Games through the Lens of Routine Activities Theory

Researchers (Chen et al, 2005, 250; Elliot 2008, 5–7; Regli, Mitkus, and D'Ovidio 2012, 3–6), the mass media (Cavalli 2009; Edwards 2010; Tiemann 2007), and government entities (Barroso et al. 2008, 25–50; Interpol 2010, 30–55) have all documented the occurrence of real crimes involving video games and video game devices. Regli, Mitkus, and D'Ovidio (2012, 4–5) categorize crimes involving video games based on the adverse consequences caused by the criminal activity. Namely, crimes that produce social harm, or crimes that have "negative physical, psychological or emotional consequences that cannot be readily expressed in cash terms," are differentiated from crimes that produce economic harm, or crimes that have "negative effects on an individual, community, business, institution, or government that can readily be expressed in cash terms" (Criminal Intelligence Services Canada [CISC] 2007, 10).

Economically, harmful crimes occurring in and targeting video games include, according to Regli, Mitkus, and D'Ovidio (2012, 5), identity theft, phishing, money laundering, virtual goods theft, software and server piracy, and network intrusions (Baker and Finkle 2011; Boxer 2011; Graft 2010; Tiemann 2007). Stickney (2012), for example, reports on a recent email phishing scam designed to trick World of Warcraft players into giving over their game account credentials by promising them beta access to a forthcoming game expansion. Upon getting access to a victim's account, the criminals behind the phishing attack can easily sell off the weapons, game currency, and other items collected during the game for

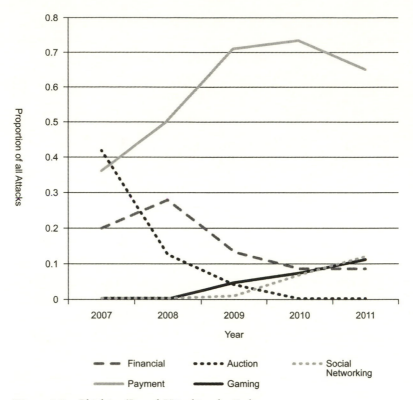

Figure 3.6 Phishing/Brand Hijacking by Industry

real-world currency through numerous gray-market websites dealing in virtual video game goods.

Based on valid phishing attacks reported to the PhishTank website, Figure 3.6 provides a look at phishing victimization in the financial, consumer payment platform, online auction, video game, and social networking industries from 2007 to 2011. The data indicate the current attractiveness of video games to criminals looking to obtain personal identifiers and account credentials through phishing, relative to other industries. Phishing attacks against video games brands have been increasing since 2008, whereas attacks against the financial, consumer payment platform, and online auction industries have been decreasing.

Routine activities theory can provide insight into the attractiveness of video games to criminals looking to cause economic harm. Grabosky, Smith, and Dempsey (2001, 3) have linked theft and fraud in cyberspace to increased connectivity and the widespread adoption of online commerce. They claim that the increasing use of online services for commerce produces a subsequent increase in the number of suitable targets for victimization from fraud. As such, we should look at the number of people who play video games and the volume of commerce in the industry as an indicator of the suitability of players for victimization. With video games being played in 72 percent of U.S. households (*Essential Facts* 2011), industry trends moving toward more digital downloads and online transactions, and annual consumer spending in the video game industry reaching $24.75 billion (*Essential Facts* 2012), there is little question that game players surely represent an economic opportunity for criminals.

As criminals continue to target video games and gaming devices, consideration must be given to the capacity of the law enforcement community to successfully investigate these types of crimes. Successful investigations require, in part, that law enforcement professionals have access to digital forensics tools that are compatible with the computing devices on which video games are played. Digital forensics tools for examining traditional computing devices (i.e., desktop computers and laptop computer)—such as Access Data's FTK and Guidance Software's Encase—and those for examining cell phones—such as Access Data's MPE+ and BK Forensics CPA—are readily available. These tools are, however, not compatible with popular video game devices (e.g., Xbox 360, PlayStation 3, DSi, Vita) due to the use of proprietary file systems and operating systems and disk encryption. Podhradsky, D'Ovidio, and Casey (2011) found, for example, that the FTK software was unsuccessful at imaging the Xbox 360 hard drive because of the use of the FATX file structure in the gaming console. Additionally, tools for dedicated gaming systems are scarce, if they exist at all, and provide nowhere near the forensic capability provided by the forensics tools for traditional computing devices. Future research addressing crime and video games should, therefore, include the development of forensics tools that are compatible with video game devices and that mirror the capabilities of the tools used to examine traditional computing devices.

Notes

This essay was supported by Grant No. 2009-D2-BX-K005 awarded by the Bureau of Justice Assistance. The Bureau of Justice Assistance is a component of the Office of Justice Programs, which also includes the Bureau of Justice Statistics, the National Institute of Justice, the Office of Juvenile Justice and Delinquency Prevention, the SMART Office, and the Office for Victims of Crime. Points of view or opinions in this essay are those of the authors and do not represent the official position or policies of the U.S. Department of Justice.

References

Baker, L. B., and J. Finkle. "Sony PlayStation Suffers Massive Data Breach." *Reuters*, April 26, 2011. http://www.reuters .com/article/2011/04/26/us-sony-stoldendata-idUSTRE 73P6WB20110426. Accessed November 5, 2012.

Barroso, D., R. Bartle, P. Chazerand, M. de Zwart, J. Doumen, S. Gorniak, E. Guamundsson, et al. *Virtual Worlds, Real Money: Security and Privacy in Massively-Multiplayer Online Games and Social and Corporate Virtual Worlds,* edited by Giles Hogben, 80. Greece: European Network and Information Security Agency, 2008.

Boxer, S. "Xbox Live Users Hit by Phishing Attacks." *The Guardian*, November 22, 2011. http://www.guardian.co.uk/ technology/2011/nov/22/xbox-live-users-phishing-attacks. Accessed November 5, 2012.

Cavalli, E. "World of Warcraft Phishing Attempts on the Rise." *Wired*, April 29, 2009. http://www.wired.com/gamelife/2009/04/world-of-warcraft-phishing-attempts-on-the-rise/. Accessed November 4, 2012.

Chatfield, T. "Videogames Now Outperform Hollywood Movies." *The Observer*, September 26, 2009. http://www.guardian.co.uk/ technology/gamesblog/2009/sep/27/videogames-hollywood. Accessed November 3, 2012.

Chen, Y. C., P. S. Chen, J. J. Hwang, L. Korba, R. Song, and G. Yee. "An Analysis of Online Gaming Crime Characteristics." *Internet Research* 15, no. 3 (2005): 246–261.

Criminal Intelligence Services Canada (CISC). *Integrated Threat Assessment Methodology*, 29. Criminal Intelligence Services Canada, 2007.

Edwards, A. L. "Former Disney Worker Used Xbox Gaming System to Solicit Nude Pics of Kids." *Orlando Sentinel*, August 27, 2010. http://articles.orlandosentinel.com/2010-08-27/news/os-xbox-child-pornography-arrest-20100827_1_xbox-system-nude-photos-child-pornography. Accessed November 3, 2012.

Elliot, J. "Help—Somebody Robbed My Second Life Avatar!" *Journal of Virtual Worlds Research* 1, no. 1 (2008): 1–11.

Essential Facts about the Computer and Video Game Industry, 16. Washington, DC: Entertainment Software Association, 2011.

Essential Facts about the Computer and Video Game Industry, 16. Washington, DC: Entertainment Software Association, 2012.

Grabosky, P., R. G. Smith, and G. Dempsey. *Electronic Theft: Unlawful Acquisition in Cyberspace*. Cambridge: Cambridge University Press, 2001.

Graft, K. "Blizzard Wins $88M Judgment against WoW Private Server Owner." *Gamasutra*, August 16, 2010.

http://www.gamasutra.com/view/news/29936/Blizzard
_Wins_88M_Judgment_Against_WoW_Private_Server
_Owner.php#.UJiD6LSD3d4. Accessed November 5, 2012.

Hines, A. "Modern Warfare 3: While Movie Industry
Struggles, Gaming Thrives." *AOL Daily Finance*,
November 10, 2011. http://www.dailyfinance.com/2011/
11/10/what-to-make-of-modern-warfare-3s-record
-breaking-sales/. Accessed November 3, 2012.

Interpol. *Crime and Policing in Virtual Worlds*, 85. France:
Interpol Working Party on IT Crime, 2010.

Podhradsky, A., R. D'Ovidio, and C. Casey. "The Practitioners
Guide to the Forensic Investigation of Xbox 360 Gaming
Consoles." In *The Conference on Digital Forensics, Security,
and Law (ADFSL)*, 173–191. VA: Association of Digital
Forensics, Security, and Law, ISSN 1931-7379, 2011.

Reahard, J. "Entropia Universe Player Drops $2.5 Million on
Virtual Land Deeds." *Joystiq*, April 4, 2012. http://massively
.joystiq.com/2012/04/04/entropia-universe-player-drops-2-5
-million-on-virtual-land-deed/2. Accessed November 4, 2012.

Regli, B., M. Mitkus, and R. D'Ovidio. *Real Crimes in Virtual
Worlds*, 10. Drakontas, LLC, and Drexel University, 2012.

Smith, D. "Behind the Quiet Success of the Video Game
Industry." *Inc.*, April 28, 2011. http://www.inc.com/
articles/201104/behind-the-quiet-success-of-the-video
-game-industry.html. Accessed November 3, 2012.

Stickney, A. "Watch out for Mists of Pandaria Beta Invite
Scams." *Joystiq*, March 22, 2012. http://wow.joystiq.com/
2012/03/22/reminder-watch-out-for-mists-of-pandaria
-beta-invite-scams/. Accessed November 5, 2012.

Tassi, P. "Virtual Entropia Universe Property Sells for $335K
Real Dollars." *Forbes*, November 10, 2010. http://www
.forbes.com/sites/insertcoin/2010/11/10/virtual-entropia
-universe-property-sells-for-335k-real-dollars/. Accessed
November 4, 2012.

Tiemann, A. "Virtual Theft Results in Real-Life Arrest." *CNET*, November 15, 2007. http://news.cnet.com/8301 -13507_3-9817894-18.html. Accessed November 4, 2012.

Westaway, L. "Virtual Space Club Sold for $635,000." *CNET*, November 19, 2010. http://news.cnet.com/8301-17938 _105-20023429-1/virtual-space-club-sold-for-$635000/. Accessed November 4, 2012.

Rob D'Ovidio, PhD, is an associate professor in the Criminal Justice Program at Drexel University in Philadelphia, Pennsylvania. Correspondence regarding this paper can be sent to his attention at rd64@drexel.edu.

Murugan Anandarajan, PhD, is a professor of Management Information Science at Drexel University in Philadelphia, Pennsylvania.

Alex Jenkins is a PhD student in culture and communication at Drexel University in Philadelphia, Pennsylvania.

BK

8 29384 09·08·90

LOS ANGELES POLICE = JAIL·J

2600: The Hacker Quarterly

2600: The Hacker Quarterly is a magazine that is highly regarded in the hacker community for its information and coverage of issues pertaining to the hacker underground. The title comes from the tone used by phreaks—2600—to control telephony. First published in 1984 by Eric Corley (also known as Emmanuel Goldstein) and David Ruderman, the magazine is released four times per year. Its focus is on applications of hacking that extend technology beyond its limits, and articles tend to be devoid of the notions of ethical or malicious hacking.

2600 is still very popular with hackers today and is considered by many to be controversial in nature—in a cognitively complex "nice" sort of way. Eric Corley remains the editor-in-chief of the magazine, and Ed Cummings (also known as Bernie S.) is a regular contributor and collaborator (Schell and Martin 2006). The magazine has covered many notable issues, including the Kevin Mitnick trial and free speech issues related to technology in

---

Kevin Poulsen is booked in Los Angeles, California on September 8, 1990. After serving a short prison term for his "black hat" exploits, Poulsen, like many former hackers, parlayed his expertise into an alternate career, reporting on technology issues, and eventually becoming the senior editor for *Wired News*. (AP/Wide World Photos)

general, and to the Digital Millennium Copyright Act (DMCA) in particular.

The DMCA copyright case actually involved *2600* and Universal Studios; it occurred over allegations by Universal Studios that *2600* had infringed the DMCA. This intriguing case arose in November 1999 from *2600*'s publication of and linking to a computer program called DeCSS as part of its news coverage about DVD decryption software that could be used to unscramble digital video discs. In January 2000, Universal Studios and other members of the Motion Picture Association of America filed suit against the hacker magazine; they sought an order that *2600* no longer publish the said contents. In particular, the complainants objected to the publication of DeCSS because, they argued, it could be used as part of a process to infringe copyrights on DVD movies. The magazine, represented by Eric Corley, argued in its defense that decryption of DVD movies is necessary for a number of reasons, including to make "fair use" of movies and to play DVD movies on computers running the Linux operating system (Schell and Dodge, with Moutsatsos 2002). In the end, *2600* lost the case. Upon hearing the court's decision, the head of the Motion Picture Association of America declared that the decision "nailed down an indispensable constitutional and congressional truth. It's wrong to help others steal creative works" (Dixon 2001, B22).

In addition to its role as a magazine, *2600* also serves as a rallying point for hackers in the real world by supporting meetings held in locales around the world on the first Friday of every month. The magazine also sponsors the Hackers on Planet Earth (HOPE) conference, which is held biannually in New York City. This is one of the oldest hacker conferences in the world; it started in 1994 and is typically held at the Hotel Pennsylvania (which has "HOPE" embedded in its name). Famous hackers and phreakers from the past and present often network and share hacking stories at HOPE. For example, at the H2K conference in New York City in July 2000, phreaker John Draper made an appearance on "The Old-Timer Panel" with fellow phreakers Cheshire Catalyst and Bootleg. Another speaker was modern-day phreaker Bernie S. Besides being active in *2600*, Bernie S. was sent to federal prison in 1995 for his phreaking exploits—the first person to be imprisoned without bail for using a modified Radio Shack speed dialer to make free telephone calls using public telephones. To this day, Bernie S. maintains that the tones and information in his possession were very easy to obtain (Schell and Dodge, with Moutsatsos 2002).

At the HOPE convention in 2008, Emmanuel Goldstein sold his book, *The Best of 2600: A Hacker Odyssey*. This 888-page book collects some of the most interesting and often the most controversial articles ranging from the year *2600* was first published until the present—all from a hacker's perspective. The book contains stories about the creation of the infamous tone dialer "red box," which allowed hackers to make free phone calls from payphones without paying a cent; the founding of the Electronic Frontier Foundation (EFF), an organization that began in the summer of 1990 primarily in reaction to threats to free speech and continues to provide legal counsel to hackers charged with various infractions; and the "insecurity" of modern locks designed to keep burglars out of real, rather than virtual, doors. In 2009, Goldstein released his 912-page *Collector's Edition* with the same title.

Subscriptions to the magazine, back issues, and other merchandise are available from the *2600* online store or by consulting its price list and sending money to *2600 Magazine*, P.O. Box 75, Middle Island, New York 11953. Nowadays, the magazine is available in paper or digital forms. The magazine's website is http://www.2600.org.

Abene, Mark (Phiber Optik) (1972–)

Mark Abene is a notorious phreaker who enjoyed breaking into telephone systems using a common telephone receiver. A former member of the Legion of Doom hacker group and later the founder of the hacker group called Masters of Deception, Abene was held accountable for the American Telephone and Telegraph system crash back in 1990—though it was later discovered that the crash was actually caused by a computer bug not of Abene's doing. The next year, Abene was investigated by the U.S. Secret Service and indicted for his phone hacking exploits involving Southwestern Bell, New York Telephone, Pacific Bell, US West, and the Martin Marietta Electronics Information and Missile Group. He served 10 months in a U.S. prison—and during his incarceration was visited by so many journalists that his fellow prisoners called him "CNN." After his release from prison, Abene worked on penetration tests (a technical service aimed at compromising a security company's network from outside to search for vulnerabilities) for an accounting firm and created the now-defunct security company Crossbar Security (Schell and Martin 2004).

According to his LinkedIn webpage, Abene is currently the chief technical officer and founder of TraceVector, Inc. He resides in New York City and has as his professional identity "Security Guru."

Adams, Douglas (1952–2001)

Douglas Adams was a man of many talents. He is an author, for example, whose book *The Hitchhiker's Guide to the Galaxy* became a household name when the cult science-fiction novel was turned into a British Broadcast Corporation television series. Adams was also extremely well respected in the computer underground, in part because his book demonstrated much of the Zen-like thinking so common among hackers. In fact, the book was so popular in the mainstream and in the computer underground that it sold more than 14 million copies worldwide. In 2005, a film of the same title was produced by Buena Vista Pictures. In essence, *The Hitchhiker's Guide to the Galaxy* details the universal journey of Ford Prefect, an alien, and Arthur Dent, a human, in a period following the destruction of Planet Earth. More deeply, the story focused on the search for an answer to life and to the universe—with 42 being the sought-after number.

Some of the terminology used by Adams in his books (he also wrote *The Restaurant at the End of the Universe; Life, the Universe, and Everything;* and *So Long and Thanks for All the Fish, Mostly Harmless*) made its way into hacker jargon. The word "bogon," as one case in point, was used incorrectly by Arthur Dent to describe the Vogons, a race of aliens. In the hacker community, "bogon" has been used to describe the erratic behavior of network equipment. A common expression is "the network is emitting bogons."

Another creative pursuit of Adams was the h2g2 website—itself groundbreaking in that it enabled an online encyclopedia to be developed "by the people and for the people"—as Adams used to say. Educated at Cambridge University's St John's College, Adams was also considered to be an Internet pioneer who believed that something powerful could be created when people pooled their experiences and information—which is what Adams claimed the Internet did. Adams presented a series on the greatness of the Internet on BBC radio until his sudden death in 2001 at age 49 (Schell and Martin 2006).

Anonymous

Anonymous is the name used to refer to a loose collective of actors who have engaged in hacking-related attacks against various targets around the world. Their activities go back to the group 4chan and other online communities where individuals share images and information in a relatively anonymous fashion. Exactly *what* Anonymous is remains somewhat of a mystery, but hackers in this clan have brought down the Vatican's website, taunted cabinet ministers whose policies they did not like, and inserted themselves into online national debates without being invited. But is Anonymous an agitprop activist group, or is it truly an international security threat? Could the group be an online "cover-up" for governments wanting to meddle in other governments' affairs, or is the group just a bunch of hactivists whose anarchy bent has gone "viral" online?

What IT security experts know is that Anonymous is not centralized anywhere, but rather acts as a nebulous collection of cells and splinter groups that tend to coordinate their efforts in online chat rooms. Consistent with the Hacker Manifesto, Anonymous members are committed to anonymity, the free flow of information, and transparency. Beyond this point, Anonymous seems to embody a culture of online "creative disturbance" (Tossell 2012).

In February 2012, Anonymous turned its virtual attention to Canada's Public Safety Minister Vic Toews. Members of Anonymous went on YouTube and called on Toews to drop the federal government's controversial Internet surveillance bill, which was touted as protecting children online by allowing police to access personal information about Internet users without first obtaining a search warrant. The intent, of course, was to nab online child pornographers. The speaker in the YouTube video purported to "know all about" the Public Safety Minister and threatened to release this information online if the bill were not dropped. Since its appearance in the virtual world, the video has since been removed from YouTube. In 2011, Anonymous gained prominence after it launched cyberattacks on PayPal and Visa. Members also had a key role in the Occupy Wall Street movement (D'Aliesio 2012).

Opposition to the proposed Canadian bill focusing on the federal government's "lawful access" continued to grow once the YouTube video was released. Internet privacy advocates viewed it as an unnecessary intrusion into Canadians' lives. Responding to such criticisms, Minister Toews declared that opponents of the bill were either "with the Conservatives supporting the bill" or "with the child pornographers"—a proclamation that prompted even greater indignation (Mackrael 2012).

A similar online protest—one of the biggest online protests in history—was launched by hackers in January 2012 as a means of stopping two pieces of controversial U.S. legislation before the U.S House of Representatives and Senate, respectively: the Stop Online Piracy Act (SOPA) and the Protect Intellectual Property Act (PIPA). As a result of the protest, some of the most popular websites in the world, including Wikipedia and Reddit, became difficult or impossible to access (El Akkad, January 19, 2012).

Not long after these events, the YouTube Anonymous video appeared. It showed a headless man in a black suit under a red maple leaf as a computer-generated voice demanded Toews' resignation (Canadian Press 2012).

Anonymous made media headlines worldwide when it was announced by Interpol on February 28, 2012, that that 25 suspected members of the loose-knit hacker movement had been arrested in Europe and South America. Interpol further said that the arrests made in Argentina, Chile, Colombia, and Spain had been completed by law enforcement officers working with the support of Interpol's Latin America Working Group of Experts on Information Technology Crime. The suspects ranged in age from 17 to 40 years. The suspects were held accountable for planning coordinated cyberattacks against Colombia's defense ministry and presidential websites, Chile's Endesa electricity company and national library, and other targets. There was immediate Internet noise suggesting that a distributed denial-of-service (DDoS) attack likely would be launched against Interpol's website by members of Anonymous. There is little question that many of the hacktivist activities of Anonymous have increased since the global clampdown on music piracy and the international controversy caused by the secret-spilling website known as WikiLeaks—which Anonymous members seem to identify with (Keller 2012).

On March 7, 2012, the media announced that Hector Xavier Monsegur, one of the purported leaders of the Lulz

Security hacker group affiliated with Anonymous, had been assisting the Federal Bureau of Investigation (FBI) in the United States for months in an attempt to track down hackers (allegedly Ryan Ackroyd, Jake Davis, Darren Martyn, Donncha O'Cearrbhail, and Jeremy Hammond) who had recorded a private conference call between members of the FBI and Scotland Yard. Operating under the moniker Sabu, Monsegur was well known and respected in hacking circles, but when word got out in the computer underground that he had helped the FBI snag fellow hackers, ripples of mistrust among hackers once again surfaced in the virtual world. Meanwhile, in an effort to quiet the unrest, an Anonymous affiliated group argued online: "#Anonymous is an idea, not a group. There is no leader, there is no head. It will survive, before, during and after this time" (El Akkad, March 7, 2012).

Assange, Julian Paul (1971–)

Julian Paul Assange is currently the editor-in-chief and founder of the whistleblowing website WikiLeaks. During his youth in Australia, he was involved with the hacker group the International Subversives and used the handle Mendax (Greenberg 2010). Police caught Assange in 1991 after he hacked into systems of the communications company Nortel. He was also associated with hack attacks against universities and U.S. government systems, and was charged with 31 counts of hacking and related offenses. In 1995, he pled guilty to 25 of the counts and was released with a small fine and no additional time served (Assange 2011). The judge for this case indicated that Assange's attacks were not malicious, but rather a consequence of his intelligence and curiosity. Thus, the judge decided, Assange did not merit more substantive punitive sanctions. Upon his release, he began working as a computer programmer and author, and created various freeware programs designed to protect data (Assange 2011).

In 2006, Assange founded WikiLeaks to provide an outlet
for promoting regime change and open information sharing
to expose injustice and abuses of power (Greenberg 2010).
The site has published materials related to the Church of
Scientology, the U.S. military's operations at Guantanamo
Bay, military strikes, and classified documents around the
world. WikiLeaks is perhaps most famous for its acquisition
and publication of 251,000 U.S. diplomatic cables that range
from unclassified to secret documents (Greenberg 2010). A
U.S. Army soldier named Bradley Manning, who downloaded
the materials while stationed in Iraq, obtained this information.
He then provided the materials to WikiLeaks, which chose to
release these materials in batches over two years with cooperation from major news outlets such as *The New York
Times* and *Der Spiegel* (Harrell 2010).

The release of these cables caused massive controversy and
embarrassment for the U.S. government due to the sensitive
nature of the information they contained. In fact, a distributed
denial-of-service attack was launched against the WikiLeaks
site shortly after the first release—taking the site offline.
Subsequently, the companies that provided funding and infrastructure for WikiLeaks, such as PayPal, pulled their support.
As a consequence, the group Anonymous began DDoS attacks
against the financial service providers to punish them for their
actions. The controversy over these documents led some in
the United States to call for the arrest of Assange, and even
his execution, in some cases (O'Brien 2010). He was arrested
in 2010 in the United Kingdom on charges related to rape
and sexual assault in Sweden. Assange has been fighting an
extradition order from the Swedish government since then,
and applied for political asylum in Ecuador in June 2012
(BBC 2012).

In mid-August 2012, after Assange had spent two months
in the Ecuadorean embassy in London, Ricardo Patino, the
Foreign Minister of Ecuador, announced that Assange would

be granted diplomatic asylum. It was interesting that in his announcement, Patino spoke not of Sweden but of the United States. While rumors have surfaced that an American grand jury is investigating Assange for possible charges related to treason, he is currently not on the lam from any U.S. legal proceedings. While Ecuador has no tradition of giving refuge to political exiles, apparently President Rafael Correa enjoys annoying the United States. For his part, Assange appears to have no qualms about invoking state power and international law when he does not want to face his day in Swedish court over charges unrelated to hacking (Stackhouse, August 17, 2012).

It is also interesting to note that President Correa was the reason that the director of Ecuador's primary opposition newspaper sought asylum earlier in 2012, hiding away in Panama's embassy for two weeks when Ecuador's high court upheld a criminal defamation ruling against him and other high-ranking editors. Correa later pardoned them and forgave a $42 million damage award against the newspaper, but free press and human rights activists maintain that Correa remains a threat to any speech not of his view (Bajak 2012).

On August 19, 2012, Assange made headlines again when he spoke to the media outside the Ecuadorean embassy in London. He stood on the balcony and called on U.S. President Barack Obama to abandon what he called a "witch hunt" against WikiLeaks. He went on to say that an alleged FBI investigation against his whistleblowing website should be "dissolved" and that the United States should return to its "revolutionary" values. Assange also demanded that Bradley Manning, the U.S. army intelligence analyst suspected of leaking confidential information, should be released—calling Manning a hero and "an example to all of us." Although Assange's supporters argue that if Assange is sent to Sweden to face allegations of sexual misconduct, he is in danger of being extradited to the United States to be charged with espionage (though the 41-year-old is an Australian), Sweden has openly and vehemently denied this supposition. Assange closed his balcony speech by saying that with all of these escapades, his children are being denied contact with their father—a rare mention of his family by this seemingly narcissistic individual (Harding and Quinn 2012, A3).

Baker, Jake (1974–)

Jake Baker was an undergraduate student at the University of Michigan when he used the Internet to disseminate obnoxious and potentially harmful messages. The criminal case associated with this activity began in 1995 and garnered much attention from the press in 1997 after a U.S. appellate court dismissed the case against Baker and his exploits, provoking mixed reactions from many regarding the First Amendment. In 1995, Baker was arrested and charged with interstate transmission of threats over the Internet after he posted a story involving a detailed rape and torture depiction of a woman who had the same full name as one of Jake Baker's classmates in his university Japanese course. As a result, the University of Michigan suspended Baker indefinitely, and at the time of his charges, Baker spent a month in prison. Besides First Amendment controversies, other online issues related to cyberstalking were raised by Gloria Allred, the attorney for O. J. Simpson's murdered wife Nicole Simpson. Basically, Allred argued that the Baker case was a prime example of cyberstalking—and that by letting him walk free, law officials were not treating cyberstalking cases and the harm that they produced seriously enough (Schell and Martin 2006).

Stories written by Jake Baker are found on this website: http://www.mit.edu/activities/safe/cases/umich-baker-story/Baker/jakedisclaimer.html.

Baker, Mitchell (1957–)

Mitchell Baker is a White Hat hacker who was inducted into the Internet Hall of Fame in the spring of 2012. Her claim to fame in the virtual world resulted from her pioneering work

in the development of Mozilla, which Netscape Communications Corporation first launched as a worthwhile project
in 1998. Through her talented engagement in this project,
Baker helped to legitimize open-source Internet applications,
as Mozilla demonstrated that clients could enter the market
through open-source means rather than through private firms.
Many online users today rely on Firefox, the free and open
web browser that was developed and managed by Mozilla
(Internet Society, "Mitchell Baker," 2012).

Berners-Lee, Tim (Sir Timothy John Burners-Lee) (1955–)

A graduate of Oxford University in England, Tim Berners-Lee in
1989 invented the World Wide Web, an Internet-based hyper-
media start-up for information sharing on a wide-ranging scale.
This brilliant scholar holds the prestigious 3Com Founder's
Chair at Massachusetts Institute of Technology (MIT), and he
directs the World Wide Web Consortium, a group of companies
and agencies interested in capitalizing on the World Wide Web's
potential. In 1999, Berners-Lee's book (along with coauthor
Mark Fischetti) *Weaving the Web* was released by Harper
Publishers in San Francisco (Schell 2007).

Burners-Lee has been awarded a number of prestigious prizes,
including the Japan Prize, the Prince of Asturias Foundation
Prize, the Millennium Technology Prize, and Germany's Die
Quadriga Award. In 2004, Berners-Lee was knighted by Queen
Elizabeth, and in 2007, he was awarded the Order of Merit.

Bernie S. (Edward Cummings) (1963–)

In 1995, "Bernie S." of the virtual world, also known as Edward
Cummings in the grounded world, was sent to U.S. federal prison
for his phreaking exploits. Bernie S. is a modern-day phreaker and
co-leader with Emmanuel Goldstein of *2600: The Hacker
Quarterly*; like Goldstein, he has a cult following in the computer

underground. Born in Pennsylvania, Bernie S had the distinction of being the first person sent to prison for using a modified Radio Shack speed dialer to make free telephone calls using public telephones. While imprisoned, he was severely beaten by a prisoner who, ironically, was anxious to use a telephone that Bernie S. was speaking on. The case of Bernie S., detailed in the book *The Hacking of America: Who's Doing It, Why, and How* (Schell and Dodge, with Moutsatsos 2002), graphically illustrates the rough kind of treatment that charged and convicted hackers have notoriously received when placed behind prison walls. Some would say that imprisoned hackers are treated no differently from rapists and serial killers—a point made by Cummings himself in the case study and following his imprisonment from the spring of 1995 until September 13, 1996. In the proceedings that led to his imprisonment, he was convicted of possession of a computer and software that could be used to modify a cellular phone.

The case of Bernie S. is seen as significant by hackers because if the U.S. government was able to charge, convict, and sentence Bernie S. on such crimes, any other hackers could also be successfully prosecuted for similar offenses. In fact, the way that hackers see it, the tones and information in Bernie's possession are very easy to get—and in their minds, there was not any solid evidence that Bernie S. was then or is now a criminal. At the time that Bernie S. was charged and convicted, a U.S. federal law had just been passed making it a federal felony to possess "hardware or software for the modification of telecommunications instruments for the unauthorized access to telecommunications services." Bernie S. and fellow phreakers at the time claimed that this vague law could be applied to any electronics hobbyist, computer enthusiast, or ham radio operator, as no showing of actual wrongdoing with such commonplace hardware or software needed to be presented for the authorities to arrest or convict someone (Schell and Dodge, with Moutsatsos 2002).

In 1994, Bernie S. lectured about and distributed the software needed for phreaking at the HOPE Conference. He also sold a booklet explaining how to construct the necessary cables needed to program a cellular phone with a computer running this software so that it could function as an extension of one's original cell phone. At the time, cellular phone carriers were charging upward of $30 per month for individuals wanting to have a second cell phone; thus this software enabled cell phone users to "roll their own" extension—much like individuals could plug an extra phone into their home telephone lines—which was actually illegal in the United States until the early 1980s.

Every two years, Bernie S. and other hackers gather in New York City for the Hackers on Planet Earth (HOPE) conferences. Typically, the hackers gather at Hotel Pennsylvania. Bernie S. is a frequent presenter at the conference, along with fellow phreakers from the present and the past. At the HOPE 5 conference held in July 2004, for example, Bernie S. and Barry "The Key" Wells spoke about "hacking more of the invisible world"—a discussion of TSCM (technical surveillance countermeasures), the art of evading electronic surveillance, and various intercepts and equipment demonstrations (Schell and Martin 2006).

Black Hat and DefCon Hacker Conferences

The Black Hat and DefCon hacker conventions have been held each summer in Las Vegas, Nevada, since the early 1990s. The Black Hat conference is meant for legal and IT security professionals and is held at the Caesar's Palace Hotel; entry into this conference carries a much heftier price tag compared to that for entry into DefCon, which is held later in the same week at a different hotel and is intended for students interested in the same topics but having little money to put toward the ticket. The visionary behind the hacker conferences is Jeff Moss (also known as The Dark Tangent).

Both hacker conferences have always been open to the public, with attendees ranging from members of law enforcement to technophiles. Because of its huge popularity, the Black Hat conference has changed substantially since its start as a regional hacker conference. Besides the Las Vegas event, Black Hat conferences are also held in Europe and Abu Dhabi.

While attendees at the Black Hat conference typically receive an insignia backpack, a CD, and excellent food following registration with a likely professional or press title, attendees at DefCon tend to receive a convention program, a bumper sticker, and a data disk containing data and files for panels, events, and other conference-related materials. An official conference identification badge is also furnished, with a different design each year. No identifying information is required from attendees at DefCon; however, the conference identification badge must be worn at all times within the hotel to enter panels and events. Numerous events are held during DefCon, ranging from very complex technical presentations to a coffee-making contest. Panel presentations go on throughout the day on security issues, hardware hacking, phreaking, privacy, law, and more abstract technical applications. Presenters come from diverse backgrounds and include PhDs, security professionals, government agents, and hackers with specific interests. In fact, many of the speakers at Black Hat often speak without payment at DefCon.

Both Black Hat and DefCon are as much social functions as educational events, providing a wealth of unique opportunities to observe hackers and hacking—and to network "in real time" with like-minded folks. More details about Black Hat can be found at http://www.blackhat.com/usa/. More details about DefCon can be found at www.defcon.org.

Bray, Tim (1955–)

Tim Bray, a White Hat Canadian who went to the University of Guelph in Ontario, Canada, is credited with making online auctions such as those held on eBay a virtual reality. An entrepreneur by nature, Bray was employed by computer companies such as DEC, and in 1987, he accepted the unique job of managing the online transfer of the Oxford English Dictionary at the University of Waterloo, also in Ontario. From 1989 through

1996, he was the co-founder and senior vice president of the Open Text Corporation in Waterloo. It was during this period that Bray invented and built the Open Text Index of the World Wide Web—one of the first popular web search engines. Bray says on his online resume that he served as the Open Text Corporation's leading evangelist, speaking and giving keynote addresses at many conferences. A gifted businessman and elite geek, Bray also participated in three rounds of venture capital investment and a $65 million NASDAQ initial public offering (IPO) during these years (Textuality Services, Inc. 2012).

From 1996 through 2003, Bray acted as an independent consultant who was invited as an expert in computer science to the World Wide Web Consortium. This work eventually led to his creation of XML (Extensible Markup Language), which permits programmers to attach "tags" or universal codes to differentiate, say, a business name from a telephone number. The impact on electronic commerce was extensive, because with the application of XML, purchase orders and invoices could be universally read and routed to the right applications. Nowadays, XML lets online users play games, buy books online, and partake in online auctions like those held on eBay (Schell 2007).

Bray wanted to be a high school math teacher after graduating from university, but at the time there were no jobs available, so he searched for other opportunities in the IT field. His entrepreneurial and visionary spirit led him to become the founder and chief technology officer for Antarctica Systems, based in Vancouver, British Columbia, Canada, during the period 1999–2003. Besides raising two rounds of venture capital financing at this time, he designed and implemented very unique data visualization software. From 2004 through 2009, Bray was a distinguished engineer and director of web technologies at Sun Microsystems in Santa Clara, California, where he led the company's movement toward embracing dynamic languages on and off the Java platform. In 2010, Bray joined Google in Mountain View, California, where he has the role of developer advocate for the Android Group and serves as the editor of the Android Developers blog, which had a readership of 100,000 individuals in 2012 (Textuality Services, Inc. 2012).

Burns, Eric (Zyklon) (1980–)

Eric Burns, whose online moniker was Zyklon, made media headlines when in 1999, a U.S. grand jury in Virginia indicted him (then aged 19) on three counts of computer intrusion. Burns was thought to be a member of a hacker group that claimed responsibility for attacks on the White House and U.S. Senate websites. He was charged with illegally cracking a computer used by the U.S. Information Agency between August 1998 and January 1999. He was also accused of cracking two other networks: one owned by LaserNet in Virginia and the other owned by Issue Dynamics, Inc., in Washington, D.C. What is more, Burns appeared to be attracted to a student at school named Crystal—who was actually being cyberstalked by him without her being upset about it because she did not perceive that any harm was being done. In the end, Crystal—along with a tip from an Internet informant—led the FBI agents to figure out who Zyklon was. The agents went to Burns' apartment, where he lived with his mother. Although the agents did not arrest Burns that morning, they did raid his apartment and seized a cache of incriminating evidence, along with his computer. The judge hearing the case eventually ruled that Burns should spend 15 months in federal prison, pay more than $36,000 in restitution, and not be allowed to touch a computer for up to three years following his release from prison (Schell and Dodge, with Moutsatsos 2002; Schell and Martin 2006).

Caffrey, Aaron (1982–)

Aaron Caffrey, an Englishman, made media headlines in September 2001, when at age 19 he was charged under the

Computer Misuse Act of 1990 in Britain, accused of unleashing a flood of data that closed the Houston, Texas, seaport—the sixth largest seaport in the world. Caffrey denied the charges, arguing in court that although the cyberattack was apparently triggered from his computer, he was not the actual person committing the exploit. In his own defense before the Southward Crown Court, Caffrey gave a technical description of how Black Hat hackers could assume the identities of unsuspecting computer users through mal-inclined tricks such as "fishing out" security passwords to steal online identities. Although he could have spent five years behind prison bars if found guilty, the jury hearing the case accepted his arguments. Caffrey was found not guilty of the cracking charge. (Schell and Martin 2004).

According to a 2012 LinkedIn profile page, there is an Aaron Caffrey who is currently working on a computer software degree at the University of Greenwich. Could this be the same Aaron Caffrey?

Calce, Michael (Mafiaboy) (1985–)

Michael Demon Calce was involved in one of the most famous cracker attacks in Canadian history as a youth. Calce received his first computer as a gift from his father at the age of six and became extremely interested in technology at that point. While a 15-year-old high school student, he engaged in an attack against Yahoo, which he called "Rivolta" or "riot" in Italian. Specifically, he initiated a denial-of-service attack that knocked Yahoo offline for approximately an hour.

Mafiaboy used this same tool to attack multiple high-profile company websites, including eBay, CNN, and Dell. Calce's involvement in the attacks was discovered, in part, as a result of his claims in IRC chat rooms that he was responsible for the attacks against Dell. As a result of a joint investigation by the FBI in the United States and the Royal Canadian Mounted Police, Calce was arrested and pleaded guilty to 56 charges of mischief to data (Schell and Dodge, with Moutsatsos 2002). He was tried in the Montreal Youth Court, where he was sentenced on September 12, 2001, to eight months in a youth detention center, one year of probation to follow, and a $250 fine. This sentence paled in comparison to the economic harm he caused, which was thought to be approximately $7.5 million (Canadian dollars).

As is typical with most young hackers facing the prospect of a long and expensive trial, Calce admitted his part in the denial-of-service attacks. Subsequent to his arrest, Calce dropped out of high school and worked as a steakhouse busboy. In a statement made to the media, his lawyer expressed a common theme of regret among caught and convicted hackers (Schell and Dodge, with Moutsatsos 2002, 253): "If today, if placed in the same position, he would have contacted the companies and told them there was a major flaw in their security. At the time, it was the last thing on his mind. It was more of a challenge. It was not to willfully cause damage. He had difficulty believing that such companies as Yahoo had not put in place security measures to stop him. He got results."

Today, Calce works as a computer security writer and consultant. He has authored a book titled *Mafiaboy: A Portrait of the Hacker as a Young Man.* Mafiaboy has also written high-tech pieces for Canoe, an online news and information company based in Toronto, Canada. One of his interesting columns, entitled "Hacking Becoming Even Easier," detailed his strategy for the exploits that got his detention time (Schell and Martin 2006).

Cerf, Vinton ("Father of the Internet") (1943–)

Known to many as "the Father of the Internet," Vinton Cerf was the designer—along with Robert Kahn—of the TCP/IP protocols and the architecture of the Internet. For their important contribution to society, in 1997 this pair of White Hats was presented with the U.S. National Medal of Technology by President Bill Clinton. Furthermore, in 2004, the pair was honored with the prestigious ACM Alan M. Turing Award, considered by many in the IT field to be the equivalent of the Nobel Prize (Schell 2007).

Since 2005, Cert has served as vice president and chief Internet evangelist for Google, Inc. In this role, he is responsible for identifying new enabling technologies that aid in supporting the development of Internet-based products and services for Google. Many would say, in fact, that Cert is the very active public face for Google in the virtual world. He is also the chair of the board of the Internet Corporation for Assigned Names and Numbers (ICANN, 2012).

Conficker (also known as Downup, Downadup, and Kido)

Conficker is a piece of malicious software that was first found in November 2008 attacking the Windows operating system. This malware functions in part as a worm by spreading through systems using dictionary attacks to determine and exploit user passwords. At the same time, it serves as a botnet that will take commands and can be remotely managed (Keizer 2009). The malware, or some variant, has been found in more than 200 countries and affected government and end-user computers alike. In fact, Conficker was identified in computer systems of the English, French, and German military, as well as the U.K. police (Leder and Werner 2009). This program is extremely difficult to detect, as it combines multiple obfuscation tools to conceal its location and vulnerabilities. In addition, recent variants of the malware enable it to send out spam and fake antivirus messages (Keizer 2009). It is unclear who created this program or the reasons for its creation.

Due to the substantive concern over this malware, a research consortium was formed to develop mechanisms to detect and remove it. The group combined experts from private industry, academia, and governments around the world who were able to create various scanners and tools to detect the presence of Conficker (Leder and Werner 2009). These tools have been integrated into various commercial antivirus applications, and can also be downloaded from various websites to protect users from compromise. Despite the best efforts of these groups, the program is still operating and infecting systems. Thus Conficker remains an active threat.

Cook, Stephen (1939–)

Stephen Cook was born in the United States in 1939, but migrated to Canada in 1970 to become an associate professor at the University of Toronto. After receiving his graduate degrees from Harvard University, he became an assistant professor at the University of California, Berkeley. A mathematics professor, Cook published in 1971 a rather esoteric work known as *The Complexity of Theorem Proving Procedures*—also known succinctly as *Cook's Theorem*. This theorem identified a large group of computational search problems that would typically take even the most powerful computers millions of years to compute. The theorem is said to be a strong contributor to the field of cryptography; without the latter, online transactions as the world has come to know and trust them would not be secure. Cook is the only Canadian professor to have won the Association for Computing Machinery's Alan M. Turing Award (Schell 2007).

Now a distinguished full professor, Cook is a fellow of the Royal Society of London and the Royal Society of Canada. He was elected to membership in the National Academy of Sciences in the United States as well as to the American Academy of Arts and Sciences. About 30 students have completed a PhD under his supervision (Computer Science University of Toronto 2012).

Corporate Hacking

Corporate hacking generally involves hacking into the networks of targeted companies to illegally obtain proprietary information or company secrets. In earlier chapters, we detailed the

News International phone hacking debacle, which eventually cost Rupert Murdoch, chairman and CEO of News Corporation, £645,000 (plus costs) to settle with victims of the tabloid phone hacking scandal (Houpt 2012). However, targeted corporate hacking has become a major problem in recent years, with affected companies trying to play down these incidents to maintain consumer trust and to protect their corporate brand. Nevertheless, sometimes even the best-kept secrets eventually find their way into media headlines. For example, in December 2011, it was reported that a trio of computer hackers had "jail broken" Research in Motion Ltd.'s (RIM's) PlayBook tablet computer, gaining root access to operating system files and raising questions about IT security as the company marketed its PlayBook to corporate and government clients (Marlow, December 1, 2011).

Chris Wade, an Australian technology specialist working in New York City, said in an interview that it was relatively easy to hack into the BlackBerry tablet, and that likely the primary reason that someone had not bothered to hack it before is that the RIM device lacked the type of market share that would make it worth hacking. To save face, RIM spokespersons said that they were not aware of a jail break being leveraged by anyone other than the three hacker researchers, who claimed to have performed the jail break on their own tablets only. RIM officials also said that they would follow their standard response process of developing and releasing a software update designed to minimize the adverse impact on their customers (Marlow, December 1, 2011).

In 2012, the media ran headlines suggesting that the demise of Nortel Networks, one of Canada's crown jewels in the technology sector, which eventually declared bankruptcy, may have been caused by hackers who breached Nortel's security by stealing passwords and installing spy software. The more interesting question is whether costly industrial espionage involved stolen intellectual property of Nortel Networks. In February 2012, *The Wall Street Journal* ran a story in which a former senior systems security advisor at Nortel, Brian Shields, admitted that hackers "had access to everything" in the network for almost a decade—with perhaps the ring being operated out of China (Marlow, February 15, 2012, B5). In fact, telecommunications, along with oil and gas and defense, are sectors that are favorite targets for industrial espionage, much of which is argued is coming from China and Russia. However, Chris Wade, the security expert mentioned earlier, expressed doubt that a major corporation like Nortel could be a consistent hack for a decade, given that computers are replaced and passwords expire. He concluded by saying, "I find it hard to believe that the company's source code and every valuable piece of information they had was available all from one network. A targeted 10-year-attack sounds way too coordinated, like something out of a movie" (Marlow, February 15, 2012, B5).

Draper, John (Cap'n Crunch) (1943–)

John Draper, widely regarded as one of the founders of the phreaking community, is a key figure in the hacker scene in general. Draper served in the Air Force during the mid-1960s, and upon his discharge, worked for employers in the San Francisco Bay Area. Draper began to operate pirate radio stations out of a van during this period and took an interest in the counterculture of the time. Due to his interest in technology and radio, he was introduced to a group of phone phreaks, many of whom were blind. Their knowledge of the tones used in controlling and managing telephony was used by Draper to create "blue boxes"—electronic devices that could reproduce these tones. In particular, he integrated the tones used by a whistle included in boxes of Cap'n Crunch cereal because they could produce the same 2,600-megahertz tone used by AT&T and long-distance phone companies to indicate they were available for use. When either phone on the call produced this tone, it would fool the phone company's switching systems into thinking that the call had ended—which would cause all billing to cease. In this way, Draper was able to make free phone calls through the use of these devices.

Draper's exploits were detailed in part in an article printed in *Esquire* in 1971. This story brought his activities to the attention of law enforcement, which led him to be arrested on charges of toll fraud, or fraud by wire. Draper was incarcerated following his conviction, but was also soon connected to Steve Wozniak (the developer of the Apple II computer) and Steve Jobs because of the press coverage of his activities. They hired him briefly as a programmer and developer. At Apple, Draper created the program EasyWriter. EasyWriter was the first word processing program created for the Apple II, and the program was then sold by IBM with its computer systems (Schell and Martin 2006). Draper, an inventor by nature, also developed the Crunchbox Firewall program and a Voice Over IP (VOIP) telephony application.

Draper is still a frequent attendee and speaker at hacker conferences held in the United States. At the Hackers on Planet Earth (HOPE) conference in New York City in July 2000, he made an appearance on "The Old-Timer Panel" with fellow phreakers Cheshire Catalyst and Bootleg (Schell and Dodge, with Moutsatsos 2002).

Facebook Team: Mark Zuckerberg (1985–) and Eduardo Saverin (1982–)

The 27-year-old CEO of Facebook Inc., Mark Zuckerberg is a familiar face to the general public, as he is at the helm of the number one social networking site and its $1 billion acquisition, Instagram. In May 2012, Zuckerberg made media headlines when the young but very wealthy CEO kick-started a road show to promote Facebook's $10 billion initial public offering (IPO). The large size of the IPO reflects the company's rapid growth and bullish expectations about making huge amounts of money as a hub for advertising and e-commerce. Zuckerberg, who had about 57 percent voting control after the IPO, said that he personally made the $1 billion deal with mobile application maker Instagram (a small, photo-based web service) in just a few days with little involvement from the board of directors at Facebook. Founded less than two years ago, San Francisco-based Instagram allows users to quickly edit and share the photos they take on their mobile devices; considering the immense growth in the mobile device market that is predicted in the years to come, Instagram sounds like a wise investment (El Akkad, April 10, 2012). Though a seemingly young IT billionaire, Zuckerberg is clearly an independent thinker and entrepreneur who is not afraid of taking risks if there is a sound opportunity for a major return on that investment (Reuters 2012).

Less well known to the public is Facebook's other founder, 30-year-old Eduardo Saverin, whose name and popularity are big in Singapore. Saverin is a former business partner and friend of Zuckerberg. In fact, the Brazilian-born billionaire became a household name in 2010 after his fights with Zuckerberg over the future of Facebook. These fights were further publicized in the Hollywood film *The Social Network*, where Saverin was depicted as a nice but naïve young entrepreneur who was overruled by the more aggressive Zuckerberg. Apparently, Saverin was pushed out of the Facebook dynasty early on, with his stake in the Internet giant diluted to 10 percent from 34 percent. As of May 5, 2012, his stake in the company was roughly 2 percent, following the sale of some of his shares. However, considering that Facebook is valued at about $95 billion, even a 2 percent share can buy a lot in Singapore. Saverin has not given up on his unassuming but sharp business prowess. He has invested more than $6.5 million in a number of IT start-ups mostly in the United States, including Shopsavvy, a price-comparison mobile application; Qwiki, a multimedia video website; and Jumio, a mobile payments company (Mahtani 2012).

While the money-making potential for Zuckerberg and Saverin from Facebook is hugely impressive, in February, 2012, Facebook took a hit in the media after it was publicized by reporters that although many of the company's more than 800 million users are women, onlookers would not recognize this reality by looking at the board of directors of Facebook. All seven directors are male. This overt "disconnect" between the makeup of the client base in the virtual world and that of the company's board of directors puts the company at odds with other organizations in the social networking sector that have at least one female director—including LinkedIn Corporation and Google Inc. Facebook was created just eight years ago in a Harvard University dorm room, and by 2011 it had sales of $3.7 billion. A whopping 58 percent of its users are women, according to a 2010 survey by the Pew Internet and American Life Project (Bloomberg 2012).

A month after the news release about the lack of women on Facebook's board of directors, another press release talked about a 2010 lawsuit filed by Paul Ceglia, who said that he commissioned Zuckerberg to work on a website in 2003, and that he allegedly had a contract that entitled him to 84 percent of Facebook. Ceglia later amended his claim to 50 percent of his stake in the company. Facebook spokespersons called the claims "a fraud and a lie" and framed the story to depict Ceglia as someone desperate for money that was not his. In fact, Facebook's motion said that Ceglia was arrested and charged for defrauding customers out of $200,000 during the promotional period for the 2010 movie *The Social Network*, which focused on the origins of Facebook. Apparently Zuckerberg and Ceglia met through Craigslist in 2003 when Zuckerberg was a freshman at Harvard University. Zuckerberg apparently responded to an online posting to build a website for Ceglia called StreetFax.com. Although apparently the two signed a contract in the spring of 2003, the contents of that contract are currently under dispute (Raice 2012).

Feinler, Elizabeth "Jake" (1933?–)

Born in West Virginia and a 1954 alumna of West Liberty University, Elizabeth Feinler was named an inductee to the Internet Hall of Fame in spring 2012, along with 33 of the

Internet's most influential engineers, pioneers, and entrepreneurs, including the likes of Vinton Cerf, Tim Berners-Lee, and Phil Zimmerman. That a woman appears in the list as a pioneer of the Internet gives further credence to the fact that White Hat hackers have included women right from the beginning. Known to her family and friends as "Jake," Feinler was at the forefront of the development of the Internet and is credited with devising the term and context of "dot com."

Although Feinler originally got an undergraduate degree in science and a master's degree in biochemistry from Purdue University in Indiana, her career commitment involved the cultivation of computer information services for government agencies, universities, and private companies. She ran the Network Information Center for the Science Research Center, which created the earliest Internet search engines, the idea of menu-driven computer interfaces, and the ways and means to display and compose email offline even prior to the development of Windows or Macintosh. Feinler's team also created the naming registry for World Wide Web domains, resulting in the now familiar and widely used .com designation behind web addresses (West Liberty University 2012).

It is important to note that the Internet Hall of Fame recognized Feinler as a pioneer of the Internet who managed first the ARPAnet and then the Defense Data Network (DDN), as well as network information centers (NICs) under contract to the U.S. Department of Defense. As noted in earlier chapters, these early networks were the forerunners of today's Internet (Internet Society, "Elizabeth Feinler," 2012).

Gates, William H. (1955–)

According to the Time Inc. website, Microsoft's market capitalization was valued at $257 billion in 2012 (Gustin 2012). This hugely successful software company had its origins in 1975, as the creative brainchild of William ("Bill") H. Gates and Steve Allen. A White Hat hacker by nature, Gates has said that he began programming when he was 11 years old. In 1973, he went to Harvard University, where he met Steve Ballmer, who has been the CEO of Microsoft since 2000. To more effectively run his company, however, Gates decided to drop out of Harvard in his third year of undergraduate studies.

Besides being a hugely successful businessman, Gates is an accomplished writer. In 1995, his book *The Road Ahead* was released. In this book, Gates, then CEO of Microsoft, laid out his vision of an interconnected world built around the Internet. He drew on his experience at the center of the personal computer revolution to share his insights with readers on the growth, evolution, and impact of technology. In 1999, Gates wrote the book *Business @ the Speed of Thought*, which focused on how computer technology can solve complex business problems in unique ways. The book made it to *The New York Times* best-seller list, was sold in more than 60 countries, and was translated into at least 25 different languages. In May 2010, Gates wrote the foreword to his father's book called *Showing Up for Life*. In this book, Bill Gates, Sr., presented a deeply personal view of the values that he instilled in his children and that he continues to put into practice as the co-chair of the Bill and Melinda Gates Foundation—a charitable organization founded by Bill Gates, Jr., and his wife Melinda Gates.

On the Bill and Melinda Gates Foundation website, Gates and his wife note that their friend and co-trustee Warren Buffet once gave them some great advice about philanthropy: "Don't just go for safe projects. Take on the really tough problems." To this end, the foundation started by the Gates teams up with partners around the world to tackle extreme poverty and poor health in developing countries, as well as the failures of the educational system in the United States. For each issue to which large sums of money are donated, innovative ideas for removing barriers are sought—such as finding novel techniques to help farmers produce better crops in developing nations as well as producing new methods that can be more effective in teaching students who tend to struggle in school (Bill and Melinda Gates Foundation 2012).

Gonzalez, Albert (1981–)

Late one night in July 2003, just before midnight, a New York police detective, while on call investigating a wave of car thefts in upper Manhattan, followed a young man with long, stringy hair and a nose ring into a bank's ATM lobby. Pretending to make his own cash withdrawal, the detective watched as the young man pulled a debit card from his wallet and withdrew hundreds of dollars. The young man then repeated the act a number of times with various debit cards. The detective realized that the young man was not stealing cards but was stealing cash—likely from illegally obtained debit cards. Later, the young man of 22 years admitted to the authorities that he was "cashing out." He had programmed a stack of blank credit cards with stolen card numbers and was withdrawing as much cash as he could from each account. He was doing this just before 12 A.M., because that time is when daily withdrawal limits end, and a "casher" can double his or her "take" by making another maximum withdrawal a few minutes later (Verini 2010).

The young man's name was Albert Gonzalez. He had a number of monikers on the Internet, including cumbajohny, segvec, and soupnazi—his favorite, it seems. Actually, as the police later discovered, Gonzalez was more than a casher. He was a moderator and a rising star on www.Shadowcrew.com, a criminal cyberbazaar that started during the e-commerce boom in the early 2000s. Its users trafficked in databases of stolen card accounts and devices such as magnetic strip encoders and card embossers. They also posted online tips about vulnerable banks and stores, and advice on how to complete an effective email scam. The Black Hat website was created by a part-time student in Arizona and a former New Jersey mortgage broker. Later, it had hundreds of members in the United States, Europe, and Asia. While Gonzalez agreed to help the authorities "rat out" fellow

Shadowcrewers to avoid prison, he was also gaining access to about 180 million payment card accounts from the customer databases of the T.J. Maxx and Marshalls clothing chains, Barnes & Noble, and JCPenney, to name just a few. In March 2010, Gonzalez received two concurrent 20-year terms behind bars, the longest sentence ever handed down to an American for computer-generated crimes (Verini 2010).

Readers interested in knowing more about the language of carders—those who engage in the illegal acquisition, sale, and exchange of sensitive information—should consult the book chapter by Thomas J. Holt (2011) entitled, "Examining the Language of Carders."

Google, Inc. Team: Sergey Brin (1973–) and Larry Page (1973–)

Sergey Brin, born in 1973 in Russia, and Larry Page, born the same year in the United States, are two Stanford University PhD dropouts who started Google, Inc., the hugely popular Internet search engine company that made this pair billionaires. Before the Brin and Page team launched Google, Internet searches often returned more useless than useful information. Users had to wade through all of the useless information to find something worthwhile—a huge waste of resources and time. The Internet pioneers Brin and Page streamlined the search process to such a degree that their search engine took the world by storm.

Brin's father was a Russian professor who moved to the United States to teach at the University of Maryland, and his mother worked for that National Aeronautics and Space Administration (NASA). (Page's father was also a professor who was employed by Michigan State University.) When Brin was nine years old, his father presented him with his first computer, a Commodore 64. Both Brin and Page attended Montessori schools, where, they note, their young minds were fueled by creativity and free-thinking thoughts. Page says that when he and Brin were working on their PhDs, they really had no interest in being entrepreneurs. Even so, when their computer science research produced a faster kind of search engine than any other currently available, the team abandoned academia and took up the entrepreneurial spirit.

By 2006, Brin and Page were worth about $11 billion and were ranked as the second-richest Americans younger than the age of 40. Like other billionaires who capitalized on creative technologies and keen marketing skills, the Brin and Page team wanted to give back to the collective good of society. To that end, in 2006, they announced that Dr. Larry Brilliant, a former high-tech executive and physician who specializes in global health, would head the Google.org philanthropic arm (Schell 2007).

Running a hugely successful global company is not easy, and challenges for the team started making media headlines within five years of this philanthropic news release. For example, in April 2011, Google co-founder Larry Page announced that he would take over as CEO, promising that he would shake up the Internet search engine giant to increase the response time of responsible corporate decision making. However, serious challenges have accumulated for Page since he assumed the role. Some of these challenges have included a broad U.S. anti-trust probe of the company's practices; a protracted criminal investigation into Google's advertising business practices; and emerging industry forces that led Page to buy mobile device maker Motorola Mobility Holdings, Inc., for $12.5 million. In August 2011, U.S. federal prosecutors informed Google that they had reviewed the company's practice of allowing ads from illegal online pharmacies on its web-search engine since 2003; the prosecutors "singled out" Page as being the individual with the knowledge that Google was guilty of the crime and failing to prevent it. To avoid criminal charges, Google paid a fee of $500 million (Efrati 2011).

For the 38-year-old billionaire Brin, his main challenge has stemmed from his recent comments regarding web freedom and threats against it by China, Saudi Arabia, and Iran. He has publicly espoused the view that these countries are needlessly censoring and restricting the use of the Internet. In an interview with reporters, Brin warned that there were "very powerful forces that have lined up against the open Internet on all sides and around the world" (Katz 2012, A9). He claimed that the threat to the freedom of the Internet comes from a combination of governments wanting to control access and communication by their citizens, the entertainment industry's attempts to crack down on piracy, and the increase in "restrictive" walled gardens such as Facebook and Apple—which tightly control the software that can be released on their platforms and risk stifling innovation and balkanizing the Web. According to Brin, he and cofounder Page would not have been able to create Google if the Internet had been dominated by Facebook—a point that is sure to anger the CEO at Facebook.

Brin has also criticized U.S. legislation. He affirmed that Google was sometimes forced to hand over personal data to the authorities and was sometimes prevented by legal restrictions from notifying users that it had done so. He concluded: "We push back a lot; we are able to turn down a lot of these requests. We do everything possible to protect the data. If we could wave a magic wand and not be subject to U.S. law, that would be great. If we could be in some magical jurisdiction that everyone in the world trusted, that would be great . . . We're doing it as well as can be done" (Katz 2012, A9).

Brin and Page made media headlines again in July 2012, when Google agreed to pay $22.5 million to settle charges related to its bypassing the privacy settings of millions of Apple Inc. users, according to officials. The fine is believed to be the largest penalty ever levied on a single company by the U.S. Federal Trade Commission (FTC). This fine was viewed as a sign of the FTC's tougher policing of online privacy violations—just six months after *The Wall Street Journal* published a piece about Google's practices. This kind of bad press for Google can undermine users' trust in its services.

Gorman, Sean (1974–)

In 2003, Sean Gorman's name made media headlines when he produced for his doctoral dissertation in public policy a set of charts that delineated the communication networks binding together the United States and its critical infrastructure. Gorman, who was then a George Mason University PhD student, mapped every business and industrial sector in the United States and layered on top of this mapping the fiber-optic network that connected them. In essence, the charts could be viewed as treasure maps for terrorists wanting to attack the critical infrastructure as a means of destroying the U.S. economy. Using math formulas, Gorman probed for critical links as a way of answering the intriguing question, "If I were Osama bin Laden, where would I want to attack?" (Schell and Martin 2004).

Nowadays, Gorman is the CEO and founder (in 2005) of a company called FortiusOne. He is also a member of the company's board of directors. The goal of the company is to bring advanced geospatial technologies to the marketplace—Gorman is a recognized expert in geospatial analysis and visualization. Besides being a sought-after speaker at IT conferences, Gorman has made his White Hat views known worldwide in media such as *Der Spiegel, Washington Post, Business 2.0,* and CNN. He has also served as a valuable consultant to the U.S. Critical Infrastructure Task Force and the Homeland Security Advisory Council. Prior to starting FortiusOne, Gorman served as vice president of research and development for GeoTel, a telecommunications mapping firm (Conversations Network 2012).

Gosling, James ("World's Greatest Programmer") (1955–)

A Canadian by birth, James Gosling, also known as "the Software Wizard" and "the World's Greatest Programmer," is the developer of the programming language and environment known as Java. The main advantage of Java is that it can convert the one-dimensional and very noninteractive Web into a system permitting software on any operating system (e.g., Microsoft Windows, UNIX, Macintosh) to communicate by streaming bits of information that are universally translatable. In fact, the highly interactive Internet that adults and children utilize daily is as user-friendly as it is because of the wonderful invention called Java (Schell 2007).

Java was invented in 1994 by a team working at Sun Microsystems in the United States. Originally called "Oak," the writing of Java began in December 1990 as part of the Green project—which included the talented White Hats James Gosling, Mike Sheridan, and Patrick Naughton. Their goal was to figure out "the next wave" in computing (Bellis 2012).

Gosling received his undergraduate degree from the University of Calgary in Canada in 1977 and his PhD from Carnegie Mellon University in the United States in 1983. He has lived and worked in the United States since that time. Gosling began employment with Sun Microsystems in 1984 (Schell 2007). He remained at Sun until April 2010, when the company was acquired by Oracle Corporation.

In March 2011, Gosling announced on his blog that he had been hired by Google, Inc. Less than six months later, he joined a start-up company called Liquid Robotics. Gosling is also listed as an advisor to another start-up company called Typesafe, launched in May 2011.

Headley, Susan (Susan Thunder) (1959–)

Susan Headley, better known as Susan Thunder in the computer underground, was an early phreaker. Along with Kevin Mitnick (one of the 10 most wanted crackers), Headley allegedly broke into telephone lines in the 1970s and early 1980s, much to the ire of Ma Bell. Headley then and now exploded the myth that only men are actively engaged in phreaking and hacking exploits. While Kevin Mitnick and his brother Ron were eventually arrested and charged of illegal phreaking and hacking, Headley was apparently allowed to walk free of a prison sentence as long as she agreed to serve as a witness against both Mitnick brothers. Later, she called herself an IT security expert and was known to brag about how she could single-handedly crack military networks. Some in the computer underground suggest that because Headley was an attractive woman, she was especially good at pulling off her social engineering. After her stint as a phreaker, rumor has it that she turned her skill set to becoming a professional poker player (Schell and Dodge, with Moutsatsos 2002).

Deemed by many to be a tall blonde prostitute, advocates believe that Headley showed the world that Black Hat hacking could threaten national security. Rumor also has it that she was a member of a hacker gang named after her boyfriend: the Roscoe gang (MrCracker 2012).

Hotz, George (1990–)

In 2007, Apple released its market-appealing iPhone, in partnership with American Telephone and Telegraph. At the time, 17-year-old George Hotz from Glen Rock, New Jersey, was a T-Mobile subscriber—though he really wanted an iPhone. He also wanted to make telephone calls using his existing network. So Hotz did what any self-respecting hacker would do: he "jail broke" his phone. Also, on his personal computer, he wrote a program that enabled the iPhone to work on any wireless carrier. Hotz made a video boasting of his feat as the first person to "crack" the iPhone and posted it on YouTube—resulting in about 2 million views. After one of his appearances in the media, Steve Wozniak, co-founder of Apple (who was also a hacker in his teen years), reportedly sent Hotz a congratulatory email. It needs to be emphasized that while unlocking a phone was not illegal at the time of this incident, it could enable piracy.

After the iPhone, Hotz turned his attention and talents to jail breaking the PlayStation 3 gaming console, which purportedly was impenetrable. Sony responded by releasing an update to deal with the vulnerability that Hotz capitalized on. In January 2011, Hotz received an email from Sony saying that a lawsuit was being launched against him for the exploit, noting that he was in violation of the Computer Fraud and Abuse Act. The company wanted his "circumvention devices," and they wanted him to remove any online "hacking how-to" information. In fact, a California court granted Sony the restraining order that it was seeking against Hotz, stopping him from disseminating even more details about the Sony machines. In retaliation, Hotz took his cause online—which got him the attention and support of the Anonymous collective. Members of this cell went online and published the Sony executives' home telephone numbers and addresses. On April 19, 2011, the security experts at Sony noticed that their networks had been hacked.

By the summer of 2011, LulzSec joined the online fray, and companies such as Nintendo, Sega, Electronic Arts, News Corporation, Booz Allen Hamilton, the North Atlantic Treaty Organization (NATO), and the Central Intelligence Agency (CIA) found that their networks had been hacked. Although Hotz said that he did not intend to spark a hacker war, he openly admitted that he did not have any regrets about cracking the iPhone and the PlayStation 3. Although he now works for Facebook, Sony engineers apparently invited Hotz to their headquarters in recent years so that he could share with them his means of cracking the PlayStation 3 (Kushner 2012).

Jaynes, Jeremy (Gaven Stubberfield) (1974–)

In April 2005, a spammer from Raleigh, North Carolina, who was also known as Gaven Stubberfield, was sentenced to nine years in prison in Virginia for his spamming exploits. Described by prosecutors as being among the top 10 spammers worldwide, the offender—real name: Jeremy Jaynes—was given an unusually lengthy jail sentence. In fact, this case was considered to be a landmark because it represented the first successful felony prosecution in the United States for transmitting spam over the Internet. The Virginia jury ruled that Jaynes should spend a lot of time behind prison bars because he transmitted 10 million emails daily, used 16 high-speed lines, and earned as much as $750,000 per month on from operation. Jaynes decided to appeal his conviction (Schell and Martin 2006).

On September 13, 2008, the nine-year prison sentence was overturned when Virginia's high court ruled that the state's tough anti-spam law violated the First Amendment. In fact, the court unanimously agreed that Virginia's anti-spam law was overbroad from a constitutional perspective because it banned *all* unsolicited bulk email with false or misleading addresses, commercial as well as noncommercial. The law considered "unsolicited bulk email" to be a felony if more than 10,000 recipients were emailed over a 24-hour period. It is important to note that if this case had been tried after the CAN-SPAM Act was passed in the United States, Jaynes' commercial spamming exploits would violate this act. However, because this legislation was passed after he committed his spamming acts, it cannot be applied retroactively. Because his spamming campaign flooded America Online's servers, Jaynes was initially prosecuted in the state of Virginia, where the Internet provider was headquartered (Modine 2008).

Jobs, Steve (1955–2011)

Along with Steve Wozniak, Steve Jobs as a young adult started the well-known company Apple Computer, Inc. After studying physics, literature, and poetry at Reed College in Oregon, Jobs sold his Volkswagen minibus in 1976 so that he could have start-up money to begin his computer company. Four years after start-up, the business was successful, to the point that Jobs and Wozniak were able to take their company public at an initial price of $22 per share. By 1984, the creative and entrepreneurial pair reinvented the personal computer by launching the Macintosh.

Jobs left Apple from 1986 through 1997, at which time he founded and ran another company called NeXT Software, Inc. This firm created hardware to exploit the full potential of object-oriented technologies. Jobs sold NeXT Software to Apple in 1997, at which time he reassociated himself with Apple Computer, Inc.

Forever the entrepreneur and visionary, Jobs discovered and bought an animation company called Pixar Animation Studios in 1986. This company became the creator and producer of such top-grossing animated films as *A Bug's Life*; *Monsters, Inc.*; *Toy Story*; and *Toy Story 2*. After his return to the company in 1997, Jobs also helped Apple produce and bring to market such innovative products as the iMac, the iBook, the iMovie, the iPod, and the iPad. Perhaps less well known is the fact that Jobs was part of the "brain team" that positioned Apple to venture onto the Internet (Schell and Martin 2006).

In January 2011, the media began writing articles about the difficulties Jobs was having with his health. At the end of August 2011, feeling that he was unable to continue as CEO of Apple as a result of his deteriorating health, Jobs resigned from the company. At this point, the world felt that his resignation closed the book on one of the most successful and iconic leadership stints in U.S. corporate history. The 56-year-old cofounder of today's second-most valuable company in the world left his post with these closing words: "I have always said if there ever came a day when I could no longer meet my duties and expectations as Apple's CEO, I would be the first to let you know. Unfortunately, that day has come" (El Akkad 2011, A1).

The very positive creative vision that Jobs had for Apple included the move into the mobile market with the iPad and the iPhone—still the best-selling and highest-profit devices in the highly competitive mobile market, despite dozens of competing products released by Microsoft and Hewlett-Packard since 2010. At the time of his departure from Apple as CEO, Jobs recommended that Tim Cook—the company's chief operating officer—be named as his successor, for much of Apple's success, note modern-day business gurus, is a result of the company's ability to keep costs low. And, affirmed Jobs, much of that financial discipline resulted from the recommendations and sharp mindset of Cook (El Akkad 2011).

Cook, the small-town football fanatic-turned-CEO of Apple, has said that he wondered whether he had the same remarkable vision as his predecessor. But as Apple's chief operating officer at the time that Jobs was CEO, Cook found that the pair with different styles of management and behavioral mannerisms seemed to balance each other extremely well. People who worked with Cook over the last 20 years describe him as "brilliant" and "phenomenal." He is also called a supply chain genius at a company that values efficiency as much as design.

How Cook joined Apple is part of Apple legend. In 1997, Jobs, newly returned to Apple, had turned down several applicants to the company in a rather brusque fashion, including walking out during one interview. When Cook was interviewed, he was told by Jobs that he would be a fool to leave Compaq for an also-ran, on-the-verge-bankruptcy company like Apple. Nevertheless, Cook took to Jobs and accepted the job offer. The pair worked beautifully together: whereas Jobs was known for his explosive temper and his New Age interest in vegetarianism and spirituality, Cook was known for his soft-spoken manner and his love for Auburn University football (Adegoke 2011).

After Jobs' death in 2011, Walter Isaacson produced a stimulating biography of Jobs with the motivation of having readers consider which insightful messages they could draw to enhance their leadership and entrepreneurial potential. Here is a short list of the traits that Isaacson details of Jobs in the book: Jobs made the best use of his Zen training, being able to focus on key ideas and relentlessly filter out unnecessary distractions. Moreover, Jobs' urge to focus on the important was enhanced by his ability to simplify things, zeroing in on the essence and rejecting the unnecessary. When Apple fell behind the competition on any kind of computing innovation, Jobs' uplifting philosophy was to not merely catch up to the competition with similar product lines but to leapfrog over them with products that were truly compelling, innovative, and market attractive. "My passion has been to build an enduring company where people were motivated to make great products. Everything else was secondary," Jobs once told Isaacson (Schachter 2012, B7).

Finally, unlike most people on planet Earth, Jobs was able to bend reality. In a fabled *Star Trek* episode, aliens created an alternative reality through sheer mental force. Jobs often did the same, imposing tough deadlines on colleagues and vendors, assuring them all the while that if they wanted to, they could succeed (Schachter 2012).

Under Cook's new leadership, Apple will likely continue to evolve. There is little doubt that in Jobs's absence, Apple will change, not only because the company is operating in a new technology landscape, but also because the company must now shift, financial analysts maintain, by wisely managing international expansion and bringing to market cheaper prices, while pushing deeper into cloud computing.

Johansen, Jon Lech (DVD-Jon) (1983–)

Jon Johansen, also known as DVD-Jon, was born to a Polish mother and a Norwegian father in 1983 in Norway. A bright student, in 2000 he received the Karoline Award in high school because of his excellent marks (he had a 5.75 average from a 6.0 maximum) and his positive contributions to society. Bored with the structured high school curriculum, Johansen dropped out of high school in June 2000.

A year earlier, Johansen and two other European computer programmers had coauthored the DeCSS decryption program. Known as DVD-Jon at the young age of 15, Johansen's moniker was derived from the 1999 exploit in which the hacker cracked a DVD-access code and published his decryption program on the Internet. As a result, he was sued by the U.S. DVD Copy Control Association and the Norwegian National

Authority for the Investigation and Prosecution of Economic and Environmental Crime Although Johansen was charged by Norwegian police with computer crime, two courts in Norway ruled that his decryption program did not breach Norwegian law. As a result, Johansen was acquitted of all charges. To his credit, in 2002 Johansen accepted the Electronic Frontier Foundation's Pioneer Award for his contributions in the development of DeCSS. Ten years later, Johansen—a self-trained software engineer—continues to produce creative software with other more conventionally trained engineers in the San Diego, California, geographic area (Schell 2007).

Johansen was featured in the 2004 film *Info Wars*, whose focus was the wonders of media hacking and online information warfare.

Kahn, Robert (1938–)

In 2012, Robert Kahn was inducted into the Internet Hall of Fame for being the co-inventor of the TCP/IP protocols. Kahn was also the White Hat hacker who originated DARPA's Internet program. For this reason, he is revered as one of the "Fathers of the Internet." Also, at the International Computer Communication Conference, Kahn showed attendees a demonstration of ARPAnet by connecting 20 computers—which helped onlookers to begin to understand the importance of packet-switching technology. In 1997, President Bill Clinton gave Khan and Vinton Cerf the U.S. National Medal of Technology for their work in founding and developing the Internet (Internet Society, "Robert Khan," 2012).

Kutt, Mers (1933–)

Mers Kutt is a White Hat Canadian hacker who is credited with being the inventor of the world's first personal computer, known as the MCM/70. The MCM/70 was a small desktop microcomputer designed to provide the APL programming language environment for various applications—scientific, educational, and business.

Born in Winnipeg, Manitoba, Canada, Kutt is a brilliant mathematician and inventor who in 1973 founded the Toronto-based company Micro Computer Machines, Inc. (Schell 2007). In October 2001, he delivered a lecture at York University in Ontario titled "The Coming of the First Microcomputer," in which he urged other entrepreneurial and gifted White Hat hackers in the audience to follow in his footsteps. His Toronto company is now called All Computers Inc.

Levin, Vladimir (1971–)

Vladimir Levin was graduated from St. Petersburg Technology University in Russia. A talented mathematician, in 1994 he allegedly was a Black Hat hacker who masterminded the Russian hacker gang that "tricked" Citibank's computers into relinquishing $10 million. At the time, Levin was accused of using his laptop computer in London, England, to illegally access the Citibank network and obtain a list of customer codes and passwords—which gave the gang access to numerous bank accounts. Also, Levin was held accountable for logging on 18 times over a period of several weeks and transferring money through wire transfers to accounts that his hacker group controlled in the United States, Finland, the Netherlands, Germany, and Israel. Levin was arrested by Interpol at Heathrow Airport in 1995 and was sent to prison in the United States for three years. He was also ordered to pay back almost $250,000 to Citibank, apparently his share of the stolen funds (Schell and Martin 2004).

At Levin's trial in the United States in 1997, he was described as being the pioneer who successfully executed the first Internet bank raid. The reality is that Levin's ability to transfer illegally obtained funds to his accounts was accomplished through stolen account numbers and personal identification numbers. Back in 1994, the bulk of remote banking relied on client access to banking systems through dial-up connections, whereby clients' account information was coded through the telephone number keypad. In other words, Levin's so-called pioneering efforts amounted to a simple interception of a client's call while recording the punched-in numbers (Wood 2011).

Mitnick, Kevin (Condor) (1963–)

Kevin David Mitnick, brother to Ron Mitnick and former friend of female phreaker Susan Thunder (Susan Headley), is an IT security book author, a hacker with a cult following in the computer underground, a computer security professional, and, at one point, the U.S. Federal Bureau of Investigation's "most wanted" criminal. Mitnick, whose online moniker is Condor, began his criminal career by engaging in social engineering to acquire free bus rides in Los Angeles in the late 1970s. The skills that he developed were soon applied to various computer-based targets to gather user names, passwords, and other data. His first unauthorized attack against a computer network occurred in 1979 against the Digital Equipment Corporation (DEC), when he copied the company's software. Mitnick was charged and convicted of this compromise in 1988; for this infraction, he received a 12-month prison sentence and three years of probation.

In 1992, Mitnick violated the terms of his supervised release by hacking into Pacific Bell to access voice mail systems; soon thereafter, he went into hiding as a fugitive. He was on the lam for three years. During this period, Mitnick cloned multiple cell phones and hacked multiple companies, including Nokia, Motorola, and Sun Microsystems. He was able to hide his location through the use of cloned cell phones and multiple fake identity documents. However, Mitnick was eventually found by authorities and arrested in February 1995, thanks to the efforts of the FBI and Tsutomu Shimomura, a security researcher at the San Diego Supercomputing Center (Schell 2007).

When arrested in North Carolina, Mitnick faced 25 charges of hacking, wire fraud, and computer fraud. In 1999, he agreed

Kevin Mitnick, one of the world's most famous hackers, delivers a speech to 6,000 fans in Valencia, Spain in July 2011. (Kai Foersterling/EPA/Corbis)

to a plea bargain in federal court and was sentenced to 46 months in prison, as well as an additional 22 months for violating the terms of his parole agreement. During this time, the hacker community rallied around Mitnick as an example of "the unjust persecution of hackers." Many contributed to his legal defense fund, and the campaigners even made bumper stickers reading "Free Kevin." Mitnick served five years in prison, during which time he spent eight months in solitary confinement over concerns that he would be able to cause substantial harm to defense networks and government systems simply by having access to a phone. Upon his release in 2000, Mitnick received some of the most stringent conditions for supervised release ever mandated. These provisions included a prohibition against using any communications technology other than a landline telephone. In fact, the terms of his release now serve as models for other cybercriminals prosecuted in federal court for computer-related crimes (Schell and Dodge, with Moutsatsos 2002).

After his prison release, Mitnick began a computer security firm called Mitnick Security Consulting LLC. He has written multiple books on his favorite topics and well-honed skills:

hacking and social engineering. Although his transition to security consultant was questioned by many who supported his legal defense fund, his books have received substantial attention in the popular media. His most recent work, entitled *Ghost in the Wires,* details his exploits as a fugitive in the early 1990s.

Morris, Robert Tappan (rtm) (1966–)

In 1988, Robert Morris became known to the media and the public when, as a graduate student at Cornell University, he accidentally unleashed a worm that he had developed onto the Internet, infecting and crashing thousands of computers. Rumor has it that the word "cracker" was actually introduced into the vernacular as a result of this incident. Interestingly, Morris was the son of the chief scientist at the National Computer Security Center in the United States. Also of interest, when the U.S. Secret Service raided the home of a famous Legion of Doom hacker with the online moniker Bloodaxe, the agents found a copy of the source code for Morris's worm (Schell and Martin 2004).

Omidyar, Pierre (1967–)

A White Hat hacker and entrepreneur, Pierre Omidyar is known as the founder and chair of eBay, the online auction website. On Labor Day in 1995, Omidyar decided to launch the website as an experiment. His experiment—which is now worth more than $3 billion—was obviously a good idea. Today, online users continue to benefit from the experiment, which allows them to conduct online business transactions in an open and secure environment. Omidyar graduated from Tufts University in 1988 with an undergraduate degree in computer science (Schell 2007).

Rumor has it that this multibillion-dollar empire all started with a Pez candy dispenser. Omidyar was having dinner one night in 1995 with his then-girlfriend, a keen Pez collector.

When she complained about the lack of fellow Pez collectors in the San Francisco, California, area, Omidyar suggested that she should use the Internet to find other trading partners. To help her, he posted a page called "Auction Web" on his personal website, which allowed people to list items for auction online. The website attracted so many buyers and sellers that Omidyar decided to create a separate site devoted to online auctions, which he called "eBay." By charging anywhere from $0.25 to $2 to sellers for posting their items, and by taking a small percentage of the sale, the company made its fortunes simply by creating an online venue for buyers and sellers to meet. In May 1998, Omidyar was named eBay's chair; the following year, he married his girlfriend, who now has more than 400 Pez dispensers (Biography.com, 2012).

In 2004, the Omidyars created the Omidyar Network for people to invest in for-profit, nonprofit, and public policy efforts. The Omidyar Network has over the years funded a number of social areas so that more people can discover their own power to make good things happen. Projects invested in have included citizens' journalism, open-source software development, and intellectual property protection (Schell 2007).

Operation Aurora

Operation Aurora is the name given to a series of attacks originating from China in 2009. Specifically, Chinese hackers compromised multiple high-level targets, including Google, Adobe, Juniper Networks, Yahoo, Symantec, Northrop Gruman, and Dow Chemical, through the use of innovative and never-before-identified attack tools (Zetter 2010). The attackers appeared to target and compromise source code repositories within these companies (Markoff and Barboza 2010; Zetter 2010). The attacks were first made public by Google when the company revealed that it had been attacked by Chinese hackers and lost intellectual property.

The initial point of the attacks appeared to be attempts by the Chinese government to access Gmail accounts owned by Chinese dissidents to understand their communications and personal activities. Through research attempts by MacAfee and other security vendors, it was revealed that the attacks stemmed from a zero-day vulnerability in Microsoft Internet Explorer and targeted a wide range of U.S. companies (Zetter 2010). In addition, these attacks have been linked to two Chinese universities with ties to the Chinese search engine Baidu and the Chinese government (Markoff and Barboza 2010). It is not clear if they are working on behalf of the government or simply located in China. Thus Operation Aurora is an excellent example of the changing nature of cyberattacks and hacking generally.

Parson, Jeffrey Lee Case (1985–)

In August 2004, Jeffrey Lee Parson went before a judge in Seattle, Washington, and admitted to having created the B variant of the Blaster worm, which infected about 50,000 computers on the Internet during 2003. In January 2005, Parson was sent to prison for 18 months; he was also ordered to put in 10 months of community service after his release. Because Parson was only 18 years old when he committed his cybercrime, the judge sentencing him said that he would be given a lighter jail sentence; at the time when he launched the cyberattack, he appeared to be emotionally immature. Had the judge been less lenient, Parson could have been behind prison bars for a decade and given a fine of $250,000 (Schell and Martin 2006).

On March 27, 2005, Ronald Standler posted online the plea agreement in *United States v. Jeffrey Lee Parson* because (in his words):

• Prosecution and punishment of people for writing or releasing a computer virus/worm has been rare;

- This Plea Agreement avoided a trial, so the facts on pages 4–6 of this Agreement are the only facts that were legally established in *U.S. v. Parson*;
- I hope that readers will see the seriousness of writing or releasing malicious computer programs, such as a virus or worm; and
- I hope to assist professors of computer science to teach ethical behavior to their students.

Standler posted the plea agreement at the following website: http://www.rbs2.com/parson0.html.

Pinterest Social Networking Site

Pinterest, the fastest-growing new social networking site, which competes with social networking giants including Twitter and Facebook, acts like a virtual scrapbook filled with pretty pictures of outfits, recipes, and other goodies appealing to its online users. Because of its rapidly growing popularity, however, it has a growing problem with fake users spamming the site to make money from its advertising potential.

Picture this: you go to the website and a friendly-looking young woman online tells you that she loves a particular dress because the fabric is soft; interestingly, the woman has no hands. All of this to say that the Pinterest social networking site is really an e-commerce and marketing platform that links to other websites where the coveted items can be purchased. However, fake accounts created by spammers, which are formatted to push out content and drive links to illegitimate advertised products, are increasing day by day (Krashinsky 2012).

A recent tech blog called "The Daily Dot" revealed that one Pinterest spammer created multiple fake accounts to manipulate the algorithm tracking a post's "popularity" (i.e., the more that users "repin" an item, the more popular the item appears to be). In retaliation, Pinterest took on the vigilante role, deleting some of the spammer's fake accounts (Krashinsky 2012).

Postel, Jon (1943–1998)

In 2012, Jon Postel was a posthumous entry into the Internet Hall of Fame. He was such a White Hat pioneer for the Internet that it is difficult to pinpoint his strongest contribution. Many believe that perhaps his volunteering to take on and perform manually the creation of the Internet Assigned Numbers Authority (IANA) was his major contribution, as this action provided stability for the Internet's numbering and protocol management systems—two critical factors required if the Internet were to grow by leaps and bounds (as it has, indeed).

Postel was also involved technologically in the creation of a number of protocols that make the Internet functional—TCP/IP, which determines the way that information moves through the network; SMTP, which lets online users send email to one another; and the Domain Name Service (DNS), which helps online users get an understanding of how the Internet functions.

Postel got his PhD in computer science in 1974 from the University of California at Los Angeles. Afterward, he became intimately involved with the ARPAnet project, the packet-switching network that was the predecessor to the present-day Internet (Internet Society, "Jon Postel," 2012).

Poulsen, Kevin (Dark Dante) (1966–)

Kevin Poulsen's claim to hacker fame resulted from his taking over all of the telephone lines going into Los Angeles radio station KIIS-FM, thereby making sure that he was the 102nd caller and the winner of a Porsche 944S2, as well as his similar action to ensure that he was the winner of about $20,000 in prizes at another radio station. When the FBI began an investigation,

Poulsen went into hiding. After the crime was featured on the television show *Unsolved Mysteries*, Poulsen was arrested. He was charged with and convicted of criminal behavior, and spent more than 50 months behind prison bars. After his release from prison, Poulsen served as editorial director for the SecurityFocus website; he later wrote for *ZDNet*. He is now the senior editor for *Wired News* in San Francisco (Schell and Martin 2004).

Raymond, Eric Steven (1957–)

A graduate of the University of Pennsylvania, Eric Raymond has remained in Pennsylvania over the years. Annoyed by the fact that the press tends to use the word *hacker* when they really should be using the word *cracker*, Raymond wrote two popular books to inform the media and the mainstream about the difference: *The Hacker's Dictionary* and *How to Become a Hacker*. He noted that while hackers build things (generally of good use to society), crackers break them. In 2001, Raymond's book *The Cathedral and the Bazaar: Musings on Linux and Open Source by an Accidental Revolutionary* was released. Topics covered in this book include caring about the computer industry's future, the dynamics of the information economy, and details on open-source development (Schell and Martin 2004, 2006).

Ritchie, Dennis (dmr) (1941–2011)

Until his death in 2011 following a long illness, Dennis Ritchie was a major White Hat hacking contributor to the Computer Sciences Research Center at Bell Laboratories (but under the Lucent Technologies label). Ritchie joined Bell Laboratories in 1967, when the company was still known as American Telephone and Telegraph Company (AT&T). He teamed up with Ken Thompson in his early days at Bell Labs, and the pair, along with other creative talents working at Bell, created UNIX, an open operating system for minicomputers. Besides helping UNIX users with general computing, word processing, and networking, UNIX became a standard computer language. Also the creator of the popular C programming language, Ritchie received his graduate degrees in applied mathematics from Harvard University (Schell 2007).

When Steve Jobs died in 2011, the whole world grieved. But, maintained Ritchie's coworker at Bell, Rob Pike, few in the world grieved for Dennis Ritchie. But they should have, Pike maintained, because almost everything on the Web uses C and UNIX. The browsers are written in C, and the UNIX kernel—which much of the entire Internet runs on—is written in C. Furthermore, web servers are written in C, Java, or C++, all of which are C derivatives. Moreover, the network hardware running these programs also rely on C (Metz 2011).

Russian Business Network

The Russian Business Network (RBN) is a well-known cyber-crime entity operating out of Saint Petersburg, Russia (Krebs 2007). The group began as an apparently legitimate service in 2006, offering hosting activities for various businesses. In 2007, it began hosting malware, child pornography, and spam distribution services, which quickly drew in cybercriminals from around the world (Krebs 2007). During this time, the business network diversified its services, and it now operates under a variety of names around the world, including iFrame Cash; Rusouvenirs, Ltd.; Too Coin Software; and MalwareAlarm. The Russian business network is thought to have earned millions of dollars, though its legal risk may be low, primarily because the individuals who use its services engage in cybercrime (Krebs 2007). The RBN simply hosts these materials.

The RBN is extremely difficult to trace, as it has no advertisements or registrations (Krebs 2007). In addition, the operators are known only by nicknames, or handles, and minimal information can be found about these identities. For instance, the supposed creator of RBN is known by the handle Flyman and is thought to be related to Russian political actors (Krebs 2007). If this is correct, the RBN may be insulated from legal challenges and be used in nonsanctioned state attacks.

Shimomura, Tsutomu (1966–)

Born in Japan and raised in Princeton, New Jersey, Tsutomu Shimomura is best known for tracking down and outsmarting famous cracker Kevin Mitnick, a hacker on the "FBI's Most Wanted" list in the early 1990s. In December 1994, after his colleagues at the San Diego Supercomputing Center told Shimomura that someone had stolen hundreds of software programs and files from his workstation, Shimomura decided to find the perpetrator and to bring him or her to the authorities. And, in the end, he did just that. In February 1995, Shimomura led the FBI to an apartment complex in Raleigh, North Carolina, where the agents finally found and arrested Mitnick. At the time, Mitnick was on the lam.

Shimomura is a research fellow at the Supercomputer Center, and he often serves as an IT security consultant to the FBI and other U.S. agencies. In 1996, his book with John Markoff called *Takedown: The Pursuit and Capture of America's Most Wanted Computer Outlaw—By the Man Who Did It* was released and became an immediate best-seller (Schell and Martin 2004).

Sklyarov, Dmitry (1974–)

Dmitry Sklyarov is a 1970s-era, Russian-born computer programmer who made media headlines when he was arrested at the DefCon 9 hacker convention in Las Vegas—when he was about to speak about a software package that he developed for his employer Elcomsoft. Although he was arrested in the United States, it is important to note that Sklyarov's employer was housed in Russia—where the software that he invented was not illegal. Simply put, Sklyarov's software permitted Internet users to convert the so-called copy-protected Adobe eBook file format to a more freely copy-able computer file. According to U.S. authorities, Sklyarov's work violated the U.S. Digital Millennium Copyright Act (DMCA) of 1998. Whisked away from the hacker convention in handcuffs, Sklyarov was put in a federal prison in the United States. Soon after his arrest, however, the Electronic Frontier Foundation took on his case and lobbied on his behalf; it maintained that Sklyarov's activities were under the jurisdiction of Russian law, and that he did no wrong. As the case continued, even his employer was charged with violating the same U.S. law. Finally, in December 2002, both the computer programmer and his employer were cleared of all charges by the courts (Schell 2007).

Following his return to Russia to be with his wife and children, Sklyarov published a book, *Hidden Keys to Software Break-ins and Unauthorized Entry*, in February 2004. While it was intended primarily for software developers, the book is also useful for individuals wanting to understand the problems of modern data protection technologies. Also provided in the book is information on cryptography and cryptanalysis, as well as information on methods commonly used for software security. Sklyarov is also known for his development of the Advanced eBook Processor (AEBR) algorithm that allows on-line users to decrypt an e-book in a way so that the e-book can be opened in any Portable Document Format (PDF)—such as Adobe Acrobat Reader. What is more, the e-book can be opened without the usual restrictions placed on editing, copying, and printing (Schell 2007).

Smith, David L. (1968–)

The year was 1999, and a computer virus named Melissa brought down much of the Internet for days. At that time, the world had never witnessed a computer virus that moved so fast. The creator of the virus was a young man named David L. Smith. Melissa was a Microsoft Word-based virus that replicated itself through email and seemingly came out of nowhere to take over computer systems in businesses, government offices, and the military. Given the scope of the damage done by Melissa, the FBI began the biggest Internet person-hunt ever to find its developer. Eventually, the person suspected of creating the virus was found: Smith, a resident of New Jersey. In court, Smith said that he never intended to cause harm with his virus Melissa—apparently the name of a lap dancer whom he had met in Florida. In 2002, Smith was found guilty of criminal behavior, sentenced to 20 months in jail, fined $5,000, and required to perform 100 hours of community service after his prison release (Schell and Martin 2006).

Many computer security technologies, including antivirus software, firewalls, and mobile code, are based on the concept of querying the user with the question, "There is a security issue here. Are you sure that you want to continue?" In the case of the Melissa virus, every user who spread the virus was first prompted with the query: "This document contains macros; do you want to run them?" Often the users would answer, "Yes," and the damage was done (Schell and Martin 2006).

Stallman, Richard (1953–)

Richard Stallman is a White Hat hacker who went to Harvard University. Computer underground lore says that as an undergraduate, Stallman walked into the prestigious MIT Artificial Intelligence Laboratory in 1971 without any prior arrangements and got a job there. His fame relates to his founding the GNU Project (an acronym for GNU's Not UNIX), launched in 1984. Its goal was to develop the free operating system GNU. Because GNU is free software, everyone is free to copy it, redistribute it, and make changes to it. Nowadays, Linux-based variants of the GNU system are widely used (Schell and Martin 2004).

Stallman's present-day U.S.-based webpage is very politically oriented, featuring news notes and links to global news items.

On August 21, 2012, this quote appeared on Stallman's personal online page: "In the 1970s we had a name for politicians with policies like Obama's: *Republicans*. Therefore, Jill Stein for President."

Thompson, Ken (1943–)

The late Dennis Ritchie's co-inventor of the UNIX operating system is Ken Thompson, now retired from the Bell Labs Computing Research Center. He continues to reside in New Jersey. Thompson began his creative exploits at Bell Laboratories in 1966, and within three years, he worked alongside Dennis Ritchie to produce UNIX. In 1970, Thompson began to create the B programming language, the precursor to the C language. Three years later, he rewrote UNIX in C. In 1995 and 1996, Thompson served as a visiting professor at the University of California, Berkeley, where he received his undergraduate and master's degrees in electrical engineering. In 1998, Thompson and Ritchie were jointly awarded the National Medal of Technology for developing UNIX. Thompson retired from Lucent Technologies in 2000 (Schell 2006).

Tomlinson, Ray (1941–)

In 1971–1972, Ray Tomlinson helped contribute to one of the greatest inventions on the Internet: electronic mail, or email. One of the forefathers of the Internet, Tomlinson worked on ARPAnet, described in Chapter 1 of this text. Tomlinson, a Harvard University graduate, chose the @sign for email—a sign that simply meant "at." Tomlinson was not the actual inventor of email—it has been around since about 1965, when Fernando Corbato and colleagues at MIT developed a software program that allowed online users at MIT to share messages via MIT's Compatible Timesharing System (CTSS). The problem with the original program was that it let only individuals using the same computer communicate with each other. Tomlinson's contribution was that he made it possible for users to exchange messages between different computers and in different locations, even if they were located in different continents. As a result of this White Hat contribution, email as we know it today is now more than 40 years old (Schell 2007).

In 2012, Tomlinson was inducted into the Internet Hall of Fame as an innovator. Besides his significant contribution to email, he also played a key role in developing the first email standards. For example, in 1972, Tomlinson was a participant in a meeting to enhance FTP to support email; FTP was replaced in 1982 by SMTP. In September 1973, Tomlinson was coauthor of RFC 561, the first standard for Internet email message formats that defined several of the email fields in use today (From, Subject, Date) (Internet Society, "Raymond Tomlinson," 2012).

Torvalds, Linus (1969–)

Inducted into the Internet Hall of Fame in the spring of 2012, Linus Torvalds is the Finnish creator and namesake of the Linux computer operating system, the open-source software that is a major competitor to Microsoft's products in the personal computer marketplace. Torvalds coauthored a book in 2001 with Pekka Himanen (a former hacker-turned-philosophy professor at the University of Helsinki) and Manual Castells (a sociology professor at the University of California Berkeley). Called *The Hacker Ethic and the Spirit of the New Economy,* the book tends to focus on the White Hat side of hacking. In the book, the authors said that a hacker should be seen as an enthusiastic programmer who shares his or her work with others and not as some dangerous criminal who is a threat to society (Schell and Martin 2006).

Wozniak, Steve (The Other Steve) (1950–)

Steve Wozniak is a creator, White Hat, and entrepreneur with multiple names, including "The Other Steve," "Oak Toebark," and "The Wizard of Woz." Together with Steve Jobs, Wozniak made his fortune in the high-tech market with the invention of the Apple II computer decades ago. An engineer, Wozniak was always interested in stretching the limits of technology. At age 11, he built his own home radio station. Two years later, he started designing computers. When he went to university, he met Steve Jobs. There, the two Steves had fun creating "blue boxes" that would allow the pair to phreak (i.e., manipulate long-distance telephone lines to get telephone calls for free). In 2004, when Wozniak spoke at the Hackers on Planet Earth (HOPE) gathering, he focused on his fond "blue box" exploit memories from the good old days. The entrepreneurial Jobs and Wozniak started the Apple Company in California in 1976, and four years later, the company went public—creating two wealthy men. In a power struggle between the two founders, both men left Apple in 1985. Although Jobs returned to the company as CEO in 1997 and stayed with Apple until his death in 2011, the entrepreneurial Wozniak went on to found the Electronic Frontier Foundation (EFF) advocacy group, as well as the Tech Museum and the Children's Discovery Museum in San Jose (Schell 2007).

Yahoo! Inc. Team: David Filo (1967–) and Jerry Yang (1969–)

According to the 2012 theirnetworth.com website, Yahoo! Inc. is now worth $20 billion, down from its peak valuation of $60 billion in 2006. This online search engine was started by two electrical engineering doctoral candidates at Stanford University: David Filo and Jerry Yang. Like Sergey Brin and Larry Page from Google, Filo and Yang had not in their formative years thought about making a career in business. In fact, the foundation for Yahoo! was laid in a campus trailer in February 1994, with the main goal of helping the pair keep track of their personal interests on the Internet. Given that this self-chosen goal was a lot more interesting than their doctoral study assignments, Filo and Yang started spending more time on their lists of favorite links than on their dissertations. Then, when the team's lists became too large and unwieldy, they ordered them into categories and subcategories—forming the foundation for the search engine. Although the pair originally coined the phrase "Jerry's and David's Guide to the World Wide Web," they eventually changed the title to "Yahoo"— which technically means "Yet Another Hierarchical Officious Oracle." Because Filo and Yang had an obvious sense of humor, they wished the same for their search engine website. The pair also laughed that they wanted the name to indicate an entity that was simultaneously rude, unsophisticated, and uncouth—just like them (Farzad and Elgin 2005; Schell 2007).

Zero-Day Exploit

Abbreviated as "0-day exploit," the term means capitalizing on vulnerabilities right after their discovery. Thus zero-day attacks occur before the company producing the software knows about the vulnerability or has been able to distribute patches to repair it. Such exploits allow crackers to wreak maximum havoc on systems. The term actually relates to the fact that the value of exploits decreases rapidly as soon as they are announced to the public. The next day after the announcement, for example, exploits are half as valuable to crackers. By the second day after the announcement, they are one-fourth as valuable, and 10 days later, they are one-thousandth as valuable as on day 0. The reality is that today's Internet is a rather unsafe cyber-neighborhood. If someone connects a freshly loaded Windows system without patches to the Internet, in about 10 or 20 seconds following the connection, the system can be attacked. Worse, with zero-day exploits, a patch may not be available. It is for this reason that software companies typically encourage security "bug" finders to report the bugs to them immediately so that they can write a patch and distribute it to consumers. As a case in point, on May 10, 2005, the Mozilla.org company issued a public statement noting that it discovered a zero-day exploit code taking advantage of vulnerabilities in its Mozilla Firefox 1.0.3 browser (Schell and Martin 2006).

Zeus Trojan Horse

The Zeus Trojan horse is a form of malware that was first identified in 2007 after it was used to steal data from the U.S. Department of Transportation (Symantec 2010). This malware is a keystroke logger and form grabber that is used to capture information individual users enter, primarily through phishing schemes. It can also operate as a botnet connecting all infected systems together to exfiltrate captured data to single drop points (Symantec 2010). The program has been used in attacks against multiple major banks and financial service providers, as well as Verizon Wireless and Amazon. Zeus specifically targets Windows operating systems and can be purchased through the online black market from various hackers and carders (Symantec 2010). In fact, the U.S. Federal Bureau of Investigation began a crackdown on Zeus operators in 2010 that led to more than 100 people being arrested on charges ranging from bank fraud to money laundering (Bartz 2010). Due to the functionality of the Trojan horse, it is still in use today and is difficult to identify through antivirus software and security tools.

Zimmerman, Phil (1954–)

Phil Zimmerman is known as the inventor of "Pretty Good Privacy" (PGP), an encryption program that is distributed worldwide and is used by average computer users. This White Hat hacker's greatest barrier to marketing his security products involved an attempt by the U.S. government to prosecute him for the illegal export of sophisticated encryption algorithms. It is interesting to note that at the time the charges were laid against Zimmerman, only weak encryption algorithms were allowed to be exported from the United States. Zimmerman spent three prime years of his life battling the U.S. government and eventually the charges were dropped (Schell and Martin 2006).

In 2012, Zimmerman was inducted into the Internet Hall of Fame for his contribution to developing an online "human rights tool." Actually, Zimmerman designed Pretty Good Privacy to empower online users to take privacy into their own hands; he believed that with the growing social reliance on electronic communication, it was extremely important that there was a way to ensure that online users and companies could protect their intellectual property. He was apparently inspired by U.S. Senate Bill 266, a 1991 omnibus anticrime bill that would require makers of secure communications equipment to insert special "trap doors" into their products so that the government could read any online user's encrypted messages. Zimmerman believed that the danger of these trap doors was that they would be abused by business competitors, organized crime units, or foreign governments (Internet Society, "Phil Zimmerman," 2012).

References

Adegoke, Y. "From Low-key to Filling Famous Shoes." *The Globe and Mail*, August 26, 2011, p. B7.

Assange, J. *The Unauthorized Autobiography*. Edinburgh Canongate Books, 2011.

Bajak, F. "Move to House Assange a Political Gamble." *The Globe and Mail*, August 18, 2012, p. A14.

Bartz, R. "Top Hacker "Retires", Experts Brace for His Return." *Reuters*, December 16, 2010.

BBC. *WikiLeaks' Julian Assange Seeks Asylum in Ecuador Embassy*. BBC News, June 20, 2012.

Bellis, M. "History of Java and Programmer James Gosling." 2012. http://inventors.about.com/od/gstartinventors/a/James_Gosling.htm. Accessed August 14, 2012.

Bill and Melinda Gates Foundation. "Letter from Bill and Melinda Gates." 2012. http://www.gatesfoundation.org/

about/Pages/bill-melinda-gates-letter.aspx. Accessed August 14, 2012.

Biography.com. "Pierre Morad Omidyar." 2012. http://www .biography.com/print/profile/pierre-omidyar-9542205. Accessed August 14, 2012.

Bloomberg. "Facebook Keeps Women out of the Boardroom." *The Globe and Mail*, February 4, 2012, p. B10.

Canadian Press. "Toews under 'Direct Threat' by Online Collective Anonymous." *The Globe and Mail*, March 7, 2012, p. A3.

Computer Science University of Toronto. "Stephen A. Cook." 2012. http://www.cs.toronto.edu/~sacook/homepage/bio .08.html. Accessed August 9, 2012.

Conversations Network. "Sean Gorman." 2012. http://itc .conversationsnetwork.org/shows/detail3849.html. Accessed August 21, 2012.

D'Aliesio, R. "Anonymous Wants Transparency, Hides behind Name." *The Globe and Mail*, February 20, 2012, p. A4.

Dixon, G. "Hackers under Attack over Copyrights." *The Globe and Mail*, August 2, 2001, p. B22.

Efrati, A. " 'Honeymoon over' for Google's CEO." *The Globe and Mail*, August 20, 2011, p. 12.

El Akkad, O. "Hacker Crackdown." *The Globe and Mail*, March 7, 2012, p. A3.

El Akkad, O. "Online Protest Prompts Retreat on Privacy Bills." *The Globe and Mail*, January 19, 2012, p. A12.

El Akkad, O. "Unable to Continue, Apple's Jobs Steps down." *The Globe and Mail*, August 25, 2011, p. A1, A12.

El Akkad, O. "Why Facebook Paid $1-Billion for Instagram." *The Globe and Mail*, April 10, 2012, p. B3.

Emmanuel Goldstein. *The Best of 2600: Collector's Edition: A Hacker Odyssey*. Indianapolis: Wiley Publishing, 2009.

Emmanuel Goldstein. *The Best of 2600: A Hacker Odyssey*. Indianapolis: Wiley Publishing, 2008.

Farzad, R., and B. Elgin. "Googling for Gold." *Businessweek*, December 5, 2005, p. 48–52, 54.

Greenberg, A. "An Interview with WikiLeaks' Julian Assange." *Forbes,* December 16, 2010. http://www.forbes.com/sites/ andygreenberg/2010/11/29/an-interview-with-wikileaks -julian-assange/ Accessed January 11, 2011.

Gustin, S. "Apple Now Worth More Than Microsoft, Google Combined." 2012. http://business.time.com/2012/02/10/ apple-now-worth-more-than-microsoft-google-combined/. Accessed February 10, 2012.

Harding, L., and B. Quinn. "From His Ecuadorean Sanctuary, Assange Calls on U.S. to End 'Witch Hunt.' " *The Globe and Mail*, August 20, 2012, p. A3.

Harrell, E. "Defending the Leaks: Q&A with WikiLeaks' Julian Assange." *Time*, December 1, 2010. http://www.time .com/time/world/article/0,8599,2006789-2,00.html Accessed January 14, 2011.

Holt, T. J. "Examining the Language of Carders." In *Corporate Hacking and Technology-Driven Crime: Social Dynamics and Implications*, edited by T. Holt and B. Schell, 127–145). Hershey, PA: IGI Global, 2011.

Houpt, S. "News International Pays up for Phone Hacking." *The Globe and Mail*, January 20, 2012, p. A15.

ICANN. "Vinton G. Cerf, Vice President and Internet Evangelist." (2012). http://www.icann.org/en/groups/ board/cerf.htm. Accessed August 9, 2012.

Internet Society. "Elizabeth Feinler." 2012. http://www .internethalloffame.org/inductees/elizabeth-feinler. Accessed August 15, 2012.

Internet Society. "Jon Postel." 2012. http://www .internethalloffame.org/inductees/jon-postel. Accessed August 16, 2012.

Internet Society. "Mitchell Baker." 2012. http://www
    .internethalloffame.org/inductees/mitchell-baker. Accessed
    August 21, 2012.

Internet Society. "Phil Zimmermann." 2012. http://www
    .internethalloffame.org/inductees/philip-zimmermann.
    Accessed August 15, 2012.

Internet Society. "Raymond Tomlinson." 2012. http://
    internethalloffame.org/inductees/raymond-tomlinson.
    Accessed August 14, 2012.

Internet Society. "Robert Khan." 2012. http://www
    .internethalloffame.org/inductees/robert-kahn. Accessed
    August 15, 2012.

Katz, I. "Web Freedom Is Seriously Threatened, Says Google
    Co-founder." *The Globe and Mail*, April 17, 2012, p. A9.

Keizer, G. "Conficker Cashes in, Installs Spam Bots and
    Scareware." *Computerworld*, April 4, 2010. http://www
    .computerworld.com/s/article/9131380/Conficker_cashes_in
    _installs_spam_bots_and_scareware Accessed May 14, 2010.

Keller, G. "Police Sweep Nets 25 Alleged Anonymous
    Hackers." *The Globe and Mail*, February 29, 2012, p. A14.

Krashinsky, S. "Networking Site Pinterest in Battle against
    Spammers." *The Globe and Mail*, March 29, 2012, p. B6.

Krebs, B. "Shadowy Russian Firm seen as a Conduit for
    Cybercrime." *The Washington Post*, October 13, 2007.
    http://www.washingtonpost.com/wp-dyn/content/article/
    2007/10/12/AR2007101202461_2.html?sid
    =ST2007101202661 Accessed December 1, 2007.

Kushner, D. "Machine Politics." 2012. http://www.newyorker
    .com/reporting/2012/05/07/120507fa_fact_kushner
    ?currentPage=1. Accessed May 7, 2012.

Leder, F,. and Werner, T. "Know Your Enemy: Containing
    Conficker." *Know Your Enemy* Series. The Honeynet

Project, 2009. http://www.honeynet.org/files/KYE
-Conficker.pdf Accessed October 14, 2010.

Mackrael, K. "Toews Faces Personal Threats over Internet
Bill." *The Globe and Mail*, February 20, 2012, p. A4.

Mahtani, S. "Facebook's Other Founder." *The Globe and Mail*,
May 5, 2012, p. B8.

Markoff, J., and Barboza, D. (2010). "2 China Schools Said to
Be Linked to Online Attacks." *The New York Times*, May 4,
2010, A1.

Marlow, I. "Hackers Find a Way into RIM's PlayBook." *The
Globe and Mail*, December 1, 2011, p. B3.

Marlow, I. "Reported Hacking of Nortel Fuels Concerns,
Skepticism." *The Globe and Mail*, February 15, 2012, p. B5.

Metz, C. "Dennis Ritchie: The Shoulders Steve Jobs Stood
on." 2011. http://www.wired.com/wiredenterprise/2011/
10/thedennisritchieeffect/. Accessed August 14, 2012.

Modine, A. "Virginia De-convicts AOL Junk Mailer Jeremy
James." 2008. http://www.theregister.co.uk/2008/09/13/
virginia_overturns_antispam_conviction/. Accessed
August 28, 2012.

MrCracker.com. "Female Hacker." http://mrcracker.com/
2010/01/female-hacker/. Accessed August 28, 2012.

O'Brien, M. "Republican Wants WikiLeaks Labeled as a
Terrorist Group." *The Hill.com*, November 29, 2010. http://
thehill.com/blogs/blog-briefing-room/news/130863-top
-republican-designate-wikileaks-as-a-terrorist-org. Accessed
October 11, 2011.

Raice, S. "Man's Claim to Stake in Facebook 'a Fraud and a
Lie,' Company Says." *The Globe and Mail*, March 27, 2012,
p. B14.

Reuters. "Mark Zuckerberg Kicks Off Facebook's IPO Road
Show." *The Globe and Mail*, May 8, 2012, p. B2.

Schachter, H. "Six management lessons from the master leader: Steve Jobs." *The Globe and Mail*, April 15 2012, p. B7.

Schell, B. *Contemporary World Issues: The Internet and Society*. Santa Barbara: ABC-CLIO, 2007.

Schell, B., and J. Dodge, with S. Moutsatsos. *The Hacking of America: Who's Doing It, Why, and How*. Westport: Quorum Books, 2002.

Schell, B., and C. Martin. *Contemporary World Issues: Cybercrime*. Santa Barbara: ABC-CLIO, 2004.

Schell, B., and C. Martin. *Webster's New World Hacker Dictionary*. Indiana: Wiley, 2006.

Stackhouse, J. "Assange under Siege." *The Globe and Mail*, August 17, 2012, p. A10.

Symantec. *Zeus: King of the Bots*. Symantec Security, February 20, 2010.

Textuality Services, Inc. "Tim Bray's Resume." *Textuality*, 2012. http://www.textuality.com/content/tim-brays -resume. Accessed August 9, 2012.

Tossell, I. "The ABCs of Cyber-security." *The Globe and Mail Report on Business* 28 (May 10, 2012): 55–60.

Verini, J. "The Great Cyberheist." *The New York Times Magazine*, November 10, 2010, p. MM44.

West Liberty University. "Alumna Recognized for Early Internet Contributions." 2012. http://westliberty.edu/news/ news/alumna-recognized-for-early-internet-contributions/. Accessed August 15, 2012.

Wood, A. "Ten of History's Greatest Hackers." 2011. http:// betabeat.com/2011/08/ten-of-historys-greatest-hackers/. Accessed August 21, 2012.

Zetter, K. 2010. " 'Google' Hackers Had Ability to Alter Source Code." *Wired*, December 14, 2010. http://www .wired.com/threatlevel/2010/03/source-code-hacks/.

As discussed throughout this text, hacking techniques can be used to engage in various forms of cybercrime, ranging from spam mail distribution to fraud to malware infections. In addition, actors may target individual computer users, corporations, and government targets depending on their motivations and abilities. Some of the victims in these incidents may not know that they have been compromised or do not know where to report an incident should something occur. At the same time, businesses and government entities may not report an incident due to concerns about which further harms may result if this information is made public. As a consequence, it is difficult to assess the scope of hacker-related offenses that occur each year. This chapter provides an assessment of the various forms of hacker-related cybercrimes using both public and private reports from computer security groups. The information presented does not give a complete picture of the criminal use of hacking techniques, but rather illustrates trends and growing problems that demand further research over time.

Joe Stewart, director of malware research for SecureWorks (which manages security information systems for corporations worldwide), is pictured with servers in their Atlanta office on July 22, 2010. (AP Photo/John Amis)

Anti-Phishing Working Group: Phishing Activity Trends Report, Second Quarter 2012

Source: Anti-Phishing Working Group. "APWG Phishing Activity Trends Report, 2nd Quarter 2012." http://docs .apwg.org/reports/apwg_trends_report_q2_2012.pdf. Used by permission of the Anti-Phishing Working Group.

In Chapters 1 and 2, we discussed the role of hacking in data theft and fraud. The global scope of the hacker community allows individuals to compromise consumers around the world, regardless of their geographic proximity. The Anti-Phishing Working Group (APWG) emerged to document the scope of this problem through member companies in the computer security and finance industries, as well as through independent researchers and academics. Its focus is on the problem of phishing, defined as "a criminal mechanism employing both social engineering and technical subterfuge to steal consumers' personal identity data and financial account credentials" (APWG 2012, 2). This issue typically involves either the use of fraudulent email messages to persuade prospective victims to give up sensitive information, or malware that can surreptitiously steal financial information and data.

The most recent report generated by the APWG reflects phishing attempts and attacks over the first quarter of 2012. During this period, the number of phishing attacks reported peaked at 30,237 incidents in February, which was an increase over the previous month (Table 5.1). There was a minimal decrease in March to 29,762 reported campaigns. This statistic is important because it reflects the number of unique emails sent to multiple users, which then point the users toward a specific website. In addition, a substantial number of phishing websites were detected during this period based on unique IP addresses. The largest proportion of phishing websites were hosted in the United States for each month within this quarter. This may be a function of the fact that U.S. financial institutions are most commonly targeted by phishers as well as the massive number of web hosting services available in the United

Table 5.1   Statistical Highlights for First Quarter 2012

	January	February	March
Number of unique phishing email reports (campaigns) received by APWG from consumers	25,444	30,237	29,762
Number of unique phishing websites detected	53,225	56,859	53,939
Number of brands hijacked by phishing campaigns	370	392	392
Country hosting the most phishing websites	United States	United States	United States
Percentage of phishing emails containing some form of target name in URL	49.53%	45.39%	55.42%
No host name; just IP addr	1.19%	1.40%	2.09%
Percentage of sites not using port 80	1.19%	0.68%	0.26%

(Anti-Phishing Working Group, "APWG Phishing Activity Trends Report, 2nd Quarter 2012." Available at: http://docs.apwg.org/reports/apwg_trends_report _q2_2012.pdf. Used by permission of the Anti-Phishing Working Group.)

States. In addition, almost half of all phishers use the name of their target institution in the URL that they direct victims toward. This is a sensible move because phishers want to produce a convincing replica of the financial institution or service their victims use. Greater accuracy will ensure that victims believe that the request is coming from a legitimate source and, therefore, comply with any questions asked of the online user.

Considering the number of phishing campaigns that occur in the course of a given month, it is vital to understand which services are most commonly attacked. Evidence suggests that resources that handle or manage financial information are the most frequently targeted. In fact, financial service providers are the largest target of phishers (34.4%), followed by payment service providers (32.1%) and retailers (9.9%). Social network providers such as Facebook represent a much smaller proportion of the targeted service sectors (3.2%), as do government resources (1.8%). This finding is sensible, as phishers may have a higher likelihood of success when they target a wide audience whose members may or may not use a specific bank or financial service provider. Attempting to compromise government and

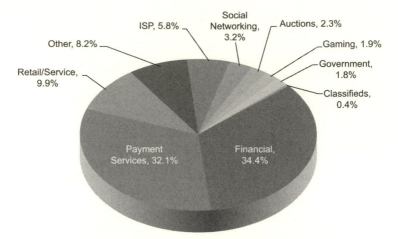

Figure 5.1   Most Targeted Industry Sectors Second Quarter 2012 (Anti-Phishing Working Group, "APWG Phishing Activity Trends Report, 2nd Quarter 2012." Available at: http://docs.apwg.org/reports/ apwg_trends_report_q2_2012.pdf. Used by permission of the Anti-Phishing Working Group)

social networking users may be less successful because of the difficulty in replicating these resources and convincing end users that their claims are legitimate.

Given the scope of phishing campaigns across the world, there is substantial value in considering how these messages are structured to entice prospective victims to enter in personal information. The most common subject lines used by phishers illustrate the role of social engineering in the hacker community (see Table 5.2). All of these messages indicate that there is an issue with the security of a user's account, such as that it has been accessed by a third party or that a user must validate his or her account details. This information may arouse fear in the message recipients and increase the likelihood that they read the entire message (Mitnick and Simon 2002). Only one message cited in the AWPG report used the name of a financial institution (LloydsTSB), which may be intentional—it may be intended to increase the likelihood that a victim reads the

Table 5.2   Subject Lines Used in Phishing Emails

From Subject
Top Phishing Sender 1: Your account has been accessed by a third party
Top Phishing Sender 2: LloydsTSB Internet banking customer service message
Top Phishing Sender 3: Security measures
Top Phishing Sender 4: Verify your activity
Top Phishing Sender 5: Account security notification

(Anti-Phishing Working Group, "APWG Phishing Activity Trends Report, 2nd Quarter 2012." Available at: http://docs.apwg.org/reports/apwg_trends_report _q2_2012.pdf. Used by permission of the Anti-Phishing Working Group.)

entire message to understand which account has been harmed. Thus phishers appear to carefully craft message content to affect users' emotions.

The Malware Domain List

Source: Malware Domain List, http://www.malwaredomain list.com/

In Chapters 1 and 2, we discussed the role of malware in the attack toolkit of hackers and attackers. Malicious software allows hackers to compromise a large number of systems around the world through common vulnerabilities and manipulate them remotely. Thus concern has arisen about the spread and use of malware around the world. One group that collects data on this phenomenon is the Malware Domain List (MDL), an archive of identified and known malware infections reported by computer security professionals and enthusiasts around the world. The site is operated as a community project with no commercial or profit-driven base. Anytime an individual identifies a web page that is hosting malware or is infected by a certain form of malware, whether a botnet or an exploit pack, he or she can report this web page to the MDL. In turn, this information is made available to the general public.

The MDL group requires that the individual provide the date the web page was identified, the domain name of the site, its IP address, its physical location at the country level, a description of the infection, and the person to whom the domain is registered for identification purposes. The public nature of this reporting is in keeping with the tradition of open information sharing within the hacker community. The more information individuals have about infections, the more likely they can protect themselves from such an attack or be aware of the spread of programs at the global level. The amount of information provided by the MDL also allows individuals to discover trends about infection rates and hotspots for attacks.

To that end, when the number of infections between January 1, 2009, and February 2, 2012, at the country level are counted, it appears that the United States was the most common victim of infections (Table 5.3). In fact, the United States had more than 19,000 infections in a 24-month period, which is three times higher than the rate in China (6,937) and Russia (6,893). This finding is surprising, given the much larger population of Internet users in China who could potentially be harmed by malware infections hosted within that country. It is important to note that the nations most commonly infected are industrialized ones with relatively substantial populations of Internet users, such as South Korea, Brazil, France, Germany, and Canada.

The variations in infection rates reported may be a function of differences in the size and scope of Internet resources within each country. For instance, the United States, China, and Russia have a large number of web hosting services available that could be easily exploited by an attacker (Central Intelligence Agency [CIA] 2011). The infection of a few dozen websites may go unnoticed by an Internet service provider (ISP) with hundreds of sites, at least until the ISP begins to receive complaints from law enforcement or customers (Brenner 2008). In addition, the inherent variations in security protocols and management make it possible for attackers to easily identify vulnerable infrastructure

Table 5.3   Malware Infections by Country from 2009 to 2012

Country	Malware Count
United States	19,559
Ukraine	9,477
China	6,937
Russia	6,893
Germany	4,890
Netherlands	4,226
Czech Republic	3,790
Latvia	2,578
Canada	2,209
Moldova	1,689
United Kingdom	1,614
France	1,441
European Union	1,302
Brazil	1,138
South Korea	1,024
Turkey	990
Bosnia and Herzegovina	715
Romania	553
Sweden	476
Egypt	452
Spain	424
Luxembourg	421
Italy	409
Azerbaijan	380
Austria	342
Taiwan	325
Malaysia	320
Poland	305
Panama	226
Singapore	186
Hong Kong	185
Lithuania	176
Israel	167
India	154
Thailand	154
Hungary	150
Japan	122

(continued)

Table 5.3 (*continued*)

Country	Malware Count
Argentina	110
Estonia	103
Bulgaria	102
Australia	90
Kazakhstan	83
Vietnam	82
Iraq	80
Denmark	67
Indonesia	60
Chile	57
Switzerland	51
Greece	46
Mexico	43
Portugal	41
Colombia	39
Croatia	29
Philippines	28
Saint Helena	28
Georgia	27
Jordan	25
Serbia	22
Belgium	20
Morocco	15
Ireland	14
Slovakia	14
South Africa	14
Belize	12
Armenia	11
New Zealand	11
Venezuela	11
Cayman Islands	10

(Malware Domain List, http://www.malwaredomainlist.com/)

that is not securely patched and up-to-date. The countries with the highest infection rates also have the largest populations of Internet users who can be readily infected by malware hosted on country-specific domains (CIA 2011). Thus attackers may be able to immediately infect a wide variety of user systems by infecting domains in these countries.

In addition, examining the infections within the United States by location provides some insight into the nature of attacks (Table 5.4). In the MDL reports mentioned earlier, California had the highest overall number of infections, followed by Texas, Pennsylvania, Illinois, and Arizona. The distribution of infections may be a function of the concentration of Internet users, because California, Texas, and Illinois are among the top five states with the largest populations of users overall (CIA 2011). Additionally, these states have a large proportion of web hosting services and internet-based companies, which may provide a greater number of targets for infection overall (Brenner 2008). Thus the likelihood of malware infections may be driven by demographic factors, as well as the presence of vulnerabilities and technical problems that can be exploited.

Table 5.4 Infections by State within the United States

State	Frequency	Percentage
CA	2,979	15.6
TX	2,723	14.3
PA	2,201	11.6
IL	1,637	8.6
AZ	1,424	7.5
UT	1,149	6.0
NJ	972	5.1
MO	720	3.8
GA	598	3.1
NY	531	2.8
VA	522	2.7
FL	484	2.5
MI	476	2.5
WA	476	2.5
DE	379	2.0
OH	330	1.7
NV	264	1.4
CO	248	1.3

(continued)

Table 5.4   *(continued)*

State	Frequency	Percentage
MT	185	1.0
NC	119	0.6
Washington, DC	113	0.6
MA	98	0.5
MD	91	0.5
OR	61	0.3
KS	54	0.3
MS	42	0.2
OK	25	0.1
WI	22	0.1
SC	20	0.1
IN	17	0.1
AK	16	0.1
NH	10	0.1
AL	8	0
KT	8	0
ND	7	0
MN	5	0
CT	4	0
ME	4	0
IA	3	0
NM	3	0
TN	3	0
RI	2	0
HI	1	0
SD	1	0
WV	1	0
Total	19,036	100.0

(Malware Domain List, http://www.malwaredomainlist.com/)

Ponemon Institute Study: 2011 Cost of Data Breach Study: United States

Source: Ponemon Institute. "2011 Cost of Date Breach Study, United States." Sponsored by Symantec. March 2012. http://www.symantec.com/content/en/us/about/media/pdfs/b -ponemon-2011-cost-of-data-breach-us.en-us.pdf?om_ext_cid

=biz_socmed_twitter_facebook_marketwire_linkedin_2012Mar _worldwide__CODB_US. Used by permission of Ponemon Institute.

As discussed in previous chapters, hackers may attempt to steal sensitive data from businesses and governments with the ultimate goal of stealing money or reselling the data for profit. The scope of these offenses can be difficult to document due to concerns over the negative consequences that may result from reporting a business has been compromised (see Chapter 3; Furnell 2002; Newman and Clarke 2003). To address this gap in our knowledge, the Ponemon Institute has conducted research to address the number of data breaches and their costs to industry in the United States. Through interviews with more than 400 individuals in 268 institutions from 49 states in the United States, it has attempted to document the problem of data breaches across various industries.

The findings from the 2011 study suggest that the cost of data breaches declined in that year for the first time since 2005 (Figure 5.2). This figure is based on the average cost of each record compromised, suggesting that data loss is generally large. In fact, while the cost decreased from 2010 to 2011, this figure is still much higher than in 2005, when the average cost was $138. Thus the general costs of data breaches are still quite large.

Similarly, the average cost of data breaches within organizations declined from 2010 to 2011 from $7,240,000 to $5,500,000 per institution. This 24 percent decline suggests there have been organizational improvements in the response to data breaches, which the Ponemon Institute report attributes to a decrease in the number of records lost or stolen, as well as a decrease in customer turnover within each institution. At the same time, these figures are quite large and support the notion that corporations suffer massive losses from these attacks generally (see Figure 5.3).

The cost of data breaches, however, is not evenly distributed across industries. For instance, communications companies and financial institutions are much more heavily impacted by data

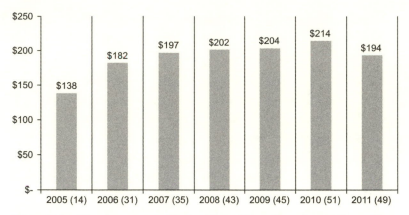

Figure 5.2   The Average per Capita Cost of Data Breach over Seven Years (Bracketed number defines the benchmark sample size. Ponemon Institute, "2011 Cost of Date Breach Study, United States." Sponsored by Symantec. March 2012. Available at: http://www.symantec.com/content/en/us/about/media/pdfs/b-ponemon-2011-cost-of-data-breach-us.en-us.pdf?om_ext_cid =biz_socmed_twitter_facebook_marketwire_linked

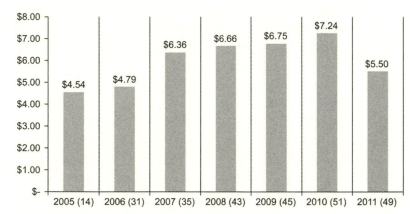

Figure 5.3   The Average Total Organizational Cost of Data Breach over Seven Years ($000,000 omitted. Ponemon Institute, "2011 Cost of Date Breach Study, United States." Sponsored by Symantec. March 2012. Available at: http://www.symantec.com/content/en/us/about/media/pdfs/b-ponemon -2011-cost-of-data-breach-us.en-us.pdf?om_ext_cid=biz_socmed_twitter_face book_marketwire_linkedin_2012Mar_worldwide__CODB_US.   Used   by permission of Ponemon Institute)

Figure 5.4 Per Capita Cost by Industry Classification of Benchmarked Companies (Ponemon Institute, "2011 Cost of Date Breach Study, United States." Sponsored by Symantec. March 2012. Available at: http://www .symantec.com/content/en/us/about/media/pdfs/b-ponemon-2011-cost-of-data-breach -us.en-us.pdf?om_ext_cid=biz_socmed_twitter_facebook_marketwire_linkedin _2012Mar_worldwide__CODB_US. Used by permission of Ponemon Institute)

breaches than are retailers and educational institutions. This may be a function of the type of data maintained across different industries. For instance, data thieves may obtain consumer account data in a breach against a financial institution, which can in turn be used to engage in fraudulent charges that must be reimbursed to the consumer. In addition, the institution may have to identify, close, and reissue accounts at no cost to the victim. Such activities may be more costly than the losses that an educational institution may experience if student information or data are acquired (see Figure 5.4).

Given the cost of breaches, it is valuable to understand the root cause of the data loss. Evidence from the Ponemon Institute study suggests that individual negligence (39%) and criminal actors (37%) are almost equal in their role in compromises. For instance, contractors and employees who lose laptops or sensitive data on

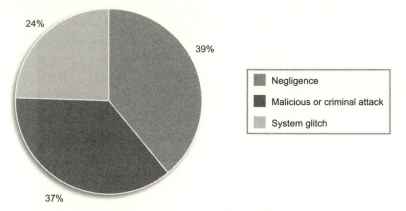

24%

39%

37%

- ■ Negligence
- ■ Malicious or criminal attack
- ▨ System glitch

Figure 5.5   Distribution of the Benchmark Sample by Root Cause of the Data Breach (Ponemon Institute, "2011 Cost of Date Breach Study, United States." Sponsored by Symantec. March 2012. Available at: http://www .symantec.com/content/en/us/about/media/pdfs/b-ponemon-2011-cost-of-data -breach-us.en-us.pdf?om_ext_cid=biz_socmed_twitter_facebook_market wire_linkedin_2012Mar_worldwide__CODB_US. Used by permission of Ponemon Institute)

flash drives play significant roles in the loss of data. However, criminal efforts to acquire information are also quite extensive, whether through the use of malware or hacking techniques (see Figure 5.5).

In light of the role of malicious and criminal attacks in data breaches, there is value in understanding the mechanisms of these attacks generally. Malware (50%) appears to be the key cause of most data breaches, with 18 companies experiencing this type of attack. Malware could take the form of a Trojan horse, worm, or virus that could be used to gather sensitive data. Criminal insiders were responsible for 33 percent of breaches in the Ponemon Institute report; such attacks could involve an employee who attempts to sell the data gathered or someone who steals the information due to a perceived grudge against the company. The use of other attack mechanisms, such as SQL injections (28%) or phishing attacks (22%), are also common, suggesting there is no one way that attackers may engage in breaches (see Figure 5.6).

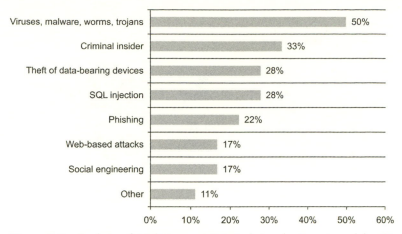

Figure 5.6 Analysis of Malicious or Criminal Attacks Experienced by 18 Companies (More than one attack type may exist for each company. Ponemon Institute, "2011 Cost of Date Breach Study, United States." Sponsored by Symantec. March 2012. Available at: http://www.symantec.com/content/en/us/about/media/pdfs/b-ponemon-2011-cost-of-data-breach-us.en-us.pdf ?om_ext_cid=biz_socmed_twitter_facebook_marketwire_linkedin_2012 Mar_worldwide__CODB_US. Used by permission of Ponemon Institute)

Symantec: Internet Security Threat Report 2011

Source: Symantec. "Internet Security Threat Report 2011 Trends, Volume 17." April 2012. http://www.symantec.com/content/en/us/enterprise/other_resources/b-istr_main_report _2011_21239364.en-us.pdf. Used by permission.

The various threats posed by hackers using different types of technologies make it difficult to understand the scope of attacks across the globe. One of the best sources of documentation of these threats is computer security companies that produce various protective products for personal and corporate entities, because they are on the cutting edge of emerging security threats. Symantec is thought to be one of the best sources for data in this area, due to its global size and operations in more than 40 countries across the world. This company produces an annual threat report based on data collected from various data sources across the globe.

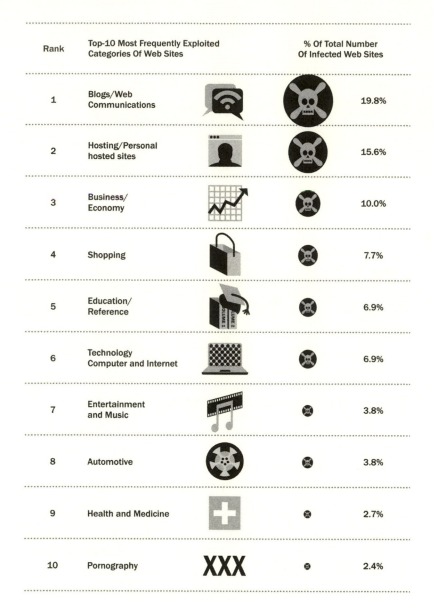

Rank	Top-10 Most Frequently Exploited Categories Of Web Sites		% Of Total Number Of Infected Web Sites
1	Blogs/Web Communications		19.8%
2	Hosting/Personal hosted sites		15.6%
3	Business/ Economy		10.0%
4	Shopping		7.7%
5	Education/ Reference		6.9%
6	Technology Computer and Internet		6.9%
7	Entertainment and Music		3.8%
8	Automotive		3.8%
9	Health and Medicine		2.7%
10	Pornography		2.4%

Figure 5.7 Most Dangerous Web Site Categories, 2011 (Symantec. "Internet Security Threat Report 2011 Trends, Vol 17." April 2012. (http://www.symantec.com/content/en/us/enterprise/other_resources/b-istr _main_report_2011_21239364.en-us.pdf). Used by permission)

Geography	2011 World Rank	2011 Malicious Code %	2010 World Rank	2010 Overall Average	Change
India	1	15.3%	2	12.6%	+2.7%
United States	2	13.3%	1	18.5%	-5.2%
Indonesia	3	8.0%	11	2.2%	+5.8%
China	4	5.1%	3	7.3%	-2.2%
United Kingdom	5	4.0%	5	3.3%	+0.7%
Vietnam	6	3.8%	12	1.9%	+1.9%
Egypt	7	3.4%	23	1.1%	+2.3%
Brazil	8	2.8%	4	3.4%	-0.6%
Russia	9	2.4%	10	2.3%	+0.1%
Bangladesh	10	2.3%	39	0.5%	+1.8%

Figure 5.8 Malicious Activity by Source: Malicious Code, 2010–2011 (Symantec. "Internet Security Threat Report 2011 Trends, Vol 17." April 2012. (http://www.symantec.com/content/en/us/enterprise/other_resources/b-istr_main_report_2011_21239364.en-us.pdf). Used by permission)

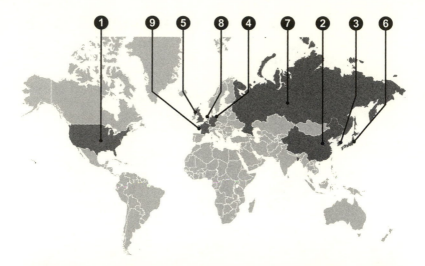

Geography	2011 Web Attacking Countries Rank	2011 Web Attacking Countries %	2010 Web Attacking Countries Rank	2010 Web Attacking Countries %	Change
United States	1	33.5%	3	7.6%	+26.0%
China	2	11.0%	1	66.9%	-55.8%
Korea, South	3	4.4%	2	12.6%	-8.2%
Germany	4	3.5%	8	0.6%	+3.0%
United Kingdom	5	2.3%	4	4.3%	-2.1%
Japan	6	2.2%	14	0.3%	+1.9%
Russia	7	2.1%	7	0.6%	+1.5%
Netherlands	8	2.0%	13	0.3%	+1.7%
France	9	1.4%	11	0.4%	+1.0%

Figure 5.9   Malicious Activity by Source: Web Attack Origins, 2010–2011 (Symantec. "Internet Security Threat Report 2011 Trends, Vol 17." April 2012. (http://www.symantec.com/content/en/us/enterprise/other_resources/ b-istr_main_report_2011_21239364.en-us.pdf). Used by permission)

One of Symantec's most critical measures relates to malware use and functionality. Its Norton Safe Web data indicate that 61 percent of sites with malware are otherwise legitimate websites that have been compromised by hackers and now host an infection. Although pornography websites are often thought to host malware, they actually represent a small proportion (2.4%) of infected sites, relative to blogs (19.8%) and personal websites (15.6%); these rates appear sensible given the dramatic increase in the use of the latter spaces by individuals. In fact, in the 2011 Symantec report, one in every 156 websites was found to contain malware based on the company's active threat scans. Many of these attacks are driven by exploit packs, or tools that contain multiple vulnerabilities that can be used to exploit computers that visit the site at any given point in time (see Figure 5.7).

The problem of malware can also be separated by country, in much the same way as the MDL data presented earlier. Symantec's data identify the geographic origin of an attack based on the source information reported to Symantec by consumers or researchers. The findings of its study support some aspects of the MDL data, particularly concerning the role of the United States in malicious code production overall. It is interesting to note, however, that India is ranked higher in terms of malicious code production, as are Indonesia, China, and the United Kingdom, relative to the MDL data source (see Figure 5.8).

Symantec's quoted rates for web attacks, are however, quite similar to those in the MDL data. Specifically, the United States and China have the highest rates of web attacks, in keeping with those rates from the self-report data provided by the Malware Domain List (see Figure 5.9).

In addition, botnet hosting appears to be differentially distributed across the globe. The United States has the highest rate of botnets, followed by Taiwan, Brazil, Italy, and Germany. This finding may be a reflection of the very large population of Internet users in the nations (see Figure 5.10).

The threat posed by malware requires researchers to identify the vulnerabilities that may be used to compromise a system. Symantec found 4,989 new vulnerabilities in 2011, which represented a decrease from 6,253 vulnerabilities in 2010. Many of these were vulnerabilities in Microsoft Windows

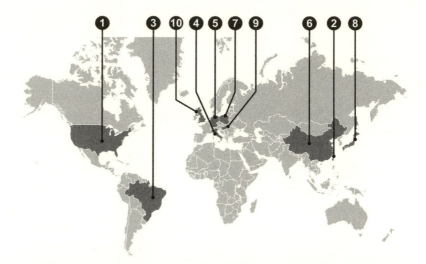

Geography	2011 Bots Rank	2011 Bots %	2010 Bots Rank	2010 Bots %	Change
United States	1	12.6%	1	13.9%	-1.3%
Taiwan	2	11.4%	3	7.8%	+3.6%
Brazil	3	8.9%	5	6.8%	+2.1%
Italy	4	8.3%	4	7.3%	+0.9%
Germany	5	7.0%	2	9.8%	-2.9%
China	6	6.6%	6	5.8%	+0.7%
Poland	7	5.4%	8	3.9%	+1.5%
Japan	8	4.6%	9	3.5%	+1.1%
Hungary	9	4.3%	11	3.1%	+1.3%
United Kingdom	10	4.3%	7	5.6%	-1.4%

Figure 5.10   Malicious Activity by Source: Bots, 2010–2011 (Symantec. "Internet Security Threat Report 2011 Trends, Vol 17." April 2012. (http://www.symantec.com/content/en/us/enterprise/other_resources/b-istr _main_report_2011_21239364.en-us.pdf). Used by permission)

products—most notably, the Microsoft Windows RPC component, which was used in more than 61 million attacks in 2011 alone. Web browser vulnerabilities were also identified in

Figure 5.11   Total Number of Vulnerabilities Identified, 2006–2011 (Symantec. "Internet Security Threat Report 2011 Trends, Vol 17." April 2012. (http://www.symantec.com/content/en/us/enterprise/other _resources/b-istr_main_report_2011_21239364.en-us.pdf). Used by permission)

Chrome, Firefox, and Internet Explorer, although they accounted for only 351 total exploits for the year (see Figure 5.11).

In 2011, spam emails accounted for 75.1 percent of all emails sent, which was a decrease from 88.5 percent in 2010. This small decline still clearly demonstrates the magnitude of the problem of spam mail, which can be used to engage in a variety of cyber-crimes. In fact, on average, 42 billion messages were sent every day, compared to 61.6 billion in 2010. Most of this spam is attributed to botnet operators, who utilize their infrastructure to send these messages. Specifically, the takedown of botnet command and control servers by U.S. law enforcement on March 16 and 17, 2011, led to a drop in spam volume from 51 million messages a day to 31.7 billion in the week immediately following the federal action (see Figure 5.12).

In addition, the overwhelming majority of the messages sent involved pharmaceuticals in some fashion. Many of these messages advertised online pharmacies that sold counterfeit products or that linked the user to malware sites. Counterfeit product spam was also common, advertising watches, jewelry, and other products. A proportion of the messages also advertised sexual services, dating sites, and casinos. Most all of these messages were in English, which is thought to be the easiest way to lure in prospective victims (see Figure 5.13).

A Closer Look at Corporate and Governmental Data Theft on a Global Basis: The 2012 Verizon Data Breach Investigations Report

Source: Verizon. 2012 Data Breach Investigations Report and Executive Summary. 2012. http://www.verizonbusiness.com/ resources/reports/rp_data-breach-investigations-report-2012_en _xg.pdf. Accessed October 3, 2012. Used by permission.

The On-Land and Online Real-World Context

In Chapters 1 and 2, we looked at the concerns of both American and Canadian systems security professionals regarding feared and real hacking threats directed toward company and government agency networks. Let us turn our attention now to the data on real breaches obtained by Verizon from a

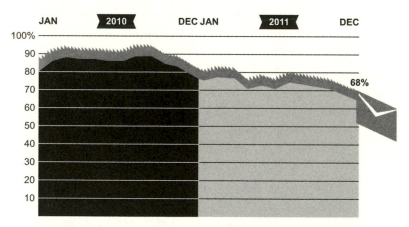

Figure 5.12   Percentage of Email Identified as Spam, 2011 (Symantec. "Internet Security Threat Report 2011 Trends, Vol 17." April 2012. (http://www.symantec.com/content/en/us/enterprise/other_resources/b-istr _main_report_2011_21239364.en-us.pdf). Used by permission)

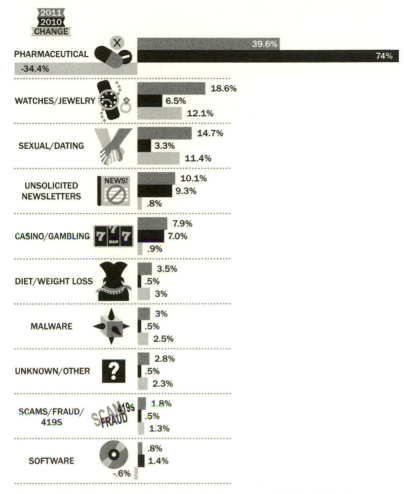

Figure 5.13 Top Ten Spam Email Categories, 2010–2011 (Symantec. "Internet Security Threat Report 2011 Trends, Vol 17." April 2012. (http://www.symantec.com/content/en/us/enterprise/other_resources/b-istr _main_report_2011_21239364.en-us.pdf). Used by permission)

study completed by the Verizon RISK Team, in partnership with the Australian Federal Police, the Dutch National High Tech Crime Unit, the Irish Reporting and Information Security Service, the Police Central e-Crime Unit, and the U.S. Secret Service. These interesting multinational findings constitute Verizon's *2012 Data Breach Investigations Report* (DBIR). But before getting into the details of this report, we must provide some real-world context for its findings.

Earlier, we talked about the very interesting cybertimes of 2011 and 2012—a period of on-land and online cultural uprisings, government overthrows (dubbed the "Arab Spring"), and online hacktivism by groups such as Anonymous. The police sweep of 25 alleged Anonymous hackers occurred at the start of 2012, with Interpol admitting that the arrests occurred in Europe and South America as a result of Interpol's Latin American Working Group of Experts on Information Technology Crime (Keller 2012). While certainly these on-land and online protests had elements of idealistic political statements and involved hacking techniques such as distributed denial-of-service attacks, network administrators found themselves staying awake at night because beyond the stated online political motives, these breaches may have resulted in the theft of proprietary industry data or personal information of selected targets.

Add to these events the recent noise resulting from the work of Julian Paul Assange, the founder and editor-in-chief of the whistleblowing website WikiLeaks. In 2006, Assange founded WikiLeaks to provide, as he said, an outlet to cause regime change and open information sharing to expose injustice and abuses of power. Although the WikiLeaks site has published materials related to the Church of Scientology, the U.S. Guantanamo Bay military base operations, military strikes, and classified documents around the world, it is perhaps most famous for the acquisition and publication of 251,000 American diplomatic cables that ranged from unclassified to secret documents. In 2010, this information was obtained by a U.S. Army soldier named Bradley Manning, who downloaded the materials while stationed in Iraq. He then provided the materials to Assange at WikiLeaks, who chose to release these materials in batches over two years with the cooperation of major news outlets such as *The New York Times* and *Der Spiegel*.

Since his arrest in Iraq in 2010, Manning has been sitting in a military jail cell. In July 2012, the U.S. government maintained in a military court in Maryland that it had proof that Manning knowingly passed state secrets to a location where the information was definitely bound to be obtained by enemy groups. Captain Joe Morrow, a member of the five-member prosecution team, said that the U.S. government would release data at court martial showing that Manning had knowingly "aided the enemy [Al-Qaida?]"—definitely the worst of the 22 charges that he faced. If Manning is found guilty of this charge, he faces the death penalty. Morrow said that the evidence would show that this soldier sent the information to "a very definite place" that he knew was the enemy (Pilkington 2012).

Besides such colorful events with considerable media coverage, 2011–2012 featured some high-volume, lower-risk hacks against selected targets. Also, there were continued hack attacks aimed at confiscating companies' trade secrets and classified proprietary information.

The Report's Main Findings

So what did those surveyed in the 2012 DBIR perceive to be the primary cyberissues of concern for that year and for the coming years? To begin, there were 855 incidents reported by the multicountry survey participants, involving 174 million compromised records, the second-highest data loss reported since Verizon began keeping track of such losses in 2004. These results were based on first-hand evidence collected during paid external forensic investigations conducted by Verizon from 2004 to 2011. The U.S. Secret Service, the Dutch National High Tech Crime Unit, the Australian Federal Police, the Irish Reporting and Information Security Service, and the Police Central e-Crime Unit of the London Metropolitan Police shared the same approach of citing first-hand evidence. All participants used VERIS as the common foundation; this framework was developed to create a common language for describing security incidents in a structured and repeatable means. It basically transforms the "who did what to what (or whom) with what result" into data that are readily digestible (Verizon 2012).

The findings in Table 5.5 are very interesting. In terms of real-world corporate hacking incidents on a global basis, outsider hackers were more dominant than insider hackers during 2011–2012, with their activities up 6 percent from the previous year. These outsider perpetrators reportedly included organized criminals as well as activist groups such as Anonymous. While the usual greed motives were commonplace, ideological dissent emerged as an important motive for 2011–2012. Indeed, relative to outsider hacks, insider hacks were less frequent, and less than 1 percent of the hack attacks were reportedly caused by business partners. Importantly, about 58 percent of all data theft seemed to be related to activist groups.

As shown in Table 5.5, it is also apparent that hacking and malware (the "hows") were up by 20 to 30 percent from the previous year, with hacking tied to nearly all of the compromised records. Given that most attacks were made by outsiders, this finding makes sense. Only about 10 percent of the breaches involved physical attacks (down by 19% from the previous year), only about 7 percent utilized social tactics (down 4% from the previous year), and only about 5 percent of the breaches resulted from misusing one's privileges (down 12% from the previous year). While in 2011–2012 many attacks circumvented authentication by combining stolen or guessed credentials to gain access

Table 5.5   The Who and How behind the Reported Data Breaches

Who			How		
Outsiders	98%	+6%	Some hacking	81%	+31%
Insiders	4%	−13%	Used malware	69%	+20%

(Verizon, 2012 Data Breach Investigations Report and Executive Summary, (2012), http://www.verizonbusiness.com/resources/reports/rp_data-breach-investigations-report-2012_en_xg.pdf (accessed October 3, 2012). Used by permission)

to the network with backdoors that allowed the attackers to retain access, there were fewer reported ATM and gas-pump skimming cases compared to the previous year.

Furthermore, Figure 5.14 indicates the kinds of commonalities that existed for 2010–2011 and 2011–2012. The findings show that target selection was based more on opportunity (i.e., network vulnerabilities discovered) than on a specific choice of target. Moreover, whether targeted or not, the bulk of victims were harmed by attacks that were not highly difficult or sophisticated; in fact, the more sophisticated attacks were reported to be found in later stages of the attack, after access was gained. Accepting this fact, most breaches appear to have been avoidable without complex or expensive countermeasures. As is typical, incidents were found by third parties and not the victims themselves—often, unfortunately, weeks or months after access to the network occurred. Finally, it must be emphasized that most of these points actually worsened in 2011–2012, relative to the previous year. Figure 5.14 shows the commonalities in breaches for the current year relative to the previous year.

Table 5.6 shows the different kinds of mitigation efforts employed by smaller and larger organizations, respectively. These findings should remind IT professionals that they have the necessary tools to prevent unwanted hack attacks if the

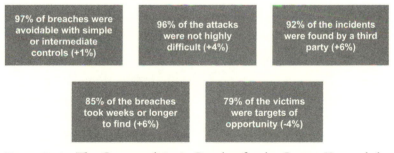

Figure 5.14 The Commonalities in Breaches for the Current Year and the Previous Year (Verizon, 2012 Data Breach Investigations Report and Executive Summary, (2012), http://www.verizonbusiness.com/resources/reports/rp_data -breach-investigations-report-2012_en_xg.pdf [accessed October 3, 2012]. Used by permission)

Table 5.6 Mitigation Efforts for Smaller and Larger Organizations

Smaller Organizations
Implement a firewall or appropriate countermeasures on remote access services.
Change default credentials of point-of-sale (POS) systems and other Internet-facing devices.
If third parties are taking care of the previously mentioned two efforts, validate these efforts to ensure prevention of future problems.
Larger Organizations
Get rid of unnecessary data and secure the remainder.
Make sure that essential controls are met and regularly check that they stay that way. Be sure to monitor and mine event logs to notice odd traffic.
Assess your threat landscape and then plan and prioritize a sound treatment strategy.

(Verizon, 2012 Data Breach Investigations Report and Executive Summary, [2012], http://www.verizonbusiness.com/resources/reports/rp_data-breach-investigations -report-2012_en_xg.pdf (accessed October 3, 2012). Used by permission)

proper precautions are implemented. The challenge for the White Hats, it seems, lies in selecting the right tools to secure the network and keeping them up-to-date so that the tools remain effective. Even when this positive set of events is enforced, however, the Black Hats are ready to tread into vulnerable waters. Because smaller and larger organizations need to implement different strategies for securing their systems, it is important to realize that larger organizations have a more diverse set of issues that must be addressed through a unique set of corrective actions.

Report Conclusions

The authors of the Verizon report concluded that many of the organizations that contributed to the report are likely not receiving the message about their security and effective countermeasures implementation. Particularly vulnerable are the smaller organizations. Problems affecting larger organizations are different in a multitude of ways from those plaguing smaller businesses. The top threats facing larger organizations include the following (Verizon 2012):

- Keyloggers and the use of stolen credentials
- Backdoors and command control
- Tampering
- Pre-texting
- Phishing
- Brute-force SQL injection

References

Anti-Phishing Working Group (APWG). "Phishing Activity Trends Report, 2nd Quarter 2012." 2012. http://docs.apwg .org/reports/apwg_trends_report_q2_2012.pdf. Accessed October 12, 2012.

Brenner, S. W. *Cyberthreats: The Emerging Fault Lines of the Nation State.* New York: Oxford University Press, 2008.

Central Intelligence Agency (CIA). *The World Factbook 2011.* Washington, DC: Central Intelligence Agency, 2011. https://www.cia.gov/library/publications/the-world -factbook/index.html. Accessed January 13, 2012.

Furnell, Steven. *Cybercrime: Vandalizing the Information Society.* Boston, MA: Addison Wesley, 2002.

Keller, G. "Police Sweep Nets 25 Alleged Anonymous Hackers." *The Globe and Mail,* February 29, 2012, p. A14.

Malware Domain List. 2012. http://www.mdl.org. Accessed May 1, 2012.

Mitnick, K. D., and W. L. Simon. *The Art of Deception: Controlling the Human Element Of Security.* New York: Wiley, 2002.

Newman, Grame, and Ronald Clarke. *Superhighway Robbery: Preventing E-Commerce Crime.* Cullompton: Willan Press, 2003.

Pilkington, E. "US Government Claims It Has Proof of Bradley Manning Aiding the Enemy. *Guardian,* 2012.

http://www.guardian.co.uk/world/2012/jul/16/bradley
-manning-aiding-the-enemy. Accessed July 21, 2012.

Ponemon Institute. "2011 Cost of Data Breach Study." 2012,
http://www.symantec.com/content/en/us/about/media/
pdfs/b-ponemon-2011-cost-of-data-breach-us.en-us.pdf?om
_ext_cid=biz_socmed_twitter_facebook_marketwire
_linkedin_2012Mar_worldwide__CODB_US. Accessed
September 15, 2012.

Symantec, "Internet Security Threat Report, Volume 17."
2012. http://www.symantec.com/content/en/us/enterprise/
other_resources/b-istr_main_report_2011_21239364.en
-us.pdf. Accessed September 25, 2012.

Verizon. "2012 Data Breach Investigations Report and
Executive Summary." 2012. http://www.verizonbusiness.
com/resources/reports/rp_data-breach-investigations-report
-2012_en_xg.pdf. Accessed October 3, 2012.

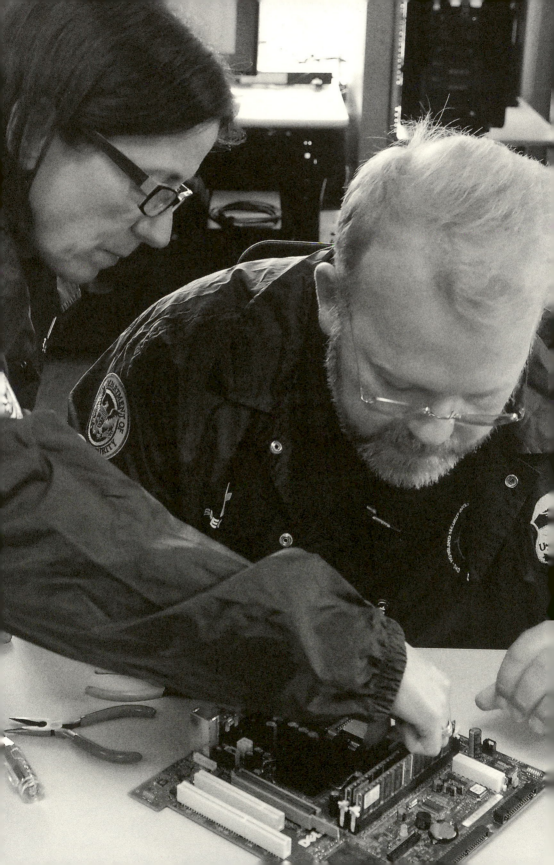

This chapter focuses on print and nonprint resources on hackers, hacking, and related topics. In the print section are IT security and various hacking books, magazines, and websites having downloadable news stories and white papers on a wide range of relevant topics. In the nonprint section are websites dealing with hacking per se; various films and videos on hackers and hacking; websites of companies offering antivirus software, firewalls, and intrusion detection systems; and government and independent agencies involved with tracking and curbing malicious hack attacks.

In addition, the U.S. Department of Justice's Computer Crime and Intellectual Property Section (CCIPS) has an email service that provides updates on various forms of computer crimes. To receive updates and to be added to the email distribution list, readers can send a message to http://www.justice.gov/govdelivery/subscribe.html?code=USDOJ.

Employees of the U.S. Immigration and Customs Enforcement's Homeland Security Investigations work in a new state-of-the-art computer forensics laboratory in Boston on October 12, 2011. The facility assists federal, state and local law enforcement authorities in New England with a wide range of forensic investigative support. (Department of Defense)

Furthermore, the CCIPS website (www.usdoj.gov/criminal/ cybercrime/index.html) has links to the following:

- Press releases from 1999 to the present (including the September 17, 2012, press release entitled "Two Romanian Nationals Plead Guilty to Participating in Multimillion Dollar Scheme to Remotely Hack into and Steal Payment Card Data from Hundreds of US Merchants' Companies")
- Manuals and reports related to computer crimes (including the *Prosecuting Computer Crimes* manual, the *Searching and Seizing Computers and Obtaining Electronic Evidence in Criminal Investigations* manual, the *Prosecuting Intellectual Property Crimes* manual, and the *Digital Forensic Analysis Methodology Flowchart* manual), as well as reports dealing with intellectual property protection
- A summary of important criminal cases (including cyber-crimes and white-collar crimes) at http://www.justice.gov/ publications/case-highlights.html
- Information on how to report Internet-related crime, including hacking and breaching intellectual property crimes

Print: Books

Arguilla, J., and D. F. Ronfeldt. *Networks and Netwars: The Future of Terror, Crime, and Militancy*. Santa Monica, CA: Rand, 2001.

This interesting book describes emerging forms of cyberconflict using the Internet. Among other topics, the book discusses netwars (conflicts involving terrorists, criminals, gangs, and ethic extremists) and various ways of coping with them.

Beaver, K. *Hacking for Dummies,* 3rd ed. New York, NY: Wiley, 2010.

This book is a good foundational one for understanding malicious hacking. Preventive measures are outlined with easy-to-understand descriptions. This book also explains ethical hacking and why it is useful in today's virtual world. The book includes a lot of useful details on web application hacking, mobile hacking, and VoIP hacking.

Berkowitz, B. D. *The New Face of War: How War Will Be Fought in the 21st Century*. New York, NY: Simon and Schuster, 2003.

This book discusses the emerging types of information wars, details on how they have revolutionized combat using the Internet, and explains how a war against cyber-terrorists could be waged.

Blane, J. V. *Cybercrime and Cyberterrorism: Current Issues*. Comack, NY: Nova Science, 2003.

This book provides an interesting approach to better understanding modern cybercrimes and various forms of cyberterrorism. It also differentiates between these two concepts.

Blunden, B. *The Rootkit Arsenal: Escape and Evasion in the Dark Corners of the System,* 2nd ed. Burlington, MA: Jones & Bartlett Learning, 2012.

This book presents comprehensive and up-to-date coverage of forensic countermeasures for network exploits. Topics include designing and deploying covert channels and ways of discovering new hack attacks.

Bright, P., N. Anderson, J. Chang, E. Bangeman, and A. Lawson. *Unmasked*. Seattle, WA: US Amazon Digital Services, Inc., 2011.

The team from ArsTechnica chronicle the Anonymous/ HB Gary saga—that is, the real-life events that unfolded after the ArsTechnica network was cracked by the Anonymous hacker cell. This e-book also details the various items and issues of interest to Anonymous that seem to motivate the group's hack attacks on government agencies and high-profile companies.

Buyya, R., J. Broberg, and A. Goscinski. *Cloud Computing: Principles and Paradigms*. New York, NY: Wiley, 2011.

This book is meant to be used by professionals and IT and business graduate students interested in having a solid grasp of the principles underlying cloud computing. It also cites research topics that relate to cloud computing.

Carvey, H. *Windows Forensics and Incident Response*. Reading, MA: Addison-Wesley Professional, 2004.

As long as Microsoft Windows systems are used by people, notes Harlan Carvey, security incidents are bound to occur. For this reason, Carvey—himself a Windows security instructor—felt compelled to write this book. Having designed his own two-day course in Windows incident response and forensic investigations, the author shares his extensive knowledge on recognizing and appropriately responding to hack attacks on Windows systems. Although the audience for this book is intended to be Windows system administrators, this book is written in easy-to-digest English. A bonus is the CD that is included; it contains numerous tools such as PERL scripts.

Casey, E. *Digital Evidence and Computer Crimes*. San Diego, CA: Academic, 2000.

This book details the law as it applies to computer networks. It also describes how evidence stored on or transmitted by computers can play a role in a wide range of crimes—including homicide, child abuse, stalking and harassment, fraud, theft, and terrorism.

Chick, D. *Steel Bolt Hacking*. TheNetworkAdministrator.com, 2004.

A best-seller upon its release, this book details the many ways and means of lockpicking, a favorite topic at hacking conventions such as DefCon and HOPE. The author has written a number of hacking-related books. He is a man of many talents: an author, computer network engineer, and entrepreneur who created TheNetworkAdministrator.com. Chick invites would-be authors with excellent ideas on hacking countermeasures to contact him for a possible book contract.

Chiesa, R., S. Ducci, and S. Ciappi. *Profiling Hackers: The Science of Criminal Profiling as Applied to the World of Hacking*. New York: Auerbach Publications, 2008.

> This book is written for a nontechnical audience and applies criminological and psychological theories to develop profiles of the hacker community with an international sample of hackers. The work is intended to provide a fundamental understanding of the behavioral and attitudinal characteristics of hackers.

Chirillo, J. *Hack Attacks Encyclopedia: A Complete History of Hacks, Phreaks, and Spies over Time*. New York, NY: Wiley, 2001.

> Written by a security expert, this book covers historic texts, program files, code snippets, hacking and security tools, and a series of more advanced topics on password programs, sniffers, spoofers, and flooders.

Clifford, R. D. *Cybercrime: The Investigation, Prosecution, and Defense of a Computer-Related Crime*. Durham, NC: Carolina Academic, 2001.

> Intended primarily for a legal audience, this book covers topics such as which conduct is considered to be a cybercrime, investigating improper kinds of cyberconduct such as malicious hacking, trying a cybercrime case as a prosecuting or defending attorney, and handling the international aspects of cybercrimes.

Cole, E., and J. Riley. *Hackers Beware: The Ultimate Guide to Network Security*. Upper Saddle River, NJ: Pearson Education, 2001.

> This book is written by experts in IT security and is intended for network security professionals. It describes UNIX and Microsoft NT vulnerabilities; protections against network intrusions; and trends and critical thoughts regarding system administration, networking, and IT security.

Davidoff, S., and J. Ham. *Network Forensics: Tracking Hackers through Cyberspace.* Upper Saddle River, NJ: Prentice Hall, 2012.

This book provides a nice foundation and roadmap for those trying to get the gist of cloud computing, advantages for businesses that move to the cloud, and concerns about IT security in the cloud. The book details the various kinds of "footprints" that hackers leave when they exploit networks.

Engebretson, P. *The Basics of Hacking and Penetration Testing: Ethical Hacking and Penetration Testing Made Easy.* Rockland, MA: Syngress Publishing, 2011.

This book provides the basics for completing a penetration test for conducting ethical hacks using such available tools as Metasploit, Whois, Google, Backtrack Linux, and Nmap. Written by an experienced penetration tester, the book takes a hands-on approach to conducting penetration testing.

Erikson, J. *Hacking: The Art of Exploitation*, 2nd ed. San Francisco, CA: No Starch Press, 2008.

Written by a hacker who believes in the power of creative hacking, this book explains how hacking techniques work. Included are basics on C programming, Linux programming, assembly language, and shell scripts. The book's hands-on approach covers such important topics as buffer overflows, bypassing protections, cracking wireless devices, and high-jacking network communications.

Furnell, S. *Cybercrime: Vandalizing the Information Society.* Reading, MA: Addison-Wesley, 2001.

Written by a British computer security expert, this book gives a thorough overview of cracking, viral code, and electronic fraud. It covers a wide range of crimes and abuses related to IT. Unlike many other hacking books on the market, this one does not require advanced technological knowledge to understand the bulk of the material covered.

Garfinkel, S., G. Spafford, and D. Russell, and A. Schwartz. *Practical Unix and Internet Security*. Sebastopol, CA: O'Reilly Media, 2003.

This is a great book covering a wide range of topics related to network security. This third edition has been revised to give network security administrators current tips and techniques for ensuring information security in business practices.

Goldstein, E. *The Best of 2600: Collector's Edition: A Hacker Odyssey*. New York, NY: Wiley, 2009.

A top seller among hackers themselves, this 912-page volume is packed with real-life hacking events and exploits written by hackers. In this large book, Emmanuel Goldstein (whose real-life name is Eric Corley) gives brilliant insights into the hacker culture and presents a series of controversial articles that depict IT security milestones and the evolution of technology over the past 25 years. As a bonus, a CD-ROM featuring some hit episodes of Goldstein's "Off the Hook" *2600* radio shows is included in the collector's edition.

Goodman, S. F., and A. D. Sofaer. *The Transnational Dimension of Cybercrime and Terrorism*. Prague: Hoover Institute, 2001.

Unlike maps showing the boundaries of countries around the globe, the Internet has no virtual boundaries. Thus this interesting book, intended for a more advanced audience, covers the important topics of transnational cybercrime and cyberterrorism.

Greenberg, A. *This Machine Kills Secrets: How WikiLeakers, Cypherpunks, and Hacktivists Aim to Free the World's Information*. Boston, MA: Dutton Adult, 2012.

This book presents the code and the characters dominating the virtual worlds of WikiLeakers, cypherpunks, and hacktivists—who are allegedly motivated by their desire to expose the well-hidden secrets of governments and industry. This novel book will appeal to both beginners and advanced experts in IT security.

Gunkel, D. J. *Hacking Cyberspace*. Boulder, CO: Westview Press, 2000.

The author, writing for an advanced audience, examines the metaphors of new technology and considers how these metaphors impact the implementation of information technology in today's world. This book combines philosophy, communication theory, and computer history to cover the topic in an innovative way.

Hadnagy, C. *Social Engineering: The Art of Human Hacking*. New York, NY: Wiley, 2010.

This books covers a lot of interesting topics related to social engineering, such as the psychological principles used and abused by hackers, steps to complete a successful social engineering exploit, and ways to capitalize on cracking cameras, GPS devices, and caller IDs for ensuring a successful hack attack.

Halpert, B. *Auditing Cloud Computing*. New York, NY: Wiley, 2011.

This book gives excellent advice to readers on the aspects involved in doing an audit for cloud computing. This book is ideal for IT security experts and auditors wanting more technical information on cloud computing.

Harper, A., S. Harris, and J. Ness. *Gray Hat Hacking: The Ethical Hackers Handbook,* 3rd ed. New York, NY: McGraw-Hill, 2011.

This book, written by experts in the field, provides useful and practical techniques for discovering and repairing security flaws. It also outlines legal disclosure methods. Penetration testing, malware, SCADA attacks, web security, social engineering, and Metasploit usage are just a few of the important topics detailed in this book.

Himanen, P., M. Castells, and L. Torvalds. *The Hacker Ethic and the Spirit of the Information Age.* New York, NY: Random House, 2001.

This is one of a few books focusing on White Hat hacking, including its values and beliefs. The underlying theme of this book is that individuals can create great things by joining forces and using information and the Internet in imaginative ways.

Hoglund, G., and J. Butler. *Rootkits: Subverting the Windows Kernel.* Addison-Wesley Professional, 2006.

The first chapter starts off with key elements in software attacks. The remaining chapters detail how rootkits work and what computer users can do to detect them or prevent them from operating on computer networks. If topics like kernel hooks, DKOM, and process hiding are of interest to you, this best-selling book is a must-read.

Holt, T. J., and B. H. Schell. *Corporate Hacking and Technology-Driven Crime: Social Dynamics and Implications.* Hershey, PA: Information Science Reference, 2011.

This book presents a series of refereed chapters on important corporate hacking issues. Experts in the field have contributed a variety of views on control systems security, the social dynamics and the future of technology-driven crime, comparisons between hackers and white-collar criminals, and the language of carders.

Howard, M., and D. E. LeBlanc. *Writing Secure Code,* 2nd ed. Redmond, WA: Microsoft Press, 2002.

Drawing on the lessons learned at Microsoft during the 2002 Windows security push, the authors offer a three-pronged strategy for securing design, defaults, and deployment of code. This book is rather advanced and is intended for experts in the programming field.

Khan, J., and A. Khwaja. *Building Secure Wireless Networks with 802.11*. New York, NY: Wiley, 2003.

> Written by two Wi-Fi experts, this book provides a ton of knowledge to help home users and system administrators secure wireless networks.

Klevinsky, T. J., A. K. Gupta, and S. Laliberte. *Hack IT: Security through Penetration Testing*. Upper Saddle River, NJ: Pearson Education, 2002.

> This book introduces the complex topic of penetration testing and cites its vital role in network security. Written for professionals, the book discusses hacking myths, potential drawbacks of penetration testing, war dialing, social engineering methods, sniffers and password crackers, and firewalls and intrusion detection systems.

Komar, B., J. Wettern, and R. Beekelaar. *Firewalls for Dummies*. New York, NJ: Wiley, 2003.

> This book presents key facts about firewalls to assist businesses and individuals wanting to protect their computer systems against hack attacks. The book is quite easy to understand, even though it was written by computer security experts.

Levy, S. *Hackers: Heroes of the Computer Revolution*. New York, NY: Penguin, 2001.

> A classic, this book was written for young people to inform them about the importance of MIT's Tech Model Railroad Club as a key pioneering effort in hacking history. This is where the White Hat hackers had their critical beginnings.

Lilley, P. *Hacked, Attacked, and Abused: Digital Crime Exposed*. London, England: Kogan Page Limited, 2003.

> This book gives practical advice to business people about how they can protect their networks against intrusions by Black Hats. The book covers topics such as organized digital

crime, website defacement, cyberlaundering, fraudulent Internet sites, viruses, identity theft, information warfare, denial of service attacks, and digital privacy.

Littman, J. *The Fugitive Game: Online with Kevin Mitnick.* Boston, MA: Little, Brown and Company, 1997.

> A great book to accompany the reading of *Ghost in the Wires,* this book details the online pranks of convicted cracker Kevin Mitnick. It is an exciting read, as it provides interviews with Mitnick while he was on the run from the FBI. Mitnick's views on the power of social engineering are especially insightful.

Littman, J. *The Watchman: The Twisted Life and Times of Serial Hacker Kevin Poulsen.* Boston, MA: Little, Brown and Company, 1997.

> This book covers the interesting exploits of former hacker and now writer Kevin Poulsen, the first man in the United States accused of carrying out espionage using a computer. By ensuring that he was the 101st caller into radio stations in the United States, Poulsen accrued two Porsches and more than $22,000 in cash. A very interesting read, indeed.

Loader, B., and T. Douglas. *Cybercrime: Security and Surveillance in the Information Age.* New York, NY: Routledge, 2000.

> These authors focus on the growing concern over the use of electronic communications for criminal activities and the appropriateness of countermeasures used to combat various forms of cybercrime. The wide range of topics includes the legal, psychological, and sociological aspects of cybercrime.

Maiwald, E. *Network Security: A Beginner's Guide.* New York, NY: McGraw-Hill, 2001.

> Despite its neophyte-focused title, this book was actually written for network administrators interested in securing their networks. Topics include antivirus software, firewalls, and intrusion detections.

McClure, S., J. Scambray, and G. Kurtz. *Hacking Exposed: Network Security Secrets and Solutions,* 6th ed. New York, NY: McGraw-Hill, 2009.

> This very popular book discusses a practical approach to network security and presents an extensive catalog of the weaponry that Black Hats utilize. Detailed explanations of concepts such as war dialing and rootkits are presented. There is also a comprehensive discussion of how to use the more powerful and popular hacking software. The language and concepts are advanced and are intended for experts such as system administrators. The authors also talk about how to locate and patch system vulnerabilities, wireless and RFID attacks, Web 2.0 vulnerabilities, and anonymous hacking tools.

McClure, S., S. Shah, and S. Shah. *Web Hacking: Attacks and Defense.* Upper Saddle River, NJ: Pearson, 2002.

> This book gives insights into what can happen when system vulnerabilities go unattended and unrepaired. It provides a useful guide to web security.

Meinel, C. P. *The Happy Hacker.* 4th ed. Tucson, AZ: American Eagle, 2001.

> This book is part of a series of hacker books written by self-proclaimed female hacker Carolyn Meinel. The basic theme in all of her books is that hacking is fun but cracking is not. This book is especially useful for neophytes interested in hacking.

Meinel, C. P. *Uberhacker II: More Ways to Break into a Computer,* 2nd ed. Port Townsend, WA: Loompanics Unlimited, 2003.

> This book discusses the weaknesses found in UNIX, Linux, and Windows, as well as various means for protecting against such intrusions. It is written in straightforward and easy-to-comprehend language.

Melnichuk, D. *The Hacker's Underground Handbook: Learn How to Hack and What It Takes to Crack Even the Most Secure Systems!* CreateSpace, 2010.

This book is perfect for hacking beginners because it talks about hacking concepts in a detailed and explicit manner and presents numerous examples to inspire readers to contemplate a career in White Hat hacking. Having been a hacker for many years, the author also runs a hacking blog and podcast at www.MrCracker.com.

Menn, J. *Fatal System Error: The Hunt for the New Crime Lords Who Are Bringing down the Internet.* New York, NY: Public Affairs, 2010.

This book focuses on the need for White Hats who can safeguard the Internet from the Black Hats. The book discusses the efforts of Barrett Lyon, an IT security guru, and Andy Crocker, a British policeman, who collaborate to find crackers who introduce worms and viruses on the Internet and who launch denial-of-service attacks on the networks of targeted companies and government agencies.

Miller, C., and D. Dai Zovi. *The Mac Hacker's Handbook.* New York, NY: Wiley, 2009.

This book gives detailed information on the steps hackers would take to exploit Mac OS X. Tips for securing Mac OS X are also given, along with the tools that are required for discovering vulnerabilities.

Miller, D., S. Harris, and A. Harper. *Security Information and Event Management (SIEM) Implementation.* New York, NY: McGraw-Hill, 2010.

Written by IT security experts, this book gives important pointers on how to identify, monitor, document, and effectively deal with network security threats. It also explains how SIEM can be effectively implemented using various products available on the market from a variety of vendors. Real-world case studies are detailed, as well as how best to utilize SIEM capabilities for business intelligence.

Mitnick, K., and W. L. Simon. *The Art of Deception: Controlling the Human Element of Security.* New York, NY: Wiley, 2002.

In this book, written by ex-convict Kevin Mitnick (whose hacking exploits put him behind prison bars a number of times), Mitnick pairs up with writer William Simon to give readers important tips about securing business computer networks and honing one's own expertise in social engineering.

Mitnick, K., and W. L. Simon. *The Art of Intrusion: The Real Stories behind the Exploits of Hackers, Intruders, and Deceivers.* New York, NY: Wiley, 2005.

This fascinating book details some interesting hacking exploits of individuals bilking Las Vegas casinos out of millions of dollars, hackers who have joined terrorist groups such as Al-Qaida to cause harm, and a prisoner who communicates with the outside world unbeknownst to prison officials with the help of his computer. Because the book avoids technical complexities, readers unfamiliar with the workings of computers will find the contents compelling and an interesting read.

Mitnick, K., S. Wozniak, and W. L. Simon. *Ghost in the Wires: My Adventures as the World's Most Wanted Hacker.* Boston, MA: Little, Brown and Company, 2011.

Written by a hacker who was once on the FBI's Most Wanted List, this book details the thinking and "outsmarting" strategies of Kevin Mitnick as he was on the run from the law for his hacking exploits into networks at Motorola, Sun Microsystems, and Pacific Bell. In and out of prison a number of times, Mitnick's other famous hacker coauthor (of the White Hat variety) is Steve Wozniak.

Nichols, R. K., and P. C. Lekkas. *Wireless Security: Models, Threats, and Solutions*. New York, NY: McGraw-Hill, 2002.

> Written for professionals, this comprehensive guide to wireless security discusses security solutions for voice, data, and mobile commerce.

Nuwere, E. *Hacker Cracker: A Journey from the Mean Streets of Brooklyn to the Frontiers of Cyberspace*. New York, NY: Morrow, William, 2002.

> Written by a then-21-year-old cracker who is now a respected IT security specialist, this book provides young readers with a look into the Black Hat world.

Olson, P. *We Are Anonymous: Inside the Hacker World of LulzSec, Anonymous, and the Global Cyber Insurgency*. Boston, MA: Little, Brown and Company, 2012.

> The author tries to document the interesting hacktivist attempts of LulzSec and Anonymous hacker cells operating on the Internet. The very interesting attacks on the Sony, Visa, and PayPal networks in retaliation for their poor treatment of WikiLeaks are described in detail.

Peterson, T. F. *Nightwork: A History of the Hacks and Pranks at MIT*. Cambridge, MA: MIT Press, 2002.

> Young readers and adults will find this book interesting, as it gives insights into the history of the pioneers at MIT who were involved in the very early stages of White Hat hacking during the 1960s and 1970s.

Pollino, D., B. Pennington, T. Bradley, and H. Dwivedi. *Hacker's Challenge 3: 20 Brand New Forensic Scenarios and Solution*. New York, NY: McGraw-Hill Osborne Media, 2006.

> This book provides critical information by experts for testing one's own computer forensics and hack attack response skills. Written by top-tier experts in the forensics field, the book is both extremely informative and

entertaining. The book cites real-world hack attack cases and explains how the experts dealt with them.

Poulsen, K. *Kingpin: How One Hacker Took over the Billion Dollar Cybercrime Underground.* New York, NY: Crown Publishers, 2011.

It is safe to say that Kevin Poulsen, who himself is a well-known participant in hackerdom history, has as an IT security reporter watched other interesting hackers in his midst. In this book, the protagonist is a White Hat hacker who turns bad. The book is well written and reads like a thriller. The pages are filled with gripping descriptions of online fraud markets, murderous Russian criminals, phishing attacks, Trojan horses, and outlandish hack attacks designed to steal billions of dollars from unsuspecting Americans.

Raymond, E. S. *The Cathedral and the Bazaar: Musings on Linux and Open Source by an Accidental Revolutionary.* Sebastopol, CA: O'Reilly and Associates, 2001.

This book, a favorite with those in the computer underground, is meant to be a good read for anyone interested in the dynamics of the information economy and particulars regarding open-source development.

Raymond, E. S. *The New Hacker's Dictionary.* Cambridge, MA: MIT Press, 1996.

This book is a classic regarding early hacking history and computer folklore. It defines the jargon used by hackers and programmers in the computer underground in the early days.

Reed, A., and S. Bennett. *Silver Clouds, Dark Linings: A Concise Guide to Cloud Computing.* Upper Saddle River, NJ: Pearson, 2010.

This book aims to explain to executives the pros and cons of adopting cloud computing. The authors define cloud computing, describe the risks involved in moving to the cloud, and emphasize the importance of a strategic approach in moving to the cloud.

Schell, B. H. *The Internet and Society: A Reference Handbook.* Santa Barbara, CA: ABC-CLIO, 2007.

This book summarizes the background and history of the Internet, provides biographical sketches of famous people who have contributed to the growth of the Internet, and gives details on various forms of U.S. pieces of legislation dealing with Internet security issues.

Schell, B. H., and J. L. Dodge, with S. S. Moutsatsos. *The Hacking of America: Who's Doing It, Why, and How.* New York, NY: Quorum, 2002.

This book describes the 2000 study of hundreds of hackers who attended the DefCon and Hackers on Planet Earth (HOPE) conferences. The study used numerous previously validated inventories to profile the personalities and behavioral traits of many self-admitted hackers in an attempt to answer the question: Is the vilification of hackers justified?

Schell, B. H., and C. Martin. *Cybercrime: A Reference Handbook.* Santa Barbara, CA: ABC-CLIO, 2004.

This book details the history and types of cybercrime; the issues, controversies, and solutions associated with computer system intrusions; a series of cybercrime legal cases; and biographical sketches of famous cyber-criminals.

Schell, B. H., and C. Martin. *Webster's New World Hacker Dictionary.* New York, NY: Wiley, 2006.

This dictionary describes almost 900 hacker terms, pieces of legislation aimed at combating malicious hack attacks, and famous hackers from the past and present.

Schneier, B. *Secrets and Lies: Digital Security in a Networked World*. New York, NY: Wiley, 2000.

> Written by an IT security expert and intended for a business audience, this book identifies what those in business need to know about computer security to help prevent exploits. The book also gives some interesting insights into the digital world and the realities of the networked society.

Schweitzer, D. *Incident Response: Computer Forensics Toolkit*. New York, NY: Wiley, 2003.

> The author is an expert in Internet security, malicious code, and computer forensics. This book provides a comprehensive discussion of topics from A to Z relating to computer security incidents.

Shimomura, T., and J. Markoff. *Takedown: The Pursuit and Capture of Kevin Mitnick, America's Most Wanted Computer Outlaw, by the Man Who Did It*. New York, NY: Warner, 1996.

> This book describes the capture of Kevin Mitnick by the authorities with the assistance of Tsutomu Shimomura. Besides giving some details on the author's personal life, the book covers some of the technical, legal, and ethical questions surrounding the hacking case that put Mitnick on the FBI's "Most Wanted" list.

Shinder, D. L., and E. Tittel. *Scene of the Cybercrime: Computer Forensics Handbook*. Rockland, MA: Syngress, 2002.

> The objective of this book is to be an informative guide on computer forensics. It would be of particular interest to law enforcement officers who want to gain an understanding of the technical aspects of cybercrime and explore how technology can be utilized to help solve such high-tech crimes.

Skoudis, E., and T. Liston. *Counter Hack Reloaded: A Step-by-Step Guide to Computer Attacks and Effective Defenses,* 2nd ed. Upper Saddle River, NJ: Prentice Hall, 2005.

This book discusses the various steps for ensuring network security by delineating countermeasures to would-be intruders. The authors also discuss how to respond to various forms of web attacks in both UNIX/Linux and Windows environments. The book describes the different approaches taken by neophyte hackers called script kiddies and differentiates these from the approaches employed by the very advanced elite hackers. In addition, it describes how hackers cover their tracks and what to do about these cover-ups.

Skoudis, E., and L. Zelster. *Malware: Fighting Malicious Code.* Upper Saddle River, NJ: Prentice Hall, 2003.

The authors have written a comprehensive work on malicious code. They provide details on what malicious code is, how it works, and how system administrators can defend themselves against it. Even beginners can gain a better understanding of this important IT security topic by reading this book. The book also provides more advanced reading topics of interest to professionals in the IT security field.

Slatella, M. *Masters of Deception: The Gang That Ruled Cyberspace.* New York, NY: Harper Perennial, 1995.

This book tells the riveting story of two cybergangs named Masters of Deception (MOD) and Legion of Doom (LOD). It reads like a bad cowboy-good cowboy tale of strikes and counterstrikes, but in this book the MOD cybergang from New York wore the Black Hats and the LOD cybergang from Texas wore the White Hats. Definitely a fun read from a virtual-world history vantage point.

Sosinsky, B. *Networking Bible*. New York, NY: Wiley, 2009.

This book covers a wide range of topics readers would want to know about setting up and maintaining networks. The authors provide a step-by-step guide to networking in general, as well as the various architectures and hardware needed to put together a functioning network. The author is the founder and chief analyst at the Sosinsky Group, consultants who focus on network design and security.

Spinello, R., and H. T. Tavani. *Readings in CyberEthics*. Sudbury, MA: Jones and Bartlett, 2001.

This book is an anthology of more than 40 essays presenting conflicting points of view about new moral and ethical questions raised by Internet usage. Topics include free speech and content controls, intellectual property protection, privacy and security protection, and professional ethics and codes of conduct regarding Internet usage.

Spitzner, L. *Honeypots: Tracking Hackers*. Upper Saddle River, NJ: Pearson Education, 2002.

Written for system administrators, this book discusses various ways of attracting, observing, and tracking crackers through the use of honeypots. Advantages and disadvantages of honeypots are discussed, as are controversial legal issues surrounding their use.

Sterling, B. *The Hacker Crackdown: Law and Disorder on the Electronic Frontier*. New York, NY: Bantam, 1993.

This classic book details the authority-generated crackdowns on hackers that occurred during the early 1990s. It explains well the paranoia that hackers have been experiencing and their fear about being caught for engaging in illegal hacker exploits.

Stoll, C. *The Cuckoo's Egg: Tracking a Spy through the Maze of Computer Espionage*. New York, NY: Gallery Books, 2005.

Originally published in 1985, this book was written by an astrophysicist who hunted down a hacker who attempted to exploit around 450 networks affiliated with U.S. national security. The hunt paid off with Stoll finding the culprit: a 25-year-old hacker from Germany named Markus Hess, who was allegedly a member of a spy ring. The book reads like a thriller and is understandable to those without a strong computer background.

Studdard, D., and Pinto, M. *The Web Application Hacker's Handbook: Finding and Exploiting Security Flaws.* New York, NY: Wiley, 2011.

This book acknowledges that web applications can be the open door to hackers bent on obtaining personal information, capitalizing on online users' naiveté, or executing fraudulent transactions online. This book discusses HTML 5, hybrid file attacks, and similar technical topics of interest.

Taylor, P. *Hackers: Crime and the Digital Sublime.* London: Routledge, 1999.

This book provides a sociological exploration of the hacker subculture using interviews with active hackers, mostly from Europe. It is well written and avoids an overly technical description of hacking to better examine the social lives of hackers over time.

U.S. Department of Justice. *21st Century Guide to Cybercrime.* Washington, DC: U.S. Department of Justice, 2003.

This resource provides extensive coverage of the Justice Department's work on computer crime and intellectual property crimes and discusses the role of the National Infrastructure Protection Center. Topics covered include searching and seizing computers in criminal investigations, legal issues in computer crime, international aspects of computer crime, cyberethics, and sound standards for prosecuting cybercriminals.

Vacca, J. R. *Computer Forensics: Computer Crime Scene Investigation*. Boston, MA: Charles River Media, 2002.

> This book offers an overview of computer forensics. Topics include seizure of data, determining the "fingerprints" of a cybercrime, and recovering from terrorist cyberattacks.

Wang, W. *Steal This Computer Book 3*. San Francisco, CA: No Starch Press, 2003.

> This book has it all: humor, IT security topic comprehensiveness, and valuable insights into the topic of personal computer security. Written for a wide-ranging audience from young to more mature readers, this book outlines key tools and techniques utilized by hackers.

Warren, H. *Hacker's Delight*, 2nd ed. Addison-Wesley Professional, 2012.

> Having had a terrific career at IBM, the author presents in this book a fine collection of programming hacks, including some remarkable algorithms, time-saving techniques, and tricks of the trade.

Winkler, V. *Securing the Cloud: Cloud Computer Security Techniques and Tactics*. London: Elsevier, 2011.

> This book is comprehensive and provides an introduction to cloud computing and IT security. It also covers cloud computing architecture; security concerns and legal issues; and securing the cloud through architecture, data security, and best practices.

Zalewski, M. *Silence on the Wire: A Field Guide to Passive Reconnaissance and Indirect Attacks*. San Francisco, CA: No Starch Press, 2005.

> There are numerous ways that potential attackers can intercept information or learn more about a target as information passes through the Internet. Although intrusion detection, antivirus software, and firewalls are designed to monitor

known or direct attacks, the author discusses in this book the many kinds of stealthy, insidious attacks that often go unnoticed by system administrators. He provides a comprehensive review of passive reconnaissance and indirect attacks and explains how to protect networks against them.

Zdziarski, J. *Hacking and Securing iOS Applications: Stealing Data, Hijacking Hardware, and How to Prevent It*. Sebastopol, CA: O'Reilly Media, 2012.

This is an excellent book for discovering how best to safeguard a company's iOS applications from hack attacks. Written by an expert who assists law enforcement in iOS forensics analysis, this book would be appreciated by application developers with a solid foundation in Objective-C.

Print: Magazines, White Papers, News, and Downloadable Articles

2600: The Hacker Quarterly

http://www.2600.com/

This website/magazine is a favorite among hackers. The proud sponsor of the Hackers on Planet Earth (HOPE) hacker conference, this often politically motivated website has two weekly live Net broadcasts: on Tuesdays "Off the Wall" and on Wednesdays "Off the Hook." Emmanuel Goldstein also has a featured book for sale called *Dear Hacker*, which contains letters sent to him by colleagues in the computer underground.

Anon News

http://anonnews.org/

Anon News is an independent, uncensored but monitored news platform for Anonymous, where anyone is welcome to post news. In October 2012, a popular news piece on this website described Anonymous's hacks of the Siemens and Fujitsu company websites.

Byte Magazine Online

http://www.byte.com

Larry Seltzer is the editorial director of *Byte*, an online magazine presenting a wide range of technology topics such as IT security and manageability. The magazine is geared to the consumerization of IT (CoIT), defined as the introduction into the enterprise (planned or not) of devices created to be consumer technologies—including smart phones, tablets, and social media.

Hakin9 IT Security Magazine

http://hakin9.org/subscription/

Readers can download for free some highly interesting features on IT security topics, such as "Eight Must-Have Features in Your Web Security Solution," "What Can a Network Scanner Do for You?" and "Why Most Web Security Training Doesn't Work." Other free downloads include topics such as "Hacking Oracle" and "Defining Best Practices for IT Security within a Cloudy World."

Infosecnews

http://www.infosecnews.com

This website presents the latest news in the IT Security world. For example, on October 12, 2012, Dan Kaplan wrote an interesting news story with this headline: "Second LulzSec Member Pleads Out in Sony Pictures Attack." Also on this date, another story by Danielle Walker was published with this headline: "Presidential Election Spurs Malware-laden CNN Spam." The website also features interesting white papers on topics such as "Privileged Password Sharing the 'Root' of All Evil." There is also a special section for Canadian IT security news. For example, a story by Danny Bradbury running on September 10, 2012, had this headline: "Canadian Energy Companies Under Threat from Anonymous, Say Agencies."

Infosecurity Magazine

http://www.infosecurity-magazine.com/

It is interesting to note that when one goes to this website, one of the first things online readers will note is a warning that the website relies on cookies (defined as small bits of data that are commonly transmitted from a web server to a web browser; they can be accessed, read, and used by malicious websites unintentionally visited by innocent online users), and that if one continues to read content online, one is consenting to the use of cookies. The website also cites details about an annual Infosecurity U.S. Fall Virtual Conference held on a particular day that presents online keynote speakers whose information security lectures' content is available to registered conference attendees. One of the keynote speakers for 2012, for example, focused on "Transforming Data into Intelligence: Big Data Analytics to Combat Breaches, Threats, and Fraud."

Infoworld

http://www.infoworld.com

This online magazine features interesting topics such as "The Nine Most Endangered Species in IT" and "Will the Future Be Entirely Written in JavaScript?" Readers can download updated white papers and articles on cloud computing, data centers, and big data explosion.

International Data Group

http://www.idg.net

This website gives up-to-date news related to information technology and information security for professionals. It has a global focus and a special research repository on IT trends such as big data, cloud computing, converged IT, safeguarding mobile devices, and the intelligent economy. There is a considerable focus on the merging of IT and business.

Java Developer's Journal

http://java.sys-con.com/

The editor of *Java Developer's Journal* is Joe Winchester. This online IT magazine is devoted to topics of interest to Java-language developers and, therefore, provides updates on the Java programming language and its applications. A featured piece in October 2012, for example, dealt with "Why Data Breaches Occur and How You Can Lessen Their Impact." Cloud computing, in general, is another highly featured topic.

Linux Journal

http://www.linuxjournal.com/

This is the original journal linked to the Linux community, with roots dating back to 1994. There are "tech tips" featured for web development and gaming, and there are trendy topics such as Linux and the cloud, embedded development, security, virtualization, and desktop development.

LulzSec

http://www.lulzsec.com

In October 2012, if an online reader logged onto this hacker cell website to get the latest news and buzz on hacking issues, one would see the following message: "This domain name has been seized by ICE—Homeland Security Investigations, pursuant to a seizure warrant issued by a United States Court." It looks as though the hackers running the website may be in a bit of trouble with the law.

News c/net

http://www.news.com

News c/net is all about information technology. Under the Security and Privacy tab for October 2012 were such timely topics as "Pre-emptive Cyberattack Possible, Panetta Warns," "Anonymous Turns Its Back on WikiLeaks after

PayPal Dispute," and "Mozilla Rereleases Firefox 16 after Fixing Critical Flaw."

PC World

http://www.pcworld.com
This IT magazine website is anything but boring. There are group chat showdowns featuring questions such as "Which instant messenger service is best?" There are also some very interesting review features, such as "Hacker Rift: Anonymous Takes Offense at WikiLeaks."

Phrack

http://www.phrack.org/
This magazine is another favorite for those in the computer underground. On the website, readers can select to see the contents of magazine issues from the initial one to the current one. As of October 2012, issues 1 through 68 were available. The editor is "The Phrack Staff." Some key writers are Taran King, Knight Lightning, Datastream Cowboy, and Phantom Phreaker. Topics in issue 68, for example, included: "Phrack World News," "Happy Hacking," and "Practical Cracking of White-Box Implementation." Some popular hacking articles making the "Stats" section include topics such as "Know Your Enemy: Facing the Cops" and "Remote Blind TCP/IP Spoofing."

Security Magazine

http://www.secmag.com
This online magazine has featured stories on current IT security issues. For example, in October 2012, the feature story was entitled "How Cloud Computing Changes Risk Management." In September 2012, a feature story was entitled, "Making a Difference in Fraud Detection." In October 2012, under the "Critical Infrastructures" tab was a featured story entitled "Secretary of Defense Says Future Cyber Attacks Could Rival 9/11."

Security Server

http://www.securityserver.com
This website features sponsored links to IT security topics such as enterprise security suites; e-commerce security; proactive cybersecurity; and network security, filters, and firewalls.

Ubiquity

http://ubiquity.acm.org/
This online magazine, an Association for Computing Machinery (ACM) information technology magazine, presents up-to-date articles and news features of interest to IT specialists. Peter J. Denning is the editor in chief. Interviews feature timely topics such as "Writing Secure Programs" and "Bringing Architecture back to Computing." Blog features include timely topics such as "How Data Became Big." There are also symposia with features such as "The Essence of Evolutionary Computation" and "Life Lessons Taught by Simulated Evolution."

Wired

https://subscribe.wired.com/subscribe/wired/69775
?source=google_int
A subscription is available for this U.S.-based high-tech magazine, which covers a wide range of topics such as how high-tech people, businesses, and technologies are transforming our lives in the 21st century. For a reasonable fee, a reader will receive an issue monthly.

ZD Net

http://www.zdnet.com
This online high-tech magazine has news, blogs, and white papers dealing with secure transactions over the Internet. Moreover, the magazine's white paper directory is purportedly one of the largest online libraries containing free information technology topic updates and numerous

case studies on data management, IT management, networking, communications, enterprise applications, and IT privacy, security, and trust issues. There is also a special section devoted to cloud computing and data centers. Under the "Security" heading are interesting timely stories such as "Hacking Google: The Three Israeli White Hats Rooting out the Web's Security Holes."

Nonprint: Hacking Websites

http://www.2600.com

> This is the website of the popular hacker magazine *2600: The Hacker Quarterly* and home of the Hackers on Planet Earth (HOPE) hacker conference.

http://www.blackhat.com/usa/bh-us-12-briefings.html

> This is the website of the popular Black Hat hacker conference held annually in Las Vegas at the end of the summer. Intended for IT security professionals, entry into the briefings and training sessions for this conference typically costs thousands of dollars—but is worth every penny. There is also Black Hat Europe and Black Hat Abu Dhabi.

http://www.defcon.org

> This is the website of DefCon, the largest hacker gathering in the world, held annually in Las Vegas at the end of the summer. For about $100, those interested in the conference get more than their money's worth in terms of the latest updates by experts in the hacker field. Because of the reasonable fee charged, the bulk of the attendees are younger hackers in their teens and early adulthood. The Black Hat conference attendees are sure to be there as well, because they view themselves as critical mentors for neophytes wanting to enter and be successful in the computer underground.

http://wikileaks.org/
    This is the controversial website for the hacking cell known as
    "WikiLeaks," whose members have a passion for publishing
    government and industry secrets online with the alleged "goal
    of bringing important news and information to the public."
    In October 2012, the upcoming U.S. presidential campaign
    was a favorite topic, with the WikiLeaks website releasing
    more than 200,000 global intelligence files (known as GI
    files).

Nonprint: Hacking-Related Films and Learn How-to-Hack Videos

The Girl Who Kicked the Hornet's Nest
Date: 2009 (Denmark)
Length: 147 Minutes
Cast: Noomi Rapace, Michael Nyqvist, and Lena Endre

Female hacker Lisbeth Salander is in a hospital awaiting her arrest
on three murder charges at the start of the film. After she is
released from the hospital, she and journalist Mikael Blomkvist
know that together they can prove her innocence, but first
Salander needs to share the sordid details of her life with the court.

The Girl Who Played with Fire
Date: 2009 (Denmark)
Length: 129 Minutes
Cast: Noomi Rapace, Michael Nyqvist, and Lena Endre

While female hacker Lisbeth Salander and journalist Mikael
Blomkvist investigate a sex trafficking ring, Lisbeth is accused
of committing three murders. While she is on the run from
the law, her journalist friend and lover helps clear her name of
any wrongdoing.

The Girl with the Dragon Tattoo
Date: 2011 (United States)

Length: 157 Minutes
Cast: Daniel Craig, Rooney Mara, Christopher Plummer, Stellan Skarsgard, and Steven Berkoff

This film story focuses on a female hacker named Lisbeth Salander, who helps journalist Mikael Blomkvist find a woman reported missing to police for 40 years and whose case was labeled "cold" because the police could not solve it. With Lisbeth's hacking prowess, the journalist and she eventually discover the truth about the woman, who is actually still alive.

Hackers
Date: 1995
Length: 107 Minutes
Cast: Jonny Lee Miller, Angelina Jolie, Fisher Stevens, and Lorraine Bracco

This film story centers on a neophyte hacker who cracks into a highly secured computer and stumbles on an embezzling scheme masked by a computer virus with the potential to destroy the world's ecosystem.

Pirates of Silicon Valley
Date: 1999
Length: 95 minutes
Cast: Anthony Michael Hall, Noah Wyle, Joey Slotnick, and John Di Maggio

This film is about the White Hat hackers who creatively made products and the innovative IT companies that gave California its label "Silicon Valley." The film focuses on the creators of Apple Computer and Microsoft, among others.

War Games
Date: 1983
Length: 114 minutes

Cast: Matthew Broderick, Dabney Coleman, John Wood, and Ally Sheedy

This film is best described as a cyberthriller. A computer hacker unwittingly taps into the U.S. Defense Department's war computer and starts a confrontation of global proportions—namely, World War III.

The White Hat Learn How to Hack Videos: Hacking 101 Beginning Pen Testing Syllabus
www.whitehackworkshop.com

This video package gives those interested in better understanding "how to hack" hands-on videos covering topics such as basic security, basic system administration, reconnaissance, scanning and mapping, vulnerability assessment, basic metasploit and exploitation, advanced exploitation, post exploitation, password cracking, wireless security, and web and database attacks. The video package also has a section on "pulling it all together."

　　Price: $300 for the standard course or $450 for the premiere course with 60 days of lab access

Nonprint: Websites of Companies Offering Antivirus Software

Two kinds of virus-scanning software exist to protect computer networks. One type is used on individual computers, while the other scans traffic going to and from the Internet at a gateway; both look for potentially harmful code. Both types of software not only try to remove any attached viruses, worms, or Trojan horses from software programs and documents, but also inform users about some actions being taken.

　　The company websites listed here offer a wide range of antivirus and antimalware products for gateway-based and local installations. These products differ primarily in their licensing and packaging schemes. These products are regularly tested by the computer security companies producing them, and the companies' website content is continually updated to reflect the findings of those tests. Most of the listed companies also provide information services to their customers as well as to the public about newly released malware on the Internet. The website content also details known countermeasures, commonly called "patches" or "fixes."

F-Secure

> http://www.f-secure.com
> The F-Secure 2013 package is part of an award-winning product line for this U.S.-based security software company. The 2013 security package guards against existing and emerging threats to computer networks—and it has gone to the cloud. The F-Secure website says that the package will keep companies' and government's networks secure using real-time cloud-based technology to guard against viruses, spyware, and other forms of malicious attacks. What is more, F-Secure has a user-friendly firewall to thwart hack attacks, block spam and phishing attacks, and prevent identity theft. For the home computer user, the F-secure protection package allows parents to block harmful sites from children or to block children's uncontrolled surfing.
> Corporate headquarters: San Jose, California, and Helsinki, Finland

Network Associates—McAfee

> http://www.mcafee.com
> The McAfee website has this clever saying: "Safety is not a privilege. It is a right." To this end, the new McAfee antivirus protection package is marketed as a total-defense protection package that has "best of breed" rootkit protection, quick-scan and one-step easy installation, and automatic scanning of USB drives. This company was founded in 1987 and continues to make technology advances every year.
> Corporate headquarters: Santa Clara, California

SafeNet

> http://www.safenet-inc.com/?aldn=true
> SafeNet is one of the largest data security companies in the world. More than 25,000 government agencies and businesses across 100 companies rely on SafeNet's products to help safeguard their networks—whether it be in the form of data protection, two-factor authentication, cloud security, cybersecurity, software security, or software licensing.
> Corporate Headquarters: Belcamp, Maryland

Sophos

> The Sophos website markets the company's suite of products as being able to effectively protect networks, servers, data, endpoints, and mobile devices. The goals of the company and its product suite are to eliminate malware, protect data on corporate and home networks, prove compliance, and protect mobile devices from hack attacks. The company claims that "We make the Internet safer and more productive." Its website also provides up-to-date IT security news and trends.
> Corporate headquarters: Abingdon, Oxford, and Burlington, Massachusetts

Symantec

> The Symantec website lets online users become better informed about the Norton Anti-virus Protection product line to help them safeguard against their networks against spyware and virus invasion. The Norton Internet Protection suite and the Norton 360 Protection product are aimed at providing the ultimate virus protection—complete with backup and 2 GB online storage. The company's website also offers online visitors interesting videos, such as one with this attention-getting message for enterprise IT security administrators: "Data center down! Is your business prepared to recover?"
> Corporate headquarters: Mountain View, California

Trend Micro

> http://www.trendmicro.com
> The Trend Micro website opens with this attention-getting sentence: "Securing your journey to the cloud." It goes on to tell online visitors: "Relax. We make it easier to secure your digital life." Founded in 1988 in the United States, Trend Micro's corporate headquarters are now in Japan. Steve Chang is the co-founder and chairman of the corporation, and Eva Chen is the co-founder and CEO.
> Corporate headquarters: Tokyo, Japan

Nonprint: Websites of Companies Offering Firewalls

Firewalls are devices used to control the data traffic flowing into and out of a corporate or government agency network. By using firewalls, companies and government agencies can try to block unwanted traffic and malware that keeps unauthorized users from gaining access to the network. Many of the available firewall products allow users to build a secure tunnel, or virtual private network, through the Internet so that two or more sites of an organization can use the Internet as a safe medium in which to communicate. Data are encrypted by one firewall before being sent, and the receiving firewall then decrypts the data. This process minimizes the risk for various crack attacks.

The firewall suppliers listed here have all provided well-designed products for these objectives. What is equally interesting is that these companies have created new technologies beyond firewalls to contend with emerging trends such as cloud computing and RFID tracking and control.

Check Point

> http://www.checkpt.com
> When one goes on the Check Point website, this company motto appears: "Helping retailers grow profitably." The company has specific IT solutions for retailers in the following market segments: apparel, food markets, warehouses,

pharmacies, hardware stores, and specialty stores. Besides providing protections, the company's solutions offer retailers in-stock information on their product line inventory.

Corporate headquarters: Thorofare, New Jersey

Cisco

http://www.cisco.com

A click on the Cisco website brings up this intriguing tag line: "The extraordinary is within reach." The company's products are wide ranging and include application networking services, data center automation and management, blade switches, networking software, physical security, routers, unified computing and servers, and video conferencing. The company's services are also wide ranging and include borderless network services, data center and virtualization services, routing and security services, storage networking services, and WebEx collaboration services.

Corporate headquarters: San Jose, California

DellSonicWALL

http://www.sonicwall.com

The home page for DellSonicWALL urges online readers to ponder these key questions: "Can your next-gen firewall pass the ultimate security and performance test? How about excelling in three?" With regard to the second question, in 2012, DellSonicWALL next-generation firewalls earned recognition for the product line from three of the industry's most influential third-party evaluators. The company's network and security products include secure remote access, antispam and email security solutions, backup and recovery solutions, management and reporting solutions, and endpoint security solutions. Originally founded in 1991 under the name SonicWALL, the company was acquired by Dell in 2012.

Corporate headquarters: San Jose, California

Nonprint: Websites of Companies Offering Intrusion-Detection Systems

Intrusion-detection systems (IDS), as noted in earlier chapters, complete the set of technical precautions that organizations typically take to keep their networks safe from malicious intruders. IDS assist system administrators in detecting whether a security breach has actually occurred. These systems typically look for unwanted changes or data transfers in the network and note any anomalies. The following companies offer reputable IDS products.

Solera Networks

http://www.soleranetworks.com

A click on the company website elicits this sage piece of advice: "The defensive capabilities of traditional security tools have been eclipsed by the capabilities of modern attackers. The evidence is in front of us every day." To help companies and government agencies deal with this very real threat, DeepSee is an award-winning security intelligence and analytics solution developed by Solera Networks to assist enterprises in more effectively preparing for advanced malware and targeted attacks by letting adopters find answers to these key questions:

- Who did this to the networks?
- How did they accomplish this exploit?
- Which systems and data were affected?
- Are we sure the attack is over?
- Can we be sure it will not happen again?

The virtual appliance is said to integrate well with other network security products such as McAfee and SourceFire. Steve Shillingford is the president and CEO.

Corporate headquarters: South Jordan, Utah

SourceFire

> http://www.sourcefire.com
> This company was founded in 2001 by Martin Roesch,
> the creator of the open-source Snort IDS, reportedly the
> world's most widely deployed IDS. To respond to a high
> demand for a commercial software product, the company
> developed the Agile Security product (based on Snort),
> which is marketed as being "as dynamic as the real world
> it protects and the attackers against which it defends." In
> short, the product is designed to provide continuous pro-
> tection to a virtual world earmarked by continual change.
> Corporate headquarters: Columbia, Maryland

Nonprint: U.S. Government Agencies and Independent Organizations Fighting Malicious Hacking

Besides the U.S. Department of Justice's Criminal Division,
the FBI, IC3, the National White Collar Crime Center
(NWC3), the Department of Homeland Security, the
National Infrastructure Protection Center (NIPC), and the
National Computer Security Center (NCSC) are involved in
the fight against malicious hacking in the United States. An independent organization with similar motivations is the U.S.
Computer Emergency Readiness Team (US-CERT). The loca-
tors for these U.S. government agencies and independent
organizations are given here.

U.S. Department of Justice

> 10th and Constitution Ave. NW
> Criminal Division
> John C. Keeney Building, Suite 600
> Washington, D.C.
> Telephone: (202) 514-1026
> http://www.cybercrime.gov
> The description for this government agency was provided
> at the beginning of this chapter.

Federal Bureau of Investigation (FBI)

http://www.fbi.gov
J. Edgar Hoover Building
935 Pennsylvania Ave. NW
Washington, D.C.
Telephone: (202) 324-2000

Internet Crime Complaint Center (IC3)

http://www.ic3.gov
The IC3 accepts complaints about online Internet crime
from either the victim or a third party representing the
victim. Many of the complaints that this government
agency deals with involve online fraud. The IC3 is a partnership between the FBI and the National White Collar
Crime Center. Its website gives Internet crime prevention
tips and outlines current reported trends (such as the
Nigerian letter scheme, also known as "419").

National White Collar Crime Center (NWC3)

http://www.nw3c.org
Telephone: (803) 273-NW3C
The NWC3 is a U.S.-based center that provides a support
system for law enforcement and regulatory agencies in the
prevention, investigation, and prosecution of high-tech
crimes. This agency conducts specialized training in computer forensics, conducts research on the many facets of
white-collar crime, and partners with the Internet Crime
Complaint Center. The NWC3 was formed in 1978; it
was then known as the Leviticus Project, and had as its
mission the investigation of crime dealing with the coal
industry. The agency name was changed to NW3C in
1992 to reflect an expanded mandate involving high-tech
crimes.

Department of Homeland Security
http://ww.dhs.gov
Homeland Security Operations Center
Washington, D.C.
Telephone: (202) 282-8101
The creation of the Department of Homeland Security (DHS) was the most significant transformation of the U.S. government since 1947, when Harry S. Truman merged the various branches of the U.S. Armed Forces with the Department of Defense to better coordinate the nation's defense against military threats. The DHS represents a similar high-tech consolidation, both in style and in substance.

In the aftermath of the terrorist attacks in September 2001, President George W. Bush decided that 22 previously disparate domestic homeland security agencies needed to be coordinated into one department to better protect the nation against threats. The new department's priority objective was to protect the nation against further terrorist attacks. Component agencies assist in analyzing threats and intelligence, guarding borders and airports, protecting critical infrastructures, and coordinating the responses to future emergencies. Besides providing a better-coordinated defense of the U.S. homeland, the DHS is dedicated to protecting the rights of American citizens and enhancing public services (such as natural disaster assistance) by dedicating offices to them.

National Infrastructure Protection Center (NIPC)
Information Analysis Infrastructure Protection
Washington, D.C.
Telephone: (202) 323-3205
Founded in 1998, NIPC was initially housed in the FBI headquarters. In 2003, it was moved to the Department of Homeland Security. NIPC is the government agency charged with safeguarding the U.S. infrastructure

networks from attack by hackers and malware. It issues three levels of infrastructure warnings:

- Level one assessments provide general information about nonspecific threats.
- Level two advisories address particular dangers requiring greater preparedness or a change in posture.
- Level three alerts warm of major and specific threats.

For example, in 2002, the NIPC issued a level one assessment warning against possible hacktivism exploits connected with upcoming meetings of the International Monetary Fund and the World Bank.

National Security Agency (NSA), National Computer Security Center (NCSC)

NSA INFOSEC Service Center (NISC)
INFOSEC Awareness, Attn: Y13
Fort George G. Meade, Maryland
Telephone: (800) 688-6115

Founded in 1981, the National Computer Security Center provides solutions, products, and services and conducts defensive information operations intended to keep the U.S. critical infrastructure safe from attack. A part of the National Security Agency, the NCSC also provides information systems security standards and solutions.

Working in partnership with industry, academic institutions, and other U.S. government agencies, the NCSC initiates needed research and develops and publishes standards and criteria for trusted information systems. It also promotes information systems security awareness, education, and technology transfer through cooperative efforts, public seminars, and an annual National Information Systems Security Conference.

U.S. Computer Emergency Readiness Team (US-CERT)
http://www.us-cert.gov
US-CERT is jointly run by the Department of Homeland
Security and CERT at Carnegie-Mellon University. Its
mission is to coordinate previously dispersed efforts to
counter threats from all forms of cybercrime. Therefore,
US-CERT does the following:

- Analyzes and attempts to reduce cyberthreats and
  vulnerabilities
- Disseminates cyberthreat warning information
- Coordinates incident responses

Individuals wanting to subscribe to CERT's mailing lists
and feeds to get the latest information on vulnerability
and threat information as well as those wanting to report a
known vulnerability are encouraged to enter this website:
http://www.kb.cert.org/vuls/html/report-a-vulnerability/.

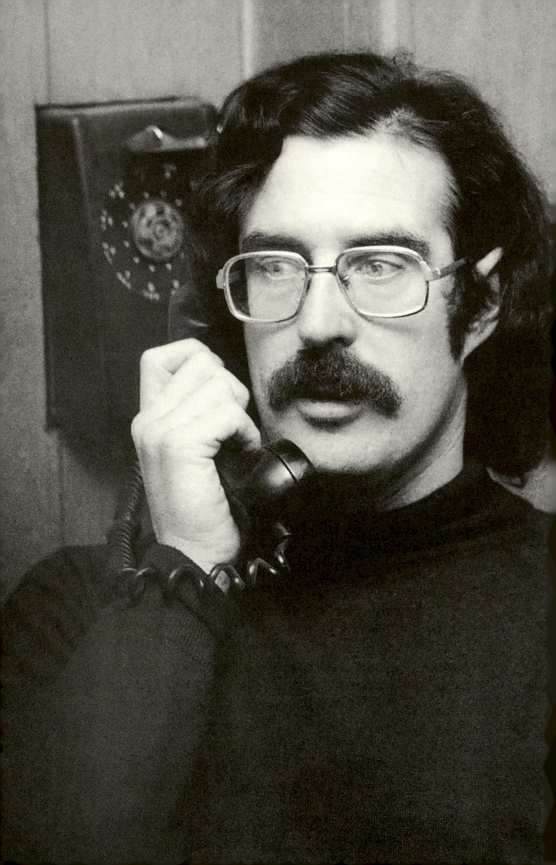

This chapter delineates in chronological order selected hacker-related events, beginning with a Prehistory (from the 1800s through about 1969); moving to the Elder Days (1970–1979), during which some of the early-school hackers began their exploits; moving next to the Golden Age (1980–1989), when hacker headlines began to be of interest to the mainstreampopulation; moving next to the Great Hacker Wars and Hacker Activism (1990–2000), when virtual wars and activism became news on an international plane; and closing with the Fear of a Cyber-Apocalypse Era (2001 to the present), as more vicious, targeted, and harmful exploits have become a real threat to property and people globally.

Prehistory (1800s–1969)

1815 to Mid-1800s

1815 Ada Byron is born to the famous poet Lord Byron. During a dinner party at friend Mary Somerville's home in 1834, Ada is introduced to a researcher named Charles

---

Phreaker John Draper in 1978. Draper was sent to prison in 1971 for using a whistle from Captain Crunch cereal to make long-distance phone calls. (AP Photo/Dave Pickoff)

Babbage, who begins discussing with her the concept of a "new calculating machine."

1841 Babbage reports on the machine development at a seminar held in Italy.

1843 AdaByron publishes her own paper on the calculating machine, adding that it could be developed to compose complex music, produce graphics, and be generally applied for a series of scientific and practical applications. About this time, Byron suggests to Babbage that he should write a plan for how the Analytical Engine might calculate Bernoulli numbers. The plan iscompleted andis considered to be the initial "computer program." (In modern days, a popular programming language called ADA is named in Ada Byron's honor.)

1920s–1950s

1921 Kay McNulty Mauchly Antonelli is born.

1942 McNulty is recruited by the U.S. Army to calculate by hand the firing trajectories of artillery. She is sort of a "human computer."

1948 McNulty marries John Mauchly, a professor and co-inventor with Presper Eckert of the first electronic computer, known as the Electrical Numerical Integrator and Calculator

1950 McNulty, Mauchly, and Eckert develop a new, faster computer called the Universal Automatic Computer, or Univac. One of its strengths is its use of magnetic tape storage to replace the clumsy punched data cards and printers.

1958–1959 Computers develop further with the use of integrated circuits, with chips having only a few transistors.

1960s During this period, the computer geeks at Massachusetts Institute of Technology (MIT) arecreatively involved in their hacking exploits. Computers are huge and capable of overheating if they are not stored in temperature-controlled spaces. Known as the PDP series, these computers' processing time is slow, so the computer geeks create what they call "hacks" or "programming shortcuts" to enable them to complete computer tasks more quickly. These White Hat creative types become the center of MIT's Artificial Intelligence (AI) Lab.

During this period, the number of transistors per unit area doubles every one and a half years, increasing computer power tremendously. This rapid evolution of circuit fabrication is known as Moore's law.

1968 The Theft Act of 1968 is passed in the United Kingdom and can be applied to individuals charged with Black Hat hacking.

1969 The Advanced Research Projects Agency Network, or ARPAnet, is created to be the initial cross-continent, high-speed computer network built by the U.S. Defense Department as a digital communications experiment. ARPAnet allows AI researchers in dispersed areas to exchange information with incredible speed and flexibility.

The standard operating system UNIX is developed by researchers Dennis Ritchie and Ken Thompson, researchers at Bell Laboratory. UNIX is considered to be a thing of beauty because its standard user and programming interface assists users with computing, word processing, and networking.

The first Computer Science Man of the Year Award is given by the Data Processing Management Association to a woman, Dr. Grace Murray Hopper, for writing the computer language COBOL.

The Elder Days (1970–1979)

1970 William Powell releases *The Anarchist Cookbook*, which promotes the message that violence is an acceptable means to effect political change. The bookupsets the more conservative elements because it includes bomb and drug recipes copied from military documents kept in the New York City Public Library.

1971 Phreaker John Draper makes long-distance telephone calls for free using the whistle from Captain Crunch cereal and is sent to prison in the United States.

The Criminal Damage Act is passed in the United Kingdom and can be applied to hackers.

Canadian Stephen Cook publishes Cook's theorem, which helps to advance the field of cryptography.

1972 The Telnet protocol is proposed as a standard.

1973 Gordon Moore, Intel's chairman, publicly announces that the number of transistors on a microchip will likely double every year and a half.

The File Transfer Protocol (FTP) is developed, simplifying the transfer of databetween networked machines.

Canadian Mers Kutt creates Micro Computer Machines, thus releasing in the market the world's first personal computer (PC).

Robert Metcalfe writes a memo to his employers at Xerox Corporation suggesting that there is huge potential in an "Ethernet."

1975 Steve Jobs and Steve Wozniak, members of California's Homebrew Computer Club, create the Apple computer. With this computer and the simplistic BASIC language, hackers see the potential for microcomputers.

Bill Gates and Paul Allen start Microsoft Corporation.

1976 Whitfield Diffie and Martin Hellman develop the Diffie-Hellman (DH) Public Key Algorithm, which is used in many secure protocols on the Internet.

David Boggs and Robert Metcalf officially announce the invention of Ethernet at the Xerox company in California.

1978 Randy Seuss and Ward Christensen from Chicago create the first computer bulletin board system (BBS), which allows hackers in the computer underground (CU) to communicate with one another.

The Transmission Control Protocol (TCP) is split into TCP and the Internet Protocol (IP), making it the TCP/IP.

By this time, counterculture Yippie guru Abbie Hoffman starts *The Youth International Party Line* newsletter, whose name is amended to *TAP* by co-publisher Al Bell. Also known as Technical Assistance Program, the newsletter publishes on such topics as phreaking, explosives, electronic sabotage blueprints, and credit card fraud. CU idiosyncrasies are introduced, such as substituting "z" for "s" and "0" for "O."

Also by the late 1970s, Dennis Ritchie's programming language C is successfully ported to several machines of varying types.

The Golden Age (1980–1989)

1981 IBM announces a new stand-alone computer dubbed the "PC" or "Personal Computer."

The Commodore 64 and the TRS-80, affectionately known as "the Commie 64" and the "Trash-S" computers, respectively, become hackers' favorite tech toys.

Two popular hacker groups, the U.S. Legion of Doom and the German Chaos Computer Club, evolve, drawing much hacker talent into their fold.

In the United Kingdom, the Forgery and Counterfeiting Act of 1981 is passed, allowing hackers who alter data in any way during their exploits to be charged with criminal offenses.

1982 Talented UNIX hackers from Stanford University and the University of California start Sun Microsystems Incorporated based on the belief that UNIX running on seemingly cheap hardware will prove to be a perfect solution for a wide range of applications—a foundation that creates high-tech millionaires.

Scott Fahlman types the first online smilie.

When ARPAnet is split into military and civilian sections, the Internet is formed.

Some White Hat hackers start leaving the MIT AI Lab, enticed by higher wages in industry.

The Simple Mail Transfer Protocol (SMTP) is published, and William Gibson coins the word "cyberspace."

1983   The Comprehensive Crime Control Act of 1983 is passed in the United States, giving jurisdiction to the U.S. Secret Service over credit card and computer fraud.

The movie *War Games* is released, exposing the public to the hidden faces of Black Hat hackers and the 414 cracker gang—the trendsetters of computer "handles" or "monikers."

The final version of the Telenet protocol is published.

1984   The U.K. Data Protection Act of 1984 is passed and is intended to be more effective at curbing cracking, at least relative to the Counterfeiting Act of 1981. Also, the Telecommunications Act of 1984 is passed in the U.K. as a means of curbing phreaking.

Steven Levy's book *Hackers: Heroes of the Computer Revolution* is released, showing the bright and creative sides of the White Hat hackers, and Fred Cohen introduces the term "computer virus."

Eric Corley (also known as Emmanual Goldstein) starts the *2600: The Hacker Quarterly* magazine.

Cisco Systems, Inc., is started by a small number of scientists at Stanford University. The company is committed to developing IP-based networking technologies—in particular, routers and switches.

Richard Stallman constructs a clone of UNIX, written in C and obtainable to the virtual world for free, calling his project GNU (a recursive acronym that stands for "GNU's Not UNIX")—a project that appeals widely to those in the CU.

In Canada, Gilles Brassard and Charles Bennett release an academic paper with details on how quantum physics can be used to create unbreakable codes using quantum cryptography.

1985   The hacker 'zine *Phrack* is published by Craig Neidorf (also known as Knight Ligtning) and Randy Tischler (also known as Taran King), and the Free Software Foundation (FSF) is founded by Richard Stallman, promoting the development and use of free software.

The U.S. Congress passes the Computer Fraud and Abuse Act to counteract fraud and associated activity aimed at or using computers.

1988   In the United Kingdom, Robert Schifreen's and Steven Gold's hacking-related convictions are set aside through appeal to the House of Lords on the grounds that the Forgery and Counterfeiting Act of 1981 is being extended beyond the appropriate boundaries.

U.S. hacker Kevin Poulsen (also known as Dark Dante) takes over telephone lines going into the radio station KIIS-FM, winning him a Porsche; he is eventually put behind prison bars for three years on phone tampering charges.

Robert Morris, Jr., becomes known to the world when, as a graduate student at Cornell University, he accidently unleashes an Internet worm that he had made. Known as "the Morris worm," it infects and subsequently crashes thousands of computers. Morris receives a sentence of three years' probation, 400 hours of community service, and a $10,500 fine.

Kevin Mitnick secretly monitors the email of MCI and DEC company officials. He is convicted of damaging computers and stealing software, and is sentenced to a year behind prison bars—the beginning of a streak of imprisonments on hacking-related charges.

The Computer Emergency Response Team (CERT) for Internet security is founded, in large part as a result of the harm caused by the Morris worm. Housed at Carnegie Mellon University, CERT's purpose is to coordinate communication among experts during security emergencies.

The U.S. Secret Service secretly videotapes attendees of the SummerConhacker convention held in St. Louis, Missouri, based on its suspicion that illegal hacker activities are occurring.

1989   West German hackers led by Karch Koch and affiliated with the Chaos Computer Club become involved in the first cyberespionage case to make international headlines, when they are arrested for cracking the U.S. government's computers and then selling operating system source code to the Soviet KGB (the State Security agency).

Herbert Zinn (also known as Shadow hawk) is the first minor to be convicted for violating the Computer Fraud and Abuse Act of 1986, after he cracks AT&T's computer systems and the Department of Defense's systems—apparently destroying files estimated to be worth about $174,000. Zinn also publishes passwords and instructions on how to exploit computer security systems. At age 16, he is sent to prison for nine months and fined $10,000.

The Great Hacker Wars and Hacker Activism (1990–2000)

1991   Linus Torvalds begins developing a free UNIX version for PCs using the Free Software Foundation's toolkit. Following feedback from creative hackers, he develops Linux, a complete version of UNIX built from free and able to be freely distributed sources.

The Pretty Good Privacy (PGP) encryption program is released by Phil Zimmerman, who is later involved in a three-year investigation by the U.S. government for allegedly being in violation of export restrictions for cryptographic software.

Until 1991, the Internet is restricted to linking the military and educational institutions in the United States, but in this year, the ban preventing Internet access for businesses is lifted.

1992   The Michelangelo virus attracts lots of media attention because of fears that it could harm data and computers—a fear that proves unfounded when this virus actually does little to no harm to the victimized computers.

The term "surfing the Net" is coined by Jean Armour Polly—getting lots of popular movement attention.

1993 Scott Chasin establishes BugTraq, a full-disclosure mailing list dedicated to issues involving computer security—vulnerabilities, means of exploitation, and fixes for vulnerabilities discovered.

With just a little more than 100 websites on the Internet, the first DefCon hacker convention is launched in Las Vegas. The sessions are held in a small hotel and organized by the Dark Tangent.

1994 The gang of crackers led by Vladimir Levin becomes famous for cracking Citibank's computers and supposedly making off with illegal transfers exceeding $10 million—putting Levin behind prison bars for three years.

The first version of the Netscape web browser is released, two Stanford University students named David Filo and Jerry Yang track their interests on the Internet by creating the start-up now known as Yahoo, and Canadian James Gosling heads a creative team at Sun Microsystems in an effort to develop a programming language that would change the simplistic, one-dimensional nature of the Web—an objective that is accomplished and becomes known as Java.

Randal Schwartz, who writes hot-selling books like *Programming Perl* and *Learning Perl*, is convicted on charges of industrial espionage and sentenced to five years' probation plus 500 hours of community work. Phreaker Ed Cummings (also known as Bernie S), the man of *2600: The Hacker Quarterly* fame and a native of Pennsylvania, is sent to prison for using a modified Radio Shack speed dialer to make free phone calls.

The first annual conference known as Hackers on Planet Earth (HOPE) is held in New York City at the Hotel Pennsylvania.

The online Cyber Angels group is founded to help track cyber-stalkers, the first online bookstore known as Amazon is launched by Jeffrey Bezos, andhacker Christopher Pile (also known as Black Baron) is convicted and sent to prison for 18 months for writing and distributing a computer virus.

1996 Kevin Mitnick is arrested again for the theft of 20,000 credit card numbers. He pleads guilty to the illegal use of cellular phones—earning him the nickname "the lost boy of cyberspace."

The National Information Infrastructure Protection Act of 1996 (NIIPA) is enacted in the United States to amend the Computer Fraud and Abuse Act (CFAA).

An insider cracker incident involving Timothy Lloyd makes headline news when Lloyd sabotages the Omega Engineering network with a logic bomb after he finds out he will be fired, costing the company about $12 million in damages.

1997 The Digital Versatile Disc (DVD) format is released, along with DVD players utilizing this format.

1998 The Digital Millennium Copyright Act of 1998 (DMCA) is passed in the United States to cope with the abuse of emerging digital technologies, members of the Boston hacker group L0pht testify before the U.S. Senate about vulnerabilities associated with the Internet, and Canadian Tim Bray helps create a computer language known as Extensible Markup Language (XML), which makes the popular online auction eBay possible.

1999 The Melissa virus hits the Internet. It is later attributed to David Smith, who pleads guilty to causing more than $80 million in damage to computers worldwide.

The Gramm-Leach-Bliley Act of 1999 is passed in the United States to provide limited protections against the sale of individuals' private financial information; the Napster music file-sharing online system developed by university students Shawn Fanning and Sean Parker attracts more than 85 million registers users before it is shut down for its alleged violation of the DCMA; and Jon Johansen becomes one of a triad of founders known as MoRE (Masters of Reverse Engineering), who make headlines after releasing the DeCSS software tool to circumvent the Content Scrambling System (CSS) of encryption-protected DVD movies.

2000 Canadian Mafiaboy makes headlines following a series of denial-of-service (DoS) attacks that bring down high-profile websites like Amazon, eBay, and Yahoo—exploits that put him behind bars in a youth prison. Cyber experts begin to question whether a cyber-apocalypse might occur as early as 2005, and the Love Bug virus is sent from the Philippines by suspects Michael Buen and Onel de Guzman.

Fear of a Cyber-Apocalypse Era (2001–Present)

2001   MIT announces that over the next decade materials for nearly all courses offered at the university will be freely available on the Internet. Peter G. Neumann writes in *The New Yorker* that he is worried about an imminent cyber-apocalypse because malicious hackers cannow get into important computer systems in minutes or seconds and can wipe out one third of the computer drives in the United States in a single day. The Code Red worm infects several hundred thousand systems worldwide and overloads the Internet's capacity—causing about $2.6 billion worth of damages worldwide.

Web defacements begin after a U.S. spy plane crashes inside Chinese airspace. Hackers in both nations target a wide range of websites to express dissent and outrage over each nation's actions in the real world.

2003   On January 24, President George W. Bush swears in Tom Ridge as the first Secretary of the Department of Homeland Security. The 24-year-old Web designer John Racine II admits that he diverted web traffic and emails from the Al-Jazeera website to another website he had designed that is known as "Let Freedom Ring" and shows the U.S. flag. In a survey of more than 1,000 U.S. adults conducted by the Pew Internet and American Life Projects, one in two adults reports being concerned about the vulnerability of the national infrastructure to terrorist attackers.

2004   The Recording Industry Association of America (RIAA) says that it has identified 532 song-swappers by the trails that their computers left when the swappers illegally downloaded music from the Internet. The worm W32. Novarg.A@mm (also known as MyDoom) spreads throughout the Internet and wreaks havoc. Sven Jaschan is arrested in Waffensen, Germany, for creating and releasing through the Internet the Sasser worm.

2005   While delivering a speech to security experts at the RSA Conference in California, Microsoft Corporation founder Bill Gates says that the company will give away software to combat spyware, adware, and other privacy-invasive cyber nuisances. A cyber war breaks out between Indonesia and Malaysia, brought on by a dispute over the Ambalat oil fields in the Sulawesi See. Documents seized from three members of the Lashkar-e Toiba (LeT) terrorist group killed in an encounter with Indian police indicate that they planned to execute a "suicide" crack attack on the networks of companies having software and chip design companies in Banlalore and Karnal Singh.

2006   Crackers deface as many as 600 Danish websites, replacing the usual information with threats and hacktivist messages such as "Danish, you'r D3ad," after a Danish newspaper publishes images from 12 cartoonists hired to create satirical drawings of the Prophet Mohammed. The U.S. investment bank Morgan Stanley offers to pay $15 million to resolve an investigation by U.S. regulators into its failure to retain email messages. Victims of a computer theft at the University of Alabama are informed that they should be on alert for identity theft.

2007   One of the first instances of cyberwar breaks out between Russian and Estonian hackers after the attempted removal of a bronze statue commemorating Russian involvement in World War II from a cemetery in Estonia in April. Physical protests begin shortly after the statute's removal is announced, and quickly escalate online through DDoS attacks and spam. The attacks become so severe that the Estonian government's computer system is taken offline and must be hosted in the United States to avoid further information loss and economic harm.

2008   The Anonymous hacker cell targets the Church of Scientology by putting its servers under hack attack.

2009   The CIA claims that cyberattackers have penetrated unnamed power grids, causing at least one blackout. The Citizen Lab uncovers a secret network that it calls Ghostnet; the network has infected at least 1,295 computers with malware that gives an unknown entity free rein to rummage through sensitive embassy and government ministry documents in real time.

2010   On January 12, Google announces that after a serious hacking incident, the company is no longer going to "play ball" with the Chinese government. The Facebook virus Koobface infects computers and then sends a lurid message to the computer owners' Facebook friends.

The computer worm Stuxnet is identified in June; it targets SCADA systems inside nuclear plants in Iran to disrupt the nation's capacity to enrich uranium. The malware is highly sophisticated and incorporates unique zero-day exploits, suggesting it was created by a nation-state, most likely the United States.

2011   After starting around 2006, the Rustock botnet is brought to an end after it is thought to enlist as many as 2.4 million machines into its network, sending an estimated 1.8 billion spam messages an hour—about a third of all global spam.

Attackers use a nasty Trojan horse that fools Android users into thinking that they are installing a regular application, though they are really installing malware that turns over personal information to a remote service and gives hackers substantial control over the phone.

2012   The AMSC engineering firm in Devens, Massachusetts, goes before China's highest court to accuse Sinoval Wind Group Ltd., China's biggest manufacturer of wind turbines, of stealing AMSC's code for software that helps run the giant machines.

/etc/password   The UNIX file that stores all of the account information, including username, password (encrypted form), the user identifier, the primary group the user belongs to, some additional information about the account (such as the real user's name or other personal information), the user's home directory, and the login shell. This file is of particular interest to crackers—if they can read files from this directory, they use the information to attack the machine.

/etc/syslog.conf   The UNIX system configuration file describing the system events to be logged either to a log file on the same machine or to a log host over the network. Information from this file is of particular interest to crackers—when they find where their actions are stored, they can forge the log files and hide their tracks.

0wn   A hacker culture term that is typically spelled with a zero, meaning to control completely. For example, a system broken into by a cracker is said to be under the 0wnership of the cracker.

2600 Hz   The tone that long-distance telephone companies such as American Telephone and Telegraph used to indicate

---

Participants work at their laptops at the 29th annual Chaos Computer Club (CCC) computer hackers' meeting on December 28, 2012 in Germany. The Chaos Computer Club is Europe's biggest network of computer hackers and its annual congress draws up to 3,000 participants. (Getty Images)

that the long-distance lines were open. This sort of knowledge was creatively used by early-day phreakers such as John Draper to make calls for free.

Access Controls The physical or logical safeguards preventing unauthorized access to information resources.

Account Harvesting A term often used to refer to spammers, individuals who try to sell or seduce others through email advertising or solicitation. Account harvesting involves using computer programs to search areas on the Internet to gather lists of email addresses. Newsgroups and chat rooms are great resources for harvesting email addresses.

Anonymous A collection of hacker cells that coordinate their efforts, to some degree, in online chat rooms. The cells have brought down the Vatican's website, teased cabinet members in numerous countries when their political messages were controversial, and released cracked emails dealing with U.S. government sensitive information. This group of hackers seems to embody a culture of creative disturbance in the pursuit of chaos, justice, and retribution.

Anonymous Digital Cash Combined with encryption and/ or anonymous remailers, a form of payment that allows criminals to make transactions with complete anonymity. The digital cash system allows a person to pay for goods or services by transmitting a number from one computer to another. Like the serial numbers on dollar bills, the digital cash numbers are unique.

Anonymous Remailers A remailer is a computer service that privatizes email and typically contains the sender's identity. Anonymous remailers send email messages that arrive in a receiver's inbox without a sender's identity.

Antivirus Software Software that detects viruses and notifies the user that a virus is present. It keeps a database of "fingerprints," a set of characteristic byes from known viruses, on file.

ARPAnet The first transcontinental, high-speed computer network built by the U.S. Defense Department as an experiment in digital communications.

Authentication A user's legitimacy to enter the network information—typically a password, a token, or a certificate.

Bacteria Also known as rabbits; viruses that do not carry a logic bomb and, therefore, are not as destructive as other known viruses. Bacteria merely replicate, consuming resources.

Beige Box A device that phone phreakers used to gain access to another's phone line to crack it. In the old days, the equivalent to the beige box would be a telephone lineperson's handset—that is, a telephone fitted out with clips to attach it to the line. Having beige boxes is not illegal in most jurisdictions, but using them to make free telephone calls at someone else's expense is illegal and considered to run counter to wiretapping laws.

Binary Numbers Numbers represented in base 2 that consist of a series of 1s and 0s. Because computers work in the binary system, hackers consider "binary" to mean "not text." In computing, every eight binary digits or bits is used to represent a byte.

BIOS Software built into the hardware of any personal computer that is used to access the operating system on the hard drive and boot or start the machine.

Black Bag Job A term used by law enforcement, referring to the practice of breaking into a computer with the goal of searching for files on the hard drive or copying files to help prosecute those believed to be guilty of cybercrimes. Wire taps and use of a keystroke logger serve similar functions—namely, collecting data for a successful prosecution.

Black Hats Hackers who engage in destructive computer exploits and are often called "crackers." They are typically motivated by revenge, sabotage, blackmail, or greed, and their exploits often result in harm to property and/or to people.

Blaster Worm Discovered in August 2003, a worm that adversely impacted computers running the Windows 2000, Windows NT, Windows Server 2003, and Windows XP operating systems. The worm was created to download the msblast.exe file to the Windows directory and then execute it. It also tried to conduct a denial-of-service attack on the Microsoft Windows Update web server to prevent the user from applying a path on his or her computer to counter the DCOM RPC vulnerability. Within just one day of its discovery, the worm had infected more than 300,000 computers.

Blended Threats   Complex cyber attacks combining the characteristics of computer worms, malicious code, and viruses with vulnerabilities found on servers and the Internet. These threats are known to spread fast and cause widespread damage, including launching denial-of-service attacks on a targeted IP address, defacing web servers, and planting Trojan horse programs to be executed at another time.

Blue Boxing   In relation to earlier phreaking exploits, the use of boxes containing electronic components to produce tones that manipulate the telephone companies' switches.

Bluejackers   A short-term event in which one person literally highjacks another person's cell phone by sending it an anonymous text message using the Bluetooth wireless networking system. In one anecdote, a group of tourists was strolling the streets of Stockholm and admiring items in a store window when one of the cell phones beeped and displayed an anonymous message saying, "Try the blue sweaters. They keep you warm in the winter." More serious concern arises when data are stolen from cell phones and used to commit identity theft scams.

Border Gateway Protocol (BGP)   One of the core routing protocols in the Internet. BGP is used in all border routers of the tens of thousands of networks making up the Internet; it takes care of forwarding data to the correct next hop on the path to the destination.

Botnet   A group of computers infected by a virus that turns them into a virtual army, falling under the control of a third party that is not visible to the computer user. Botnets can consist of hundreds or even millions of computers, making size their key weaponry. These powerful botnets or "bots" can launch distributed denial-of-service attacks or a global outflow of spam. Rustock was a botnet that may have been sending as many as 1.8 billion spam messages every hour.

Brute-Force Crack   Just as more conventional criminals might try breaking into a safe by using multitudes of number combinations, a kind of activity used by crackers to decrypt encrypted data, such as passwords, or to reveal the Data Encryption Standard (DES) keys.

Buffer   A portion of memory set aside to store data, often read from an input channel.

Buffer Overflow   An exploit that typically attacks programs written in C and C++, in which a maliciously intended application attempts to take over the program with an excessively large amount of data hiding executable code. After the overflow crashes the victimized program, the malicious code executes its purpose. The most common executions are the deletion of data and the conversion of the affected PC into a zombie, such that it transmits spam or adversely affects other computers. Buffer flow exploits were associated with the harm caused by the Blaster worm of 2003, to name just one incident involving this technique.

Bulletin Board System (BBS)   The precursor to the Internet; a computer system that ran software that allowed users to dial into the system using a phone line. Users could then download software and data, upload data, read news, or trade messages with other online users. BBSs were popular from the 1970s through the early 1990s.

C   A computer language created in the 1970s by Dennis Ritchie; a language designed to be nonconstraining and flexible. By 1978, the entire C environment was ported to computers of varying types.

Carding   The sale and distribution of stolen financial information acquired by computer hackers so as to engage in fraud and economic crimes.

Capture/Replay   An exploit in which an attacker captures a whole stream of data, with plans to replay it later in an attempt to repeat the effects. Thus a transaction might be repeated to empty the bank account of a targeted person.

Channel   An established communication link through which a message travels as it is transmitted between a sender and a receiver.

China's Involvement in Digital Warfare   Experts in IT security generally believe that China has adopted digital warfare as part of its military doctrine. On January 12, 2010, Google announced that after a serious hacking incident, the company would no longer partner with the Chinese government. Such allegations continue to be levied. For example, on October 26, 2012, U.S. engineering company AMSC, a wind turbine manufacturer based out of Devens, Massachusetts, alleged that the Sinovel Wind Group Ltd., China's biggest manufacturer of wind turbines, had committed corporate espionage against the U.S. company by stealing its software code.

Choke Points   Points where security controls can be applied to protect multiple vulnerabilities along a path or a set of paths.

Cloud Computing   Basically speaking, any company's or government agency's data and applications running on the Internet. With cloud computing, everything is stored on servers at a remote location and can be accessed from any web browser anywhere around the globe. Cloud computing commonly falls into three categories: software as a service (e.g., fee-based or free online software applications such as Google Docs), platform as a service (in which companies access virtual email or web development platforms), and infrastructure as a service (i.e., virtual machines or storage). If a data breach occurs in the cloud, the original owner of the data is accountable for the loss.

Code   The portion of the computer program that can be read, written, and modified by humans. As one case in point that caused considerable interest in the IT security field, in the spring of 2005, a crack attack exploiting some Cisco Systems equipment that powered the Internet fueled debate about whether the stolen code, which was used to support an allegedly very secure system, poses a threat, in general, to the Internet.

Code Red I and II Worm   In July, 2001, vulnerabilities in the Windows Internet Information Services Server (IIS) made headlines when the computer worms Code Red I and later Code Red II propagated within hours of each other and moved rapidly across the Internet, snagging vulnerable computers along the way. Code Red II was especially feared because it altered approximately 100,000 Windows NT and Windows 2000 web servers and personal computers, allowing any unauthorized user to log onto them and exercise total control.

Commodore 64 (Commie 64)   A computer that endeared itself to the early pioneers in the computer underground; it was released in September 1981 with only 64 kilobytes of RAM and a 40-column text screen. The 320-by-200 pixel display was typically connected to a television. Though perceived to be a technology masterpiece back then, it is clearly a dinosaur today.

Compiler   A computer science term. The compiler transforms human-readable source code into binary code that computers understand.

Compromise a Computer   To break into a computer without having authorization to do so.

Computer Underground (CU)   A concept that first emerged around 1980. The CU includes both White Hats—who commonly attempt to gain entry to a network with permission to stress-test the system for vulnerabilities—and Black Hats—who commonly gain entry to a network without authorization with the goal of causing damage, usually for personal financial gain or revenge.

Console Exploits   By definition, intrusions into a network through some vulnerability in the program interface. Over the last decade, vulnerabilities in the software installed on computers have been an effective means of spreading malware. In 2002, for example, the KlezI worm used this means of transmission to cause damage; two years after its discovery, it remained one of the most frequently detected worms on infected computers—designed to target Internet Explorer browsers.

Cookie   Small bits of data transmitted from a web server to a web browser. Though not typically dangerous in and of themselves, cookies can be accessed, read, and used by malicious websites unintentionally visited by innocent online users.

Crackers   Often called "hackers" in the media, individuals who break into other computer systems without authorization to commit crimes. Believed to be motivated by malicious intent, crackers are also labeled network hackers or Net-runners.

Cracking   Gaining unauthorized access to computer systems to commit a cybercrime.

Crash   To cause a personal computer, computer system, or network to break down or fail to operate.

Criminal Trespass   A legal term indicating that someone has entered or remains in an area in which he or she does not have legal access.

Critical Infrastructures   According to the US PATRIOT Act of 2001, the following critical sectors and resources: chemical; emergency services; information technology; postal and shipping; telecommunications; and transportation systems (including buses, flights, ships, ground systems, rail systems, and pipeline systems). Nuclear power systems are also part of this infrastructure.

Cybercrime   A crime in which technology, computers, and the Internet are used to cause harm to property or to persons.

Cybercrime and the Coincidence of Four Critical Elements   As is true forland-based crimes, for cybercrime to exist, four elements must be present: *actus reus* (the prohibited act or failing to act when one is supposed to be under duty to do so; *mens rea* (a culpable mental state); *attendant circumstances* (the existence of certain necessary conditions); and *harm* resulting to persons or property.

Cyberpunk   This term, combining *cyber* and *punk*, initially appeared as the title of a short story called "Cyberpunk," written by Bruce Bethke. The author said that he tried to find a word that would combine the notions of "punk attitudes" and "hightech" to indicate a rebellious youth segment with antisocial tendencies and having a disdain for conventional ways of using cyber tools.

Cypherpunks   A group of thinkers, programmers, and researchers dedicated to preserving individuals' freedom of speech through action. Cypherpunks believe in crypto anarchy—a term that encompasses concepts such as anonymous networks, black markets, and digital cash—along with libertarianism. These individuals write code and distribute it freely to those around the globe so that they can improve it.

Cyberterrorism   Unlawful attacks and threats of attack by terrorists against computers, networks, and the information stored within them, when done to intimidate or coerce a government or its people to further the attacker's political or social objectives.

Daemon   A process running in the background that performs some service for other computer programs.

Decode   To reverse a previously used encoding process. Normally, binary data are encoded so that the human eye can at least register them. Binary data are encoded into a readable format so that they can be transmitted by text-based protocols such as SMTP (for email) or HTTP (for the Web).

Decryption   Also called deciphering; the process of taking encrypted data that have been put in a so-called secret format called cipher text and converting those data back to the original plain text. To complete the process, a key or password is required.

Deface   To alter a website by removing or changing the message displayed. Hack tivists are often known to deface targeted companies' and government agencies' websites.

Defaults   Settings on a system prior to configuration.

Distributed Denial of Service (DDoS) Web servers can handle only so much traffic, after which the network crawls or crashes. A DDoS attack is one way of shutting down a network, by bombarding it with traffic from all directions. This can be done with a botnet, where one attacker relays a signal that causes thousands or more infected computers to bombard a targeted web server. Alternatively, in a volunteer attack, Internet users relay on software like the Low Orbit Ion Cannon, which turns computers of willing users into generators of traffic. The multiple origins of the attack make it difficult to defend against.

Driver A computer program intended to allow another program (typically, an operating system) to interact with a hardware device.

Encryption The mathematical conversion of information into a form from which the original information cannot be restored without using a special key.

Facebook A social networking website. Employers are concerned about social websites for two main reasons: they think that employees' productivity will be adversely affected by their use of such sites, and if employees use mobile devices for corporate use and then log onto Facebook, critical company information may be leaked though the social network.

File Transfer Protocol (FTP) A protocol used to transfer files between systems over a network.

Firewalls Programs used to provide additional security on networks by blocking access from the public network to certain services in the private network.

Flooding Cyberspace vandalism resulting in denial of service to authorized users.

Ghostnet In 2009, Citizen Lab discovered a secret network containing about 1,300 computers infected with malware that gave an unknown party free reign to spy in real time. The name given to this network was "Ghostnet."

Hacker A person who enjoys learning the details of computer systems and how to stretch their capabilities.

Hijacking To cut off an authenticated, authorized connection between a sender and a receiver. The attacker then takes over the connection, killing the information sent by the original sender, and sending attack data instead.

Honeypot A computer or network set up to pretend that it offers some real service to the Internet to lure crackers. This network is then closely monitored by an expert to determine how the cracker breaks into the system and what he or she does to compromise it.

Identity Theft The malicious theft of and consequent misuse of someone else's identity.

IP Address A numerical identifier that is divided into a part that identifies a network (such as a company or government agency) and another part designed to identify each computer in the network. The IP address can be thought of as a street name and house number on a real-world street.

Kernel The essential part of any operating system.

Koobface A Facebook virus discovered in 2010. The virus infected a computer and then sent out a lurid message to its owners' Facebook friends. Apparently its purpose was to trick them into downloading an infected phony software update. The virus is believed to have generated more than $2 million illegally.

Logic Bomb Hidden code that instructs a computer virus to perform some destructive action when certain criteria are met.

Malicious Code Programs such asviruses and worms that are created to exploit weaknesses in computer software by replicating and/or attaching themselves to other programs.

Malware A piece of malicious software infecting a computer network and forcing it to do an attacker's bidding. Viruses, Trojan horses, spyware, and key loggers fall into this category.

Man-in-the-Middle   An attack in which the perpetrator intercepts data and replies to them as if the data came from the intended recipient. A victim might expose private information such as bank account information, which can later be used to defraud him or her.

Network File System (NFS)   A means of sharing files across a local area network or through the Internet.

Packet   A piece of data of either fixed or variable size that is sent though a communication network like the Internet. A message is typically broken up into packets before it is sent over a network.

Phreaking   Using technology to make free telephone calls without authorization.

Piracy   Copying protected software without authorization.

Protocol   A set of rules governing how communication between two programs must take place to be considered valid.

Root Servers   On the Internet, a group of 13servers worldwide that are responsible for the basic level of the Domain Name System.

Routers   Specialized computer devices at the border of an Internet-connected network that storea specialized map of the Internet and contribute to this map by informing the network's neighbors about what it knows about its part of the Internet.

Scriptkiddies   Relatively inexperienced hackers who rely on prefabricated software to do their exploits; also called newbies.

Sniffer Program   A computer program that analyzes data on a communication network to gather intelligence, such as detecting a password that is transmitted over the network.

Social Engineering   A deceptive process whereby crackers engineer a social situation with the purpose of tricking others into allowing them access to an otherwise closed network.

Spamming   To send unsolicited emails for commercial purposes or with the intent to defraud.

SSH   A command to remotely log into a UNIX computer.

Telnet   A terminal emulation program or one based on that protocol that allows individuals to remotely log on to other computers on the Internet.

Trivial File Transfer Protocol (TFTP)   A network protocol allowing unauthenticated transfer of files.

UUCP   An acronym for UNIX-to-UNIX copy, a protocol used for the store-and-forward exchange of mail.

Virus   A computer program that replicates itself by embedding a copy of itself into other programs.

War Dialers   Simple personal computer programs that dial consecutive phone numbers looking for modems.

Worm   A self-replicating computer program considered to be self-contained and not requiring to be part of another program to propagate.

Zero-Day Attack   An attack named for the total number of days a software company has had to prepare for an onslaught by hackers, knowing that the software has vulnerabilities that could be capitalized on but for which patches have not been developed or distributed. In 2008, for example, Microsoft was overwhelmed when hackers found a flaw in Internet Explorer that had been "in hiding" for almost a decade before it was discovered by the hackers and used to steal passwords.

Zombie   A computer program that typically awaits a signal from a perpetrator to bombard a particular website. On command, thousands or more computers simultaneously send fake requests for information to a targeted website, which tries to handle these requests until it runs out of memory. The website either slows down considerably or grinds to a halt.

About the Authors

Thomas J. Holt is an Associate Professor in the School of Criminal Justice at Michigan State University. He received his undergraduate and PhD in criminology and criminal justice from the University of Missouri–Saint Louis in 2005. He has published extensively on hackers, malware, piracy, and various forms of cybercrime over the last decade, including more than 35 peer-reviewed articles in journals such as *Crime and Delinquency, Deviant Behavior, Journal of Criminal Justice, International Journal of Cyber Criminology,* and *Social Science Computer Review.* Dr. Holt also served as a co-editor of the book *Corporate Hacking and Technology-Driven Crime* with coeditor Bernadette Schell (2011); is the editor of *Crime On-Line: Correlates, Causes and Context* (2010), which is appearing in its second edition in 2013; and is a co-author of *Digital Crime and Digital Terror,* second edition (2010). He is also a regular presenter at academic and professional conferences, including local hacker conferences across the United States.

Dr. Holt has received multiple grants from the National Institute of Justice to examine the social and technical drivers of Russian malware writers, data thieves, and hackers using on-line data. In addition, he is currently completing a study of the social networks that structure the market for stolen data operating out of Russia and Eastern Europe. He is the project lead for the Spartan Devils Chapter of the international Honeynet Project, an international cybersecurity research consortium. He is also a member of the editorial board of the *International*

Journal of Cyber Criminology and the *Journal of Criminal Justice Education.*

Bernadette H. Schell is well published in the hacking and IT domain. She has coauthored books such as *The Hacking of America* (2002), *Cybercrime* (2004), *The Internet and Society* (2007), and *The Webster's New World Hacker Dictionary* (2006). In December 2011, Dr. Schell's chapter on the fictional character Lisbeth Salander as a hacker appeared in the recently published book *The Psychology of* "The Girl with the Dragon Tattoo." She has also coauthored with Dr. Tom Holt the book *Corporate Hacking and Technology-Driven Crime.* Currently the Vice-Provost at Laurentian University in Barrie, Ontario, Canada, Dr. Schell was formerly the founding dean of Business and Information Technology at the University of Ontario Institute of Technology in Oshawa, Ontario, Canada.

Index